Vocabulary
FOR
DUMMIES®

Vocabulary FOR DUMMIES®

by Laurie E. Rozakis, PhD

Wiley Publishing, Inc.

Vocabulary For Dummies®

Published by
Wiley Publishing, Inc.
111 River Street
Hoboken, NJ 07030
www.wiley.com

WILEY

About the Author

Dr. Laurie Rozakis earned her Ph.D. in English and American Literature from the State University of New York at Stony Brook. An Associate Professor of English at the State University of New York College of Technology at Farmingdale, Dr. Rozakis has published more than one hundred books and scores of articles. In addition to *Vocabulary For Dummies,* her publications include trade books, young adult books, textbooks, biographies, reference books, and articles.

Dr. Rozakis frequently appears on television, including the *CBS Morning Show;* the *Maury Povich Show;* Fox *Good Day, New York; Metro Relationships;* and Fox *Personal F/X.* Her career and books have been profiled in *The New York Times,* the New York *Daily News, Time* magazine, and the *Chicago Tribune.* Dr. Rozakis does a monthly Internet show for yo.com.

Dedication

To Robert from Long Island, my staunchest supporter and best friend.

Publisher's Acknowledgments

We're proud of this book; please send us your comments through our Online Registration Form located at www.dummies.com/register.

Some of the people who helped bring this book to market include the following:

Acquisitions, Editorial, and Media Development

Project Editor: Kathleen A. Dobie

Senior Acquisitions Editor: Gregory W. Tubach

Copy Editor: Greg Pearson

Technical Editor: Thomas La Farge

Editorial Manager: Christine Meloy Beck

Editorial Assistants: Brian Herrmann, Jennifer Young

Cover Photos: © 1999 Photodisc

Production

Project Coordinator: Nancee Reeves

Layout and Graphics: LeAndra Johnson, Jackie Nicholas, Jill Piscitelli, Jacque Schneider, Betty Schulte, Julie Trippetti, Erin Zeltner

Proofreader: Aptara

Indexer: Aptara

Special Help: Tracy Barr, Alissa Schwipps

Publishing and Editorial for Consumer Dummies

Diane Graves Steele, Vice President and Publisher, Consumer Dummies

Joyce Pepple, Acquisitions Director, Consumer Dummies

Kristin A. Cocks, Product Development Director, Consumer Dummies

Michael Spring, Vice President and Publisher, Travel

Brice Gosnell, Publishing Director, Travel

Suzanne Jannetta, Editorial Director, Travel

Publishing for Technology Dummies

Andy Cummings, Acquisitions Director

Composition Services

Gerry Fahey, Vice President, Production Services

Debbie Stailey, Director of Composition Services

Contents at a Glance

Introduction 1

Part 1: Getting Your Bearings 7

Chapter 1: Figuring Out How Words Work 9

Chapter 2: Building Your Vocabulary 17

Chapter 3: Picking Up Meaning 37

Chapter 4: Using the Right Word 51

Part 11: Mastering the Basics 63

Chapter 5: Getting to the Root of the Matter 65

Chapter 6: Starting Off with Prefixes 81

Chapter 7: Ending Well: Suffixes 101

Part 111: Expanding Your Base 119

Chapter 8: Shading Meaning: Synonyms, Antonyms, Connotations, Denotations 121

Chapter 9: Hear Your Homonyms and Homophones Here 131

Chapter 10: Compounding Words 151

Chapter 11: Romancing English: Words from French, Spanish, and Italian 167

Chapter 12: Borrowing from the Neighbors: Words from Other Languages 183

Part 1V: Getting Savvy with Vocabulary 197

Chapter 13: Trying Your Skills on Standardized Tests 199

Chapter 14: Taking Care of Business Vocabulary 215

Chapter 15: Mutterings on Money Matters 227

Chapter 16: Speaking Legalese 237

Chapter 17: Doctoring Your Words: Medical Terms 251

Chapter 18: Acquiring Shopping and Eating Language 263

Chapter 19: Expanding the Language: Recent Additions 273

Chapter 20: Exploring Words from Real and Mythical People and Places 287

Part V: The Part of Tens 301

Chapter 21: Don't Go There: Language to Avoid 303

Chapter 22: Distinctions Worth Making 307

Chapter 23: Ten Techniques for Nonnative Speakers 315

Index 321

Cartoons at a Glance

By Rich Tennant

page 119

page 301

page 7

page 197

page 63

Cartoon Information:
Fax: 978-546-7747
E-Mail: richtennant@the5thwave.com
World Wide Web: www.the5thwave.com

Table of Contents

Introduction *1*

   About This Book 1

   Conventions Used in This Book 1

   Special Features 3

   How This Book Is Organized 4

      Part I: Getting Your Bearings 4

      Part II: Mastering the Basics 4

      Part III: Expanding Your Base 4

      Part IV: Getting Savvy with Vocabulary 5

      Part V: The Part of Tens 5

   Icons Used in This Book 5

   Where to Go from Here 6

Part 1: Getting Your Bearings *7*

Chapter 1: Figuring Out How Words Work 9

   Getting an Idea of a Good Vocabulary 9

   Reaping Vocabulary's Rewards 11

   Trying to Make Sense of the English Language 12

      Borrowing words from other countries 12

      Breaking out word elements: Prefixes, roots, and suffixes 13

      Assembling blended words 14

      Figuring out English oddities, peculiarities, and quirks 14

   Improving Your Vocabulary the Easy Way 15

Chapter 2: Building Your Vocabulary 17

   Playing to Improve Your Vocabulary 17

      Carding yourself 17

      Playing those mind games: Mnemonics 18

      Wrestling with word games 19

   Reading Up on Words 20

      Diving into dictionaries 20

      Thumbing through a thesaurus 24

      Sifting through word history: Etymology 26

   Boosting Your Vocabulary for Standardized Tests 27

      Arranging words in your mind 28

      Skimming your way to comprehension 29

Pronouncing Words Correctly 29
   Seeing and saying: Pronunciation rules 29
   Handling the biggest mispronunciation problems 31
   Improving your pronunciation 35
Exercising Your New Vocabulary 36

Chapter 3: Picking Up Meaning **37**

Reading Between the Lines 37
   Saying it another way: Restatement clues 38
   Context clues after colons and dashes 40
   Context clues after transitions 40
   Inferential context clues 42
   Contrasting context clues 45
Being an Armchair Detective 46
Deciphering Words with Multiple Meanings 47

Chapter 4: Using the Right Word **51**

Choosing Your Words 51
Digging into Diction 53
   Speaking and writing formally 54
   Using standard English 55
   Employing everyday English 57
Bringing Home the Bacon: Idioms 59
Abbreviating Acronyms 62

Part II: Mastering the Basics *63*

Chapter 5: Getting to the Root of the Matter **65**

Tending to Word Roots 65
   Exploring the basics of roots 66
   Using roots to grow words 67
Getting Scientific with Greek Roots 69
   Measuring roots 69
   Describing nature 72
   Greek roots for beliefs and ideas 74
Cultivating Latin Roots 76
   Making and moving roots 77
   Sizing up other Latin roots 78

Chapter 6: Starting Off with Prefixes **81**

Going to the Head of the Word 81
Seeing Prefixes Everywhere: De-, Re-, In-, Un-, and Pre- 83
   Retooling words 84
   Deconstructing de- 85

Including in- (and em- and en- and . . .) 86
Doing and undoing with un- 86
Previewing pre- 87
Eyeing Other Common Prefixes 88
Prefixes meaning "not" and "against": A-, anti-, dis-, and more 88
Getting it together: Co-, con-, and sym-/syn- 89
Homing in on location prefixes 90
Encompassing prefixes that indicate degree 92
Counting on prefixes that show number 92
Sailing through Greek Prefixes 94
Pursuing Prefixes from Latin 97
Adding In Anglo-Saxon Prefixes 99
Acting Like a Prefix: Words that Do Double Duty 100

Chapter 7: Ending Well: Suffixes **101**
Meeting the Most Often Used Suffixes 101
Admitting my favorites: -ment, -ence/-ance,
-able/-ible, and -ion 102
Showing action: -ate, -en, -ite, and -ize 103
Changing tense: -d/-ed and -ing 104
Adding amounts: -s, -es, and others 104
Expanding Your Suffix Collection 105
Showing a state of being: -cy, -dom, -ant, -ness, and more 105
Relating to or showing likeness:
-ac, -al, -esque, -ish, and others 107
Focusing on folks 109
Designating place or condition 111
Putting Suffixes to Work 113
Figuring out a word's function 113
Comparing with suffixes 117

Part III: Expanding Your Base **119**

Chapter 8: Shading Meaning: Synonyms, Antonyms,
Connotations, Denotations **121**
Distilling Synonym Essentials 122
Sidling up to synonyms 122
Substituting synonyms 125
Analyzing Antonyms 126
Understanding Subtext: Connotation and Denotation 127
Keeping up with current connotations 128
Deciding between positive and negative connotations 128

Chapter 9: Hear Your Homonyms and Homophones Here **131**

Differentiating Homonyms and Homophones
(In Case You're Curious) 131
Dealing with Homonyms and Homophones 134
Making a Lo-o-o-ng List 134
Having Fun with Homonyms 148

Chapter 10: Compounding Words **151**

Presenting Compound Basics 151
Gathering up closed compounds 152
Separating hyphenated compounds 153
Making multiword compounds 155
Using Compounds to Build Your Vocabulary 156
Halving your options with "half" 156
Eating well: Compound words about food 157
Getting comfortable with homey compound words 159
Sunning yourself: Compound words with "sun" 160
Eyeing compound words with "eye" 161
Combing through some "hairy" compound words 163
Chilling compound words with "snow" 164
Fooling around with "play" compound words 165
Compounding a Few, Final Words 166

**Chapter 11: Romancing English: Words from French,
Spanish, and Italian** **167**

Ooo La La! English Words from French 168
Socializing with French flair 168
Dining on words 170
Entertaining words from French 171
Walking the streets 172
Ole! Words from Spanish 174
Eating words 175
Building on Spanish words 175
Getting to know you 177
Living la Dolce Vita: Words from Italian 178
Soothing the savage beast 179
Being an armchair architect 180
Invigorating Italian words (and a couple of others) 181

**Chapter 12: Borrowing from the Neighbors:
Words from Other Languages** **183**

Liking Latin 183
Using Latin every day 184
Paying attention to problematic plurals 185
Talking Blarney: Words from the Irish and Scots 187
Oy Vey! English Words from Yiddish 188

Dressing Up with Words from Arabic 190
   Trading words along with goods 190
   Changing words to gold 191
   Pursuing English-Arabic words about people 192
Lapping Up Words from Other Lands 195

Part IV: Getting Savvy with Vocabulary 197

Chapter 13: Trying Your Skills on Standardized Tests 199

Assembling the Skills You Need 199
   Knowing roots, prefixes, and suffixes 200
   Using context clues 201
   Understanding the relationship between words 201
Getting Familiar with the Types of Test Questions 202
   Analogies 203
   Antonym questions 207
   Sentence completion 208
   Reading comprehension 210
Incorporating General Test Prep Tips 212
   Make a plan of attack 213
   Don't panic 213

Chapter 14: Taking Care of Business Vocabulary 215

Talking on Company Time 215
   Writing in professional terms 216
   Keeping current with modern business lingo 217
   Doing double duty: Words with two meanings 220
Mastering Jargon 221
   Speaking of software (and hardware, too) 221
   Engineering jargon 223
   Stop the presses: Publishing and printing jargon 225

Chapter 15: Mutterings on Money Matters 227

Managing Your Money Day to Day 227
Investigating Investment Terms 230
Talking about Markets 231
Taxing Terms 233

Chapter 16: Speaking Legalese 237

Mastering Legal Terms 237
   Bellying up to the bar: General legal terms and your rights 238
   Punishing words about crime 240
   Judging the law: Words related to "judge" 242
   Courting courtroom terms 244
Hailing the Chief: Words about Government 246
   Governmental terms with multiple meanings 247
   Making sense of political terms 247

Chapter 17: Doctoring Your Words: Medical Terms **251**

Talking about Your Body 251
Choosing a Specialist 254
Determining What Ails You 257
Decoding Medical Lingo 258
   Kind and gentle medical terms 258
   Medical terms to come to terms with 259

Chapter 18: Acquiring Shopping and Eating Language **263**

Cashing In with Collectibles 263
   Collecting words, or words for collectors 264
   Cybershopping: Terms for buying and
      selling memorabilia online 265
Dressing for Success: Terms for Clothes 267
   Ordinary words for ordinary clothes 267
   Searching out named clothing 268
Chowing Down: Terms for Food 270
   Beginning at the beginning: Appetizers 270
   Enter the entrees 271
   Diving into dessert 272

Chapter 19: Expanding the Language: Recent Additions **273**

Combining Old Words to Make New Words 274
   Looking at common blended words 274
   Speaking a bit of slanguage 275
New Words Galore: Neologisms 276
   New business words 279
   Compiling new computer terms 281
   E-mailing expressions 284

**Chapter 20: Exploring Words from Real and Mythical People
and Places** **287**

What's in a Name? A Lot When It's an Eponym! 287
   A rose by any other name: Eponyms with
      positive connotations 288
   Name change, anyone? — Eponyms with negative overtones 290
   Good book, good words: Eponyms from the Bible 291
Words from Places: Toponyms 293
   Placing place names 293
   Sparkling toponyms about gems and colors 295
Talking with Words from Animals 296
Words from Myths and Literature 298

Part V: The Part of Tens 301

Chapter 21: Don't Go There: Language to Avoid 303
Ageist Vocabulary 303
Bureaucratic Language 303
Doublespeak 304
Empty Words 304
Inflated Language 304
Euphemisms 305
Language Biased Against the Handicapped 305
Jargon 305
Racist Vocabulary 306
Sexist Language 306

Chapter 22: Distinctions Worth Making 307
Sound-Alike Words 307
Accept and except 307
Conscious and conscience 308
Sit and set 308
What a Difference a Letter (Or Two) Makes 308
Affect and effect 308
Allusion and illusion 309
Beside and besides 309
Describe and prescribe 309
Farther and further 309
Immigrate and emigrate 310
Lose and loose 310
Raise and rise 310
Uninterested and disinterested 310
Words with Similar Meanings 311
Aggravate and annoy 311
Amount and number 311
Authentic and genuine 311
Between and among 312
Healthful and healthy 312
Oral and verbal 312
Precede and proceed 312
Unique and unusual 312
One Word or Two? 313

Chapter 23: Ten Techniques for Nonnative Speakers 315
A or An 315
Degree of Comparison 316
Count Nouns 316

Noncount Nouns 317
Nouns That Can Be Both Count and Noncount 317
Nouns as Adjectives 318
Plurals 318
Proper Nouns 318
The and A 319
Who, Which, That 319

Index *321*

Introduction

· ·

*W*hat's in this book? Words, words, and more words. Word roots, word suffixes, and word prefixes. And you're reading this book because you have an interest in words — how to use them, how to make the most of them, and how to figure out the meaning of new words.

Whether you're facing standardized tests and want to get your vocabulary up to snuff, or you're wanting to improve your language skills to feel more knowledgeable at work or comfortable in social situations, this is the book for you.

About This Book

In the following chapters, I introduce you to a variety of words. The words are organized in a format that helps you make sense of them. Unlike other books that aim to help you improve your vocabulary, this book isn't filled with list after list of words. Oh, I certainly include lots of tables filled with words, but I organize them by common features — the language that they came from or the root that they share, for example — so that you can remember the terms more easily.

I packed the book so full of fun and fascinating words that I'm hoping you hang on every one of them. But in case you're interested in just a few topics, I set up the book so that you can dip into the parts or the chapters that interest you and get all the information you need. And I make it easy for you to find what you want: You can check the table of contents or the index to zero in on the specific topic you want. So, whether you're interested in tips on picking up the meaning of an unfamiliar word from the surrounding text or recent additions to the language, you can find the topic and go there.

Conventions Used in This Book

Because it doesn't help if I introduce you to new words but don't tell you how to say them or how to use them, I give you the pronunciation and the part of speech for the words I put in tables. The part of speech lets you know how to use the word in a sentence: You use a noun as the subject of a sentence; a verb relays what the subject does, or what it has done to it. Adjectives and adverbs — abbreviated as *adj* and *adv,* respectively — describe nouns and verbs, respectively. The words I list fall into one of these four categories. Chapter 7 has a sidebar that gives you the rundown on all eight parts of speech that English uses.

I don't offer you pronunciation guidelines for every vocabulary word in this book. Sometimes it would be insulting your intelligence to tell you how to pronounce a word; other times the pronunciation is provided elsewhere. And, I omitted some pronunciations because I find looking up words fun and fascinating and I want you to experience the joy for yourself. (Check out Chapter 3 for advice on getting the most from dictionaries and other resources.)

Dictionaries use what can seem like a whole new language to tell you how to pronounce words — upside-down *e*'s (called *schwas*), wiggly lines above letters (called *tildes*), and two dots (called an *umlaut*) over other letters can make you feel lost before you get started. Rest assured that I don't use anything except normal letters in the pronunciation guides, which are in parentheses after the word.

I want you to be able to see the pronunciation and say the word. I did my best to be consistent in representing certain sounds — my method is set out in the following tables — but above all, I tried to represent pronunciations as simply and intuitively as I could. Hyphens separate the different sounds of a word, and the sound you stress more than others is *italicized*.

Vowel Sounds		
Sound	*Example*	*Representation*
Short a	rat	ah
Long a	rate	ay
ai	rare	ai
Short e	met	eh
Long e	meet	ee
Short i	din	ih
Long i	dine	y
Short o	look	oo
Long o	go	oh
Short u	us	uh
Long u	use	yu

The representations of short vowel sounds appear when the sound is at the end of a syllable; *a, e, i, o,* and *u* represent themselves in the middle of a syllable.

A few consonant sounds have their own representations, also. They're in the next table.

Consonants

Sound	Representation	Example	Pronunciation
hard c	k	car	kar
soft c and s	s	service	*ser*-vis
s	z	please	pleez
soft g	j	gentle	*jent*-ul
qu	kw	quite	kwyt
tion/sion	shun	tension	*ten*-shun

Notice the slash between *tion* and *sion.* I use a forward slash to separate parts of speech, word elements, and alternative pronunciations; a semicolon separates distinct definitions.

It is a strange but true fact of English (one of many) that how you pronounce a word seems to have little to do with the word's syllables. A *syllable* is simply a part of a word — and though you often pronounce a syllable as one continuous, uninterrupted sound, you don't always do so in the pronunciation guidelines included in this book. This is the long way to say that the divisions in pronunciation guidelines do *not* indicate syllable divisions — you need to consult a dictionary or your spell-check program if you want to know where syllable breaks are.

Special Features

Because I want you to be able to incorporate new words into your existing vocabulary, I put in examples and samples that can help you remember and correctly use new words.

- ✔ The Talkin' the Talk sections are sample, imaginary conversations that usually incorporate words from the tables in the surrounding text, or expand on the new vocabulary by introducing and defining related terms.

- ✔ The Before and After examples point out how you might use new, specific vocabulary in place of old, general terms.

     ✔ Occasionally I give you pointers on how to use new words correctly by giving you examples of Correct and Incorrect usage.

You don't have to make use of these features, but reading through them can help reinforce your newly acquired knowledge.

How This Book Is Organized

I organized 23 chapters into 5 parts. Each part has a theme, which I elaborate on in the following sections. From word basics to word trivia, I cover as much ground as I can, giving you what I believe is the most helpful and useful information.

Part 1: Getting Your Bearings

The chapters in this section serve as a map for your voyage to a better vocabulary. I offer a variety of methods that you can adapt to your own preferences and use to increase and improve your vocabulary. I tell you how to discover meaning — at least of new words you encounter, if not the meaning of life — and I give you pointers on choosing words to suit your audience, situation, and style.

Part 11: Mastering the Basics

If I tell you that the basic building blocks of words are roots, prefixes, and suffixes — the foundation, beginning, and ending of individual words — and that this part has three chapters, you can probably do the math.

Check out the chapters in this part for comprehensive coverage of essential tools that you can use to decipher unfamiliar words in this book and beyond.

Part 111: Expanding Your Base

These chapters take you beyond the basics and give you words that look alike, sound alike, and mean the same thing — or nearly the same thing. Chapter 10 talks about words composed of two or more other words, and Chapters 11 and 12 fill you in on some of the words English adopted from other languages.

Part IV: Getting Savvy with Vocabulary

These chapters help you broaden your knowledge by focusing on specific topics. I give you information on vocabulary in standardized tests, words about money and law, medical terms, and phrases you can use while shopping till you drop. I clue you in on recent additions to the language and how words get added into English. And, if that isn't enough, I also devote a chapter to words that come from the names of real and mythical people and places.

Part V: The Part of Tens

These short and sweet chapters warn you about phrases you shouldn't use, help you distinguish tricky word pairs, and clarify some peculiar English-related problems that may be especially unclear to folks who didn't grow up speaking this rich but often confusing language.

Icons Used in This Book

The little round things in the margins highlight information I think you may find useful or interesting (or both!) on your journey to a better vocabulary.

You may well know some or all of these nifty tidbits, but you can probably impress cocktail-party companions with the facts presented in paragraphs next to this curious fellow.

This icon sits next to text that relates the history of a word or words. The text is sometimes detailed enough to qualify as *etymology* — details of a word's origin.

General concepts to keep in mind, either in your language life or in a particular chapter, are highlighted with this classic reminder symbol.

This little bull's-eye zeroes in on especially practical bits of information that you can use to improve your vocabulary.

Advice on how to avoid linguistic pitfalls is marked with this alarming symbol.

This scholarly little owl points out definitions.

Where to Go from Here

You can jump into this book at any chapter because it's composed of self-contained units, and I put in plenty of cross-references to other chapters and sections with related information. Having said that, I recommend Chapters 5, 6, and 7 in Part II, which examine the building blocks of words — roots, prefixes, and suffixes. You can't go wrong if you start with the fundamentals.

Beyond Part II, check out Chapter 2 for methods that can help you remember and correctly use new words, and Chapter 3 for techniques you can adopt with any reading material to increase your understanding of what you read.

So, jump in where you like — the words are fine!

Part I
Getting Your Bearings

The 5th Wave   By Rich Tennant

"I'm not sure if I'm stressing the right syllable in the wrong word, or stressing the wrong syllable in the right word, but it's starting to stress me out."

In this part . . .

Navigating through a sea of new and unfamiliar words can be intimidating. But not to fear, the chapters here set you on the right path.

This is the practical part, where you pick up the tools you need to get the job done. In these chapters, I give you information on words in general and words as they relate specifically to you. I tell you where to find new words, how to figure out what they mean, how to say them, how to use them, and how to remember them.

So, grab your tools and dig in!

Chapter 1

Figuring Out How Words Work

In This Chapter

▶ Understanding what a good vocabulary is and how it benefits you

▶ A quick look at the structure of English words

▶ Ways to build your vocabulary painlessly

A h, vocabulary. The definitions. The functions. The alternative spellings. The memories of Friday afternoon vocabulary tests or of clandestinely looking up dirty words when you were supposed to be studying the list your teacher gave you. When you get right down to it, who *isn't* completely fascinated by the meaning, history, and current and past usage of words?

In two words: probably you. But there are two secrets that few English teachers let you in on:

- ✔ **Having a good vocabulary doesn't mean you have to have a stilted vocabulary.** It simply means you can communicate well with the group you're in.

- ✔ **Building a good vocabulary is actually fairly easy.** Forget the lists of words you got in school and the mind-numbing task of copying definitions. To build your vocabulary, you simply have to broaden your horizons and apply a few tricks.

Honest. This chapter gives you the basics.

Getting an Idea of a Good Vocabulary

During any typical day, you may be with your neighbors talking about things being *good,* with your colleagues talking about things being *exemplary,* and with your buddies talking about things being *cool.* If you use these words in the right way and at the right time, you show that you have a good command of vocabulary — you speak confidently and competently to the people you're with.

REMEMBER

That's all a good vocabulary is. It isn't about using big words, foreign words, or obscure words. It's about using words to convey your meaning in the way you want. The trick is knowing what words are appropriate in a situation. The following list provides the general levels of English vocabulary (head to Chapter 4 for more info) along with situations in which the levels may be used:

✔ **Formal vocabulary:** Formal vocabulary (or *formal diction*) has a very serious tone and uses specialized or elevated terms. You hear this type of vocabulary in ceremonial addresses like speeches (especially in days of yore), eulogies, and so on. You see it in such things as legal documents. You probably rarely, if ever, need to use formal English.

✔ **Standard English:** Standard English is the type of vocabulary used in most businesses and schools; it conforms to the English grammar and usage rules. You use this type of vocabulary when you're interviewing for a job, speaking with co-workers or customers, giving a presentation, or meeting your future in-laws for the first time. This is also the vocabulary you use when you write a paper or a report.

✔ **Everyday English:** You use this kind of English when you're talking informally to co-workers or gabbing with friends. It's conversational and often uses slang.

Talkin' the Talk

Adam and Alex run into each other in the break room and chat about their work. When their boss comes in, Adam demonstrates his ability to tailor his vocabulary to his audience and to the situation.

Adam:	Hey, how's it goin'?
Alex:	Fine. Pluggin' along on my presentation. How 'bout you?
Adam:	Rotten. I gotta 3 p.m. deadline, and the project's blowing up in my face. Max isn't pullin' his weight, and Delores doesn't know what the heck she's doing.
Sarah (Adam and Alex's boss):	Hi, Adam, Alex.
Adam and Alex:	Hello.
Sarah (to Adam):	I wanted to talk about your project update. Do you have a few minutes?

Alex (to Sarah):	I was just heading back to my desk. [to Adam] Later.
Sarah:	I get the impression that you're having a few problems.
Adam:	This project *has* presented some challenges.
Sarah:	Such as?
Adam:	My biggest dilemma has been finding ways to motivate individual team members. As it is, the bulk of the work is falling predominantly on a few. Another concern I have is providing the direction the team needs to be successful.

Reaping Vocabulary's Rewards

Believe it or not (and you must believe it, or you wouldn't have bought this book), having a good vocabulary is truly a good thing. It can help you move ahead, stay abreast, and fit right in:

- **Education:** The fact of the matter is that having a strong speaking and writing vocabulary can make it easier for you to do well in school. A broad vocabulary makes not only regular study easier, but it can also help you during the many standardized tests you're likely to face. Even if you manage to avoid taking standardized tests in school, more and more businesses require personality tests, competency tests, and so on in the work force. (Chapter 13 clues you in about standardized tests and vocabulary.)

- **Communication:** Having a good vocabulary strengthens your communication skills. Not only does a solid vocabulary increase the number of words you use and understand (always a plus), but it also makes you more adept at modifying your language to suit the situation.

- **Social situations:** Ever notice how many fish-out-of-water movies Hollywood makes (you know the kind, where the guy/girl finds him/her-self out of place)? Ever notice how the character reveals his or her lack of social graces in his or her dress and speech? Knowing what type of speech is appropriate in different social situations and having the vocabulary you need to speak confidently wherever you are can make you a more assured, comfortable speaker.

Trying to Make Sense of the English Language

For many reasons (most of them too ugly to go into here), English is a pretty tough language to learn. If you're a native speaker of English, you're probably familiar with the idiosyncrasies that make the language so downright mind-boggling. If you're a nonnative speaker, you may lack the familiarity that native speakers have. Either way, the following sections offer a very basic explanation for why English words are the way they are. Understanding how English words are formed and where they come from can help when you come up against unfamiliar words.

Borrowing words from other countries

One of the things that makes the English language so rich (and sometimes so overwhelming) is that English words come from — or are influenced by — lots of different languages.

The English language is essentially a Germanic language. (Other Germanic languages are German, Dutch, Flemish, and the Scandinavian languages.) English has a lot of words that reach back to its German roots: *ox, cow, meadow, grass, pig, king, knife, knight,* and *skirmish* are just a few. But, being the accommodating language that it is, English absorbed and adopted words (and parts of words) from lots of other languages, too, like Latin, Greek, French, and Spanish.

Tree, for example, comes from Old German. In English, the word *tree* means, well, "tree." We also use the word *arbor,* which is the Latin word for *tree,* to mean "tree." Arbor Day is a day for planting trees. So, in English, if you know what *tree* means, and you know that *arbor* is another word for tree, you know that anytime you see *arbor* in a word, that word has something to do with trees. What it has to do with trees depends on what prefixes and suffixes the word uses (the topic of the next section).

English has adopted numerous words from other languages. (*Garage,* for example, is actually a French word; *piano* is an Italian word.) And if English didn't adopt the whole word, as is the case with many Greek and Latin words, it probably took parts of it. *Hexagon* uses two Greek elements: *hexa* meaning "six," and *gon* meaning "angles." *Triumvirate* uses Latin elements: *trium* meaning "three," *vir* meaning "man," and *-ate,* a suffix meaning "acted upon in a specific way." A *hexagon* is a six-sided object; a *triumvirate* is a group of three people who are in power in some context. Chapters 11 and 12 offer many more examples of foreign-born English words.

Breaking out word elements: Prefixes, roots, and suffixes

A strong understanding of common prefixes, roots, and suffixes can go a long way toward improving your vocabulary. The root is a word's foundation. Prefixes and suffixes are elements that are attached to the root to shape the word's meaning. For example, one of the most common prefixes is *un-,* which means "not or against." Stick that prefix in front of almost any word, and you have that word's opposite:

patriotic → unpatriotic (not patriotic)

predictable → unpredictable (not able to be predicted)

reliable → unreliable (not reliable)

Suffixes come at the end of the word and usually indicate what part of speech the word is. (Knowing the part of speech is important, not only for defining a word but also for using it correctly.) Using the earlier example of the Latin root *arbor* (meaning "tree"), you can assemble a lot of different words simply by attaching different suffixes:

✔ *Arboreous* uses the suffix *-ous,* which means "full of." So that word means — you guessed it — "full of trees." The *-ous* suffix makes adjectives (adjectives modify people, places, or things):

Correct: The terrain was dark and arboreous.

Incorrect: If a tree falls in the arboreous and no one is around to hear, does it still make a noise?

✔ *Arboreal* means "of or relating to trees." The suffix *-al* means "of or relating to" and turns words into adjectives:

Correct: Arboreal animals live in trees.

Incorrect: The animal lives in an arboreal.

✔ An *arborist* is one who works with and cares for trees. The suffix *-ist* means "one who does." As such, *-ist* makes the word a noun.

Correct: We had to call in an arborist to help us transplant the trees in the back yard.

Incorrect: The arborist book shows all kinds of trees.

Both prefixes and suffixes modify the root. By knowing what each element means, you can get a general idea of the word's definition, which is often all you need to make sense of what's being said or read. The chapters in Part II are devoted to roots, prefixes, and suffixes.

Assembling blended words

In addition to taking words wholesale from other languages and combining roots with prefixes and suffixes to make words, English also creates words by sticking two complete words together. By knowing what each word means by itself, you can get a general idea of what the combined (or *compound*) word means. Check out these examples:

backbone = spine

freshman = first-year student

eggshell = exterior of an egg

cost-effective = economical

bedspread = comforter

Sometimes, when the words come together, a few letters get squeezed out. These types of words are called *portmanteau words:*

agriculture + business = agribusiness (business related to farming)

basket + cart = bascart (shopping cart)

cafeteria + auditorium = cafetorium (area used as both a cafeteria and an auditorium)

tangerine + lemon = tangemon (hybrid fruit of a tangerine and a lemon)

You may not use any of these hybrid words every day, but seeing how they're composed can help you decipher other portmanteau words you come across.

Figuring out English oddities, peculiarities, and quirks

Here's the rub — and it's a particularly abrasive one for people who are learning English as a second language: Sometimes, there's no way, other than context, to tell what an English word means. Why? Because English is full of oddities.

The result of such a rich linguistic heritage — English words, German words, French words, Spanish words, Greek and Latin words, word parts from everywhere, combined words, blended words, and so on — is that the English language has few rules you can rely on all the time:

✔ Many words spelled similarly don't sound alike. *Bomb, comb,* and *womb* don't rhyme with each other: You say "bom," "kohm," and "woom." Sometimes, words spelled exactly the same are pronounced differently: *tear* (teer), "a teardrop," and *tear* (tehr), "to rip," for example.

✔ Many words spelled differently *do* sound alike: *Write, right,* and *rite* are all pronounced the same but mean different things. These types of words are called *homophones.*

✔ One word can have various meanings: *Pool* (the place to swim), *pool* (the billiards game), *pool* (to put together) — and that's not even all of the definitions of pool. These types of words are called *homonyms,* and English is absolutely full of them.

These types of odd words plague all English speakers, native and otherwise. When you come up against them, the best you can do is use the context of what is being said or written, or, if you still aren't sure, head to a dictionary. For more examples of homonyms and homophones and strategies for keeping them straight, head to Chapter 9.

Improving Your Vocabulary the Easy Way

One of the best — and most enjoyable — ways to improve your vocabulary is to read. Read as much as you can from as many different sources as you can find: books (popular, classic, fiction, nonfiction), cereal boxes, magazine articles, the conversation in an online chat room, newspaper stories — you choose.

Another fun way to increase your vocabulary is to simply try new things. Take an art class and learn words like the noun *serendipity* (ser-un-*dip*-uh-tee), which means "happy accident." Go to an opera or an art film, or help out at your local theater. Join a cooking club or a book club. Take up bird watching, woodworking, or any other activity that sparks your interest. Broaden your horizons, and your vocabulary will grow as a consequence.

Of course, there are plenty of other tips and techniques that you can use to build your vocabulary (and none of them require reading a dictionary). You can keep a journal of the unfamiliar words that you hear or see; you can play all sorts of word games, like Scrabble and Boggle; you can work daily or Sunday crossword puzzles in your local newspaper; and more (Chapter 2 gives you the complete scoop).

The important thing to know is that building your vocabulary can be a lot easier and a lot more fun that you may have thought.

Chapter 2

Building Your Vocabulary

In This Chapter

▶ Playing word games

▶ Discovering word resources

▶ Gearing your vocabulary for tests

▶ Speaking well — pronunciation tips

Do you want to know the best way to increase your vocabulary? Read. Read anything and everything you can get your hands on. Read books and magazines. Read instruction manuals. Read the newspaper. Read billboards and cereal boxes (including the ingredients list). Read. Read. Read. Before you realize it, you'll know a lot more words than you did before.

Don't like to read? Then go out and do something you've never done. Travel to a place you've never been. Start a hobby. Take up music, or gourmet cooking, or art, or model aviation, or golf, or gardening, or whatever. Try things you've always wanted to experience, and expand your horizons. As your horizons expand, so will your vocabulary.

Don't have time (or the inclination) to travel, start a hobby, or experience new things? All is not lost. In this chapter, I introduce some effective and fun ways to pump up your vocabulary in just a few minutes a day.

Playing to Improve Your Vocabulary

Believe it or not, building your vocabulary doesn't have to be work (despite what many English teachers may think). It can actually be fun.

Carding yourself

Repetition is one of the most effective ways to make a word your own. Going over the word can help you master its meaning, as well as its pronunciation and usage. Try this idea:

1. **Buy a stack of 3 x 5 index cards.**

2. **As you hear or see new words, write them on the front of an index card (one word per card).**

3. **Write the definition and pronunciation of the word on the back. Be sure to note the part (or parts) of speech so that you use the word correctly.**

   You may want to add a sample sentence or two to help you. Figure 2-1 shows the front and back of a sample card.

4. **Study this card every chance you get.**

Front of card:

caprice

Back of card:

Figure 2-1:
A sample
vocabulary
flash card.

(kah-prees) n.
sudden, unpredictable
change of mind; a whim

Use these tips to get the most out of your vocabulary flash cards:

✔ Format the cards however is most helpful for you. If you find that having the pronunciation or the part of speech on the front of the card helps you remember words better, then by all means put that info on the front.

✔ Take them with you on the bus, train, and plane; hide them in your lap and sneak a peek during dull dates, meetings, and meals.

✔ Shuffle the cards so that you expose yourself to a variety of words.

Don't take a card out of the stack as soon as you learn the word. Leave it in for a while to provide a little positive reinforcement.

Playing those mind games: Mnemonics

Mnemonics are memory tricks you can use to help recall things that you have a hard time remembering or are likely to forget. The mnemonic for the Great

Lakes, for example, is *HOMES* (Huron, Ontario, Michigan, Erie, and Superior). *Roy G. Biv* is the mnemonic for the colors of the rainbow (red, orange, yellow, green, blue, indigo, and violet). A common mnemonic used to help folks spell *ie* and *ei* words is "*i* before *e* except after *c,* or when sounded like *a,* as in *neighbor* and *weigh.*"

You can use the same techniques to remember vocabulary words and to distinguish between confusing words. Consider the following examples:

- ✔ To remember that *stationary* means "standing still," stress the *a,* because both words *(stationary* and *standing)* contain an *a.* To remember that *stationery* refers to "writing materials," think *stationery* is for *letters,* because both words contain *er.*

- ✔ *Desert* and *dessert* become easier to define and use when you remember that *dessert* has a double *s,* like *strawberry shortcake.*

Create your own mnemonics to help you remember new words, as well as the easily confused words that you use every day.

Wrestling with word games

Another way to increase your vocabulary is to play word games. Although all word games expose you to words, some are better than others. Here are some of the ones that you may find most helpful in building your vocabulary:

- ✔ **Scrabble:** Scrabble is a crossword game in which you build words on a game board using lettered tiles that you select blindly. For every word you create, you score a certain number of points. Points are based on the word's length, placement, and letters. Because so few words use the letter *X,* for example, you get more points for using the X tile than for using the E tile.

  Scrabble is a great way to both test and build your vocabulary, because if anyone challenges you over a word you've created, it helps if you can define it. The word also has to appear in the dictionary. (*Xebec,* by the way, is a real word. It's a Mediterranean sailing ship — just in case you get stuck with a couple *E*'s and an *X.*)

- ✔ **Upwords:** Similar to Scrabble, Upwords adds another dimension — the letter tiles stack on top of each other so that you can build up, as well as out.

- ✔ **Boggle:** In Boggle, you form as many words as you can by linking adjacent letters. This game improves your vocabulary, because in order to make the most words, you need to think beyond the easy three- and four-letter words. The more you play, the more adept you become at creating words from nothing more than a jumble of seemingly unconnected letters.

✔ **Crossword puzzles:** Crossword puzzles help build vocabulary by exposing you to new and unusual words. The hints serve as definitions; by simply playing the game, you can find out whether you selected the right word. If you do crosswords enough, you may discover, for example, that an *epee* is a "small sword used in fencing," and a *Sten* is a submachine gun.

You can also find several vocabulary-building games and resources on the Internet. Just go to your favorite search engine and enter "Vocabulary." Here are just a few of the sites I found that offer free word games:

✔ **Word Safari:**
`http://home.earthlink.net/~ruthpett/safari/index.htm` — Guess the meaning of a word. When you get it right, you get a list of links to various places on the Web that use the word.

The Word Games and Amusements page of this site (`http://home.earthlink.net/~ruthpett/safari/megalist2.htm#Jump9`) offers links to a plethora of free word games.

✔ **Merriam-Webster's Word Game of the Day:** `www.m-w.com/mw/game/` — This site features a different word game every day. It also includes a two-month archive of past word games. The games are great vocabulary builders.

✔ **Crossword of the Day:** `www.quizland.com/cotd.htm` — This site offers a different crossword puzzle each day.

Reading Up on Words

When asked why he robbed banks, the famous bank robber Willie Sutton replied, "Because that's where the money is." When people ask why you're using a dictionary to improve your vocabulary, you can answer, "Because that's where the words are." You can say the same thing about thesauruses.

In fact, if you're serious about improving your vocabulary, you should have a good dictionary and thesaurus handy.

Diving into dictionaries

A dictionary improves your vocabulary by providing definitions, word histories, and parts of speech. It's the best source for learning new words. It's also the most effective way to find out how to pronounce new words, which is an important part of improving your vocabulary. (Head to the section "Pronouncing Words Correctly" to find out why.)

Speeding through Scrabble

"Speed Scrabble" is an alternative way to play Scrabble. You play without the board — all you need are the letter tiles and a playing surface and maybe a clock with a second hand for marking the final minute of the game.

This game can move pretty quickly because every player makes his or her own mini Scrabble grid of adjoining words at the same time. So, unlike traditional Scrabble, there's no waiting for Uncle Doug to cogitate forever before putting his word in the only space you can use — Uncle Doug makes his own word grid, and you do the same. To play, follow these steps:

1. Turn all the letter tiles face down in the middle of the playing table.

2. Each player chooses seven tiles. When all players have their tiles, one player says "Go," and everyone turns over their tiles.

3. Each player tries to assemble his or her tiles into connected words, as in a crossword puzzle. For example, the letters *e, e, i, n, r, t,* and *x* can form *exert* and *tin,* using the *t* in *exert* as the first letter in *tin.*

4. The first player to use all of her tiles to form connected words says "take two" (or "take three" if there are only two players), and every player must take two more tiles from the supply in the middle of the table, so that everyone is working with nine tiles.

5. The person who first makes a grid of connected words using her nine tiles says "take two," and every player takes two more tiles. (The player who says "take two" may change with every round — any player can say "take two," as long as all of her tiles are used in her grid.)

6. Play follows this pattern and continues until all the tiles are gone. (Because there are 100 Scrabble tiles, one tile is left over when there are three players.)

7. The first player to assemble a grid using all of her tiles says "One minute," giving the other players 60 seconds to finish their own grids.

You can rearrange your grid at any time, making completely different words every time you take more letters. However, leftover letters — those not incorporated into your mini crossword puzzle at the end of the game — count against you. You must subtract the value of each leftover letter from your total score.

Scoring favors long words: You add up the letter values of their tiles — letters used in both across words and down words are counted twice. You then add 10 points for every tile in a word after the fourth tile. For example, the word *long* scores 5 points — 1 for the *l,* 1 for the *o,* 1 for the *n,* and 2 for the *g.* It's only four letters long, so only the values on the tiles count. The score for the word *longest* is 5+33: the tile values add up to 8 — the values for *l, o, n,* and *g,* and one point each for *e, s, t* — plus 10 points each for the fifth, sixth, and seventh letters.

Count the tile values of across words and down words and jot that score down. Go back and count all the 10-point letters and then add their total to the score you just wrote down.

Knowing your prefixes and suffixes can help you build points: adding *mis-* to *align* gives you 30 more points in addition to the value of *m, i,* and *s.* Adding suffixes such as *-ing* or *-tion* can help you make longer words and build up points.

The tricky part is finding a dictionary that's right for you. Which dictionary should you purchase and use? Because more than 30,000 dictionaries are currently offered for sale online, you have some shopping to do. Here's what you need:

- All the words you're likely to encounter in your personal and professional life.

- Explanations phrased in terms that you can understand.

- A size that fits your needs. You may want to buy a hard-bound dictionary for home and a smaller paperback dictionary for work.

An *unabridged* dictionary contains all the words in the English language. It comes in many volumes, like a set of encyclopedias, or in one really large, really weighty tome. An *abridged* dictionary contains only the most common words that people use every day.

Because all dictionaries are chock-full of words listed in alphabetical order, many people mistakenly think that they are all the same. They're *not*. Different types of dictionaries fit different needs. Dictionaries have been created just for adults, college students, high school students, and elementary school students. The following list includes the best-selling general dictionaries and the Web addresses of the online versions, when available:

- *The American Heritage Dictionary of the English Language* (Houghton Mifflin Co.) — www.bartleby.com/61/

- *Merriam-Webster's Collegiate Dictionary* (Merriam-Webster, Inc.) — www.m-w.com/dictionary.htm

- *Merriam-Webster's Pocket Dictionary* (Merriam-Webster, Inc.)

- *The New Shorter Oxford English Dictionary* (Oxford University Press, Inc.)

- *The Random House Webster's College Dictionary* (Random House, Inc.)

- *Webster's 3rd New International Dictionary* (Merriam-Webster, Inc.)

- *Webster's New World College Dictionary* (Hungry Minds, Inc.)

Using a print dictionary

A good dictionary entry includes spelling, pronunciation, part of speech, irregular forms of the word, the word's meaning, and etymology (the history of the word and where it came from). An entry may also contain synonyms and antonyms; prefixes, suffixes, and other elements of word formation; and abbreviations. Figure 2-2 shows you a standard dictionary entry, which I tried to make as sweet as possible by using the word "candy."

That's one big book

The most famous scholarly dictionary is *The Oxford English Dictionary*. An unabridged dictionary, the *OED* (as it's abbreviated) contains more than 500,000 entries. Don't rush right out to buy one to stash in your bookcase, however, because the OED now contains about 60 million words in 20 volumes. However, If shelf space is an issue, and you simply can't live without an OED, online and CD-ROM versions are available. Go to www.oed.com to find out more. (Be prepared to fork over a bit of money, though. The subscription fee to access the online dictionary costs $550 a year, buying the CD-ROM version costs nearly $300, and the 20-volume print set costs about $600.)

plural

part of speech

spelling, pronunciation

etymology (word history)

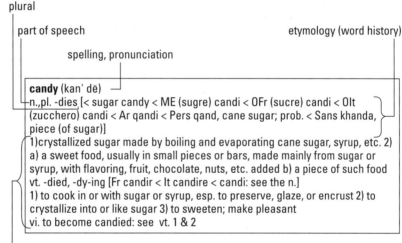

Figure 2-2:
The
*Webster's
New World
College
Dictionary*
entry for
candy.

candy (kan' dē)
n.,pl. -dies [< sugar candy < ME (sugre) candi < OFr (sucre) candi < OIt (zucchero) candi < Ar qandi < Pers qand, cane sugar; prob. < Sans khanda, piece (of sugar)]
1)crystallized sugar made by boiling and evaporating cane sugar, syrup, etc. 2) a) a sweet food, usually in small pieces or bars, made mainly from sugar or syrup, with flavoring, fruit, chocolate, nuts, etc. added b) a piece of such food
vt. -died, -dy-ing [Fr candir < It candire < candi: see the n.]
1) to cook in or with sugar or syrup, esp. to preserve, glaze, or encrust 2) to crystallize into or like sugar 3) to sweeten; make pleasant
vi. to become candied: see vt. 1 & 2

definitions

The following explains the entry in more detail:

✔ Immediately following the entry word is the pronunciation.

✔ The *n* on the second line lets you know that the word is a noun. Later, the *vt* and *vi* indicate that the word can also be a *transitive verb* (a verb that needs to be followed by an object) and an *intransitive verb* (a verb that does not require an object to complete its meaning).

✔ The *pl.* indicates how to make the word plural. In this case, you make candy plural by removing the *-y* and adding *-ies* (candies).

✔ The information in brackets is the word's etymology, or history.

According to this history, the modern English word *candy* came from the Middle English (ME) word *(sugre) candi,* which came from the Old

French (OFr) word *(sucre) candi,* which came from the Old Italian (OIt) word *(zucchero) candi,* which itself is made up of the Italian word *zucchero* and the Arabic (Ar) word *qandi* and the Persian word *qand,* which in turn probably came from the Sanskrit (Sans) word *khanda,* which means piece of sugar. And you thought candy was just a sweet treat.

✔ Following the etymology are the definitions. Candy has multiple definitions, grouped by the part of speech. The first group of definitions is for the noun (n) candy. The second and third groups of definitions are for the verbs — vt (verb transitive) and vi (verb intransitive) candy.

When you try to find a word in the dictionary, always begin by making an educated guess as to its spelling. The odds are in your favor. However, the more spelling patterns you know for a sound, the better your chances are for finding the word quickly. After you've narrowed down your search, use the *guide words,* located on the upper-corners of the pages, to guide your search as you flip through the pages. Then, follow strict alphabetical order.

Using an electronic dictionary

Nowadays, several print dictionaries come with CD-ROMs that contain the complete dictionary text. The benefit of a CD-ROM is that it makes searching for words much easier than flipping through pages. Simply type the word you want to find in the Search text box provided by the program and, without risking so much as a paper cut, you will be presented with the definition and all the other relevant information (see the preceding section).

Many dictionary CD-ROMs also enable you to perform complicated searches. If you don't know the word you want, for example, you can enter words that are likely to be found in the definition. If you want to find several words that use the same root, you can enter the appropriate search criteria to find those entries, as well.

You can also use online dictionaries (that is, dictionaries that you access from the Internet). You can find several dictionaries in several languages at www.yourdictionary.com, for example. You can also access specific online dictionaries through their publishers or presses. Although these sites don't generally give you free access to the complete dictionary, many do let you search for particular words. If you don't have a dictionary handy while you're online, these can be helpful.

An electronic dictionary can't fulfill all your needs, unless you like to tote around your laptop computer and fire it up all the time. Always have a print dictionary to use — even if you already have an online version.

Thumbing through a thesaurus

A *thesaurus* is a reference book that contains synonyms and antonyms — words that mean the same thing and words that mean the opposite. (Chapter 8 is devoted to these "-nyms.") The word *thesaurus* comes from a Greek word that means "collection" or "treasure."

A thesaurus is especially helpful when you have a word but know that it isn't quite right. You can look that word up and find the perfect word. A thesaurus is also a helpful reference when you're trying to find a better word than the one you're stuck on — or just a different one. A thesaurus helps you state exact shades of meaning rather than approximations. A thesaurus can help your vocabulary increase by leaps and bounds.

Using a print thesaurus

In a thesaurus, words with similar meanings are grouped together. If you have a really old print thesaurus, you may have to use the index at the back of the book to find specific words. But most newer editions, including online thesauruses, arrange words in alphabetical order like a dictionary.

Suppose you're writing a letter to your Aunt Agnes, and you've used the word *excitement* several times. (It was a *very* good first date.) To make your writing more interesting, you may want to use a word whose meaning is similar to *excitement*. If you look up the word *excitement* in *Webster's New World Dictionary and Thesaurus* (Hungry Minds, Inc.), you see the entry in Figure 2-3.

Figure 2-3:
A thesaurus entry for "excitement."

> **excitement [n.]**
>
> —Syn. agitation, confusion, disturbance, tumult, enthusiasm, eagerness, ferment, trepidation, turmoil, stir, excitation, animation, hurry, perturbation, excitedness, delirium, furor, rage, exhilaration, emotion, stimulation, arousal, drama, melodrama, thrill, activity, commotion, ado, fuss, hullabaloo, bother, dither, hubbub, fluster, flutter, flurry, bustle, to-do, tizzy*; see also thrill.
>
> —Ant. peace, calm, quiet.
>
> **See anger, bang, blast, desire, feeling, heat, hilarity, hysteria, interest, kick, sensation, shock**

The parts of a thesaurus entry are similar to, and yet different from, a dictionary entry:

- ✔ The *n* in brackets lets you know that the word is a noun.
- ✔ The entry right after the part of speech brackets is the word (or words) closest in meaning to the listed word.
- ✔ The asterisk (*) indicates that a word is colloquial or slang.
- ✔ *See also* gives you another closely related word to try if you don't find what you're looking for in the current list.
- ✔ *Ant.* stands for "antonym." It is followed by a list of words that mean the opposite of the listed word.

> ✔ The list of words in boldface type after *See* gives you other words and concepts to look up.
>
> Some thesauruses have a concepts feature that points you to a broad list of words related to a specific concept.

Surfing electronic thesauruses

You can find all sorts of electronic versions of thesauruses. Like dictionaries, many print thesauruses come with CD-ROMs that contain the complete text and helpful search capabilities. In addition, many word processing programs have a thesaurus built right in. Finally, you can access thesauruses on the Internet. One such service is Thesaurus.com (www.thesaurus.com), which gives you free access to Roget's online thesaurus.

In these electronic thesauruses, much of the information is the same, but it's in a different format, which you can use to easily look up a related word. If you're using a thesaurus linked with your word processor, you can replace a word with a click of the mouse or get additional help.

Some advantages and disadvantages of online thesauruses:

> ✔ Although both a print thesaurus and an online thesaurus will help you beef up your vocabulary, in general, a print thesaurus gives you more options than an online thesaurus. That's because the print versions have more words in them. Therefore, you'll need a print thesaurus even if you already have an online version. Use a print thesaurus when you need a wider variety of choices.
>
> ✔ Online thesauruses are especially useful for distinguishing among homonyms (words that are spelled alike and sound alike but have different meanings). If you're looking for a synonym for *pool* (as in body of water), for example, your online thesaurus will list *pond* (noun), *billiards* (noun), and *combine* (verb). This will help you keep your homonyms straight.
>
> ✔ Online thesauruses can also help you with homophones (words that sound alike but are spelled differently and have different meanings). For example, if you intended to type "weather" but instead entered "whether," the thesaurus will give you synonyms like *atmospheric conditions, climate, meteorology,* and *the elements.*
>
> ✔ Synonyms and antonyms rarely mean exactly the same as the word you're looking up, and thesauruses don't define the words they offer. To avoid misusing a word, check your dictionary to look up any word you find in the thesaurus unless you're sure of its meaning.

Sifting through word history: Etymology

It is easier to remember a word when you know its word history, or *etymology.* Many dictionaries include brief etymologies of words. Refer to the *candy* example (Figure 2-2) in the earlier section, "Using a print dictionary," for an example of an etymology you're likely to find in any dictionary.

There are also books dedicated solely to etymologies. The purpose of these books, which are organized like dictionaries, is to tell the history of words, including what language(s) they came from and the earliest date they appeared in writing (as best the editors can ascertain). Consider these examples:

✔ The English word *caramel,* first recorded in 1725, is actually a French word that means "burnt sugar." If you think about it, burnt sugar is a fitting description of caramel: golden brown, very sweet, and chewy.

✔ The word *disaster,* which first appeared in 1591, comes from the Middle French word *desastre,* which comes from the Italian word *disastro,* which is made up of the prefix *dis-* (without; reverse) and the root *astro* (star). This history, along with the literal translation of the word (without star), makes sense if you consider that catastrophes were once thought to be the result of stars and planets being in unfavorable positions.

Exploring the history of words can help you understand and remember many useful everyday words. But, unless you're a scholar whose life is words and word histories, you certainly don't *need* to remember a word's background to be able to define it. In some instances, however, knowing this background information can help you form an association around the word. Such an association might help you remember a definition that eludes you.

Boosting Your Vocabulary for Standardized Tests

During the years of your formal education, you face numerous standardized tests — at least in the U.S. school system. The suggestions I give you in this chapter, and in Chapter 3, can help you get your skills up to speed for the reading and language sections of these tests. I highlight a couple of variations and specialized tips in this section.

A recommendation you can use anytime, but especially when you're preparing for a test, is to keep a journal of words you think you know and new words you encounter. Boost your vocabulary by looking up each word in the dictionary and then writing each definition in the journal. The simple act of writing down the words and definitions helps fix them in your mind. (You can also use word cards, as the "Carding yourself" section, earlier in this chapter, explains.)

Practice is the best way to boost your critical reading comprehension skills — so read every minute you can. Carry a magazine, paperback book, or electronic reading device with you and make good use of the time you spend waiting in line at the bus stop, sitting in the dentist's office, or tapping your toes waiting for a late appointment. You can use all of these "lost minutes" to read. Fifteen minutes here, ten minutes there — by the end of the day, you may find that you have spent an hour sharpening your reading and vocabulary skills!

Arranging words in your mind

When you study words in this book, as well as in other sources, get in the habit of mentally arranging them into the following three categories:

- ✔ **Words you know:** You use and can define these words.
- ✔ **Words you're familiar with:** You generally use these words correctly without knowing exactly what they mean.
- ✔ **Words you don't know:** You may have seen these words once or twice, or you may be encountering them for the first time.

Pay attention to the last two categories of words as you prepare for a test. When you come across a word you're familiar with but not totally confident about or a word you haven't seen before, look it up and add it to a word journal or make a word card for it. After you become more comfortable with the word, you can move it into the "known words" category.

To make the most of your dictionary time, look up words in a dictionary that includes etymology — a detailed word history. The etymology points to the word origin, root, and any prefixes, which is knowledge you can tuck away to use when you come across another unfamiliar word built on the same word element. Some dictionaries also provide synonyms, antonyms, or both. Be sure to check those out — you often need to know synonyms on a test.

Toadying up to toadeaters

In the 1600s, people believed that toads were poisonous, and that anyone who mistakenly ate a toad's leg instead of a frog's leg would die. Rather than swear off frog's legs, people sought a cure for the "fatal" food poisoning.

Quack healers would take advantage of this search and hire an accomplice who would pretend to eat a toad. The pseudo-healer would then whip out an instant remedy and "save" his helper's life. These assistants came to be called "toadeaters." Because anyone who would consume anything as disgusting as a toad must be completely under his master's thumb, "toad-eater" or "toady" became the term for a bootlicking, fawning flatterer. And that's how the term *toady* came to be.

Skimming your way to comprehension

Skimming is a method of reading that lets you glance at a passage to get its main idea or find a key point quickly. When you're up against time limits (like you are during a test), getting information quickly is a definite advantage. Skimming boosts comprehension because it helps you focus on the important parts of the text. When you go back and read the text in detail, you can zero in on the parts you need. You won't waste time on irrelevant information.

When you skim a reading passage, first look at the title, subheadings, and any graphic elements, such as charts or graphs. Run your eyes across the page, trying to read as fast as you can. Look for the facts you need, which are often in the first and last sentences of a paragraph. Read these facts slowly. Take a moment to restate the meaning in your own words — and in your own head.

Pronouncing Words Correctly

Knowing the meaning of a word is only half the battle; you also have to know how to pronounce it. It's astonishing how many words are misunderstood and misused simply because they're mispronounced.

If you're like the average person, your "reading vocabulary" is much larger than your "spoken vocabulary." You pick up words as you read, but you may not have heard the words spoken. And, if you don't know how to say a word, you probably won't use it in conversation.

Spelling and pronunciation are easier in languages where each letter or combination of letters is always pronounced the same way. Unfortunately, English isn't one of those languages. In English, each letter and combination can be pronounced several different ways. For example, *a* is pronounced one way in *rat*, another in *rate*, and still another in *ahead*. In an example that teachers love to use to stump their students, *fish* can be spelled phonetically as "ghoti" ("gh" as in *enough,* "o" as in *women,* and "ti" as in *nation*). It's no wonder that people complain about the difficulty of learning the English language.

Check out the Introduction to this book for the pronunciation guidelines I use in this book.

Seeing and saying: Pronunciation rules

It's hard to figure out how to say some words correctly, but incorrect pronunciations can make defining the word more difficult. The pronunciation problem is especially acute with words that function as more than one part of speech. The word *ally* is a case in point. As a noun, it's pronounced "*al*-eye" (supporter in a cause). As a verb, it's pronounced "ah-*lye*" (to unite in a cause).

Here are a few pronunciation rules that may help when you encounter new or unfamiliar words. Keep in mind, though, that English is rarely this simple. Every rule that follows has a number of exceptions.

- ✔ If two vowels are together, the first vowel is sounded and the second is silent. Example: *Beat* is pronounced "beet."

- ✔ An *e* on the end of a one-syllable word makes the first vowel long, if there's only one consonant after that vowel. Example: *Mat* is pronounced "mat;" *mate* is pronounced "mayt."

- ✔ Two identical consonants following a vowel make the vowel short: *Hippy* is pronounced "*hip*-ee;" *batter* is pronounced "*bat*-ur."

- ✔ Some consonants, when together, combine their sounds — in this aspect at least English is fairly consistent — and most combinations always sound the same way (*gh* is an exception to this rule):

    - *ch* as in chart, cheek, chirp, chomp, and church

    - *fl* as in flap, flee, flip, flop, and flue

    - *gr* as in gravy, greed, grin, gross, and grueling

    - *sh* as in shampoo, sheet, shirt, short, and shunt

    - *st* as in stay, step, stigma, stop, and stun

    - *th* as in than, then, thick, thong, and thug

- ✔ When two *c*'s are together, the first *c* is hard (*k*), and the second *c* is soft (*s*). Some examples are accident (*ak*-si-dehnt) and accessory (ak-*ses*-er-ee). The word *flaccid* follows this rule, but also may be said with both *c*'s soft, as "*flas*-id."

A *diphthong* is a complex vowel sound made by gliding continuously from the position for one vowel to that for another within the same syllable. A *digraph* is a combination of two letters functioning as a unit to represent one sound.

Careless pronunciation often results in careless spelling. If you can improve your pronunciation, chances are your spelling will improve, too. Another way to improve your spelling is to become familiar with the many ways sounds are made in English. For example, the F sound can be made with *f, gh* (laugh), and *ph* (phone).

In a couple of cases, proper pronunciation of a word depends on whether the first letter is capitalized:

- ✔ *Polish* (*poh*-lish), when capitalized, refers to people and things from the country Poland; *polish* (*pawl*-ish) is the act of smoothing or brightening something, or the substance used to help you do so.

- ✔ *August,* the month after July, is pronounced with the accent, or stress, on the first syllable — "*aw*-gust." But when you say that something or someone is worthy of respect because of age, and use the word *august* to convey that, you stress the second syllable — "aw-*gust*."

In at least one case, proper pronunciation depends on meaning. When you use the adjective *content* to mean happy and satisfied, you put the accent on the second syllable — kon-*tent*. You put the accent on the first syllable when you use *content* as a noun to mean "everything contained inside something" — *kon*-tent.

Handling the biggest mispronunciation problems

Words get mispronounced in many fascinating ways. This section explains the four most common ways that we twist words out of shape. Knowing how words get mispronounced can help you pronounce them correctly. As you read this section, see which word sins you have either committed or heard committed.

If you pay attention to pronunciation, you not only say new words correctly but can often spell them correctly, too.

Dropping letters

It's astonishing how often speakers drop letters from words. For instance, the food poisoning known as *salmonella* is correctly pronounced "sal-muh-*nel*-uh." Dropping the first *l* results in "sam-uh-*nel*-uh." Sam 'n Ella may be revolting people, but they are not the same as food poisoning.

Unstressed vowels are often dropped, even in relatively common words. *Interesting* (*in*-ter-es-ting) becomes *intresting* (*in*-trehs-ting), *miniature* (*min*-ee-ah-chur) becomes *minature* (*min*-ah-chur), and *veterinarian* (vet-er-eh-*nayr*-ee-an) becomes *veternarian* (vet-er-*nayr*-ee-an).

Consonants also get lost in the shuffle. The first "r" in February is a case in point. How often have you heard *February* pronounced "*feb*-oo-ehr-ee," or even "*feb*-ree," instead of "*feb*-roo-ehr-ee?"

Table 2-1 lists words that are often misspelled because a letter is omitted in the pronunciation:

Table 2-1	Common Mispronunciations from Dropped Letters		
Word	*Proper Pronunciation*	*Dropped Letter*	*Mispronunciation*
candidate	*kan*-dih-dayt	first d	*kan*-i-dayt
diphtheria	dif-*thir*-ee-uh	first h (in *ph*)	dip-*thir*-ee-uh

(continued)

Table 2-1 *(continued)*

Word	Proper Pronunciation	Dropped Letter	Mispronunciation
government	*guv*-urn-mehnt	n	*guv*-ur-mehnt or even *guv*-ment
probably	*prahb*-eh-blee	ab	*prahb*-lee
recognize	*rek*-ehg-nize	g	*reh*-con-ize
symptom	*simp*-tuhm	p	*sim*-tuhm

Adding letters or syllables

Sometimes the problem isn't dropping letters (or sounds), but adding them. Speakers often insert an extra letter or two when they say a word. Unfortunately, this can make the word confusing or even unrecognizable. Consider the following examples:

LANGUAGE LORE

You say toh-may-toh, I say toh-mah-toh

Some words are hard to mispronounce, because any way you say them is okay. People whose religious beliefs compelled them to live the simple life long before it became a fad in the United States are called *Amish.* You can say "*ah*-mish" or "*ay*-mish" — either way is acceptable. Likewise, you can say *Celtic,* indicating Irish or Scottish traditions, with the first *c* hard, as in "*kel*-tik," or soft, as in "*sel*-tik." Following are a few other forgiving English words that you can gleefully wrap your tongue around.

- **Buoy:** As a noun meaning "a floating hazard marker," it's pronounced "*boo*-ee." As a verb meaning "to keep afloat" or "encourage," it's more often pronounced "boy."

- **Febrile** (feverish) can be pronounced either "*fee*-brul" or "*feb*-rul."

- **Fracas** (noisy fight; loud quarrel) can be pronounced "*fray*-kis" or "*frah*-kis."

- **Hegemony** (leadership; dominance, especially of one nation over others) can be pronounced "heh-*jem*-uh-nee" or "hehj-eh-*moh*-nee."

- **Insouciant** (untroubled; carefree) is pronounced "in-*soo*-see-ent" or "in-*soo*-shent."

- **Macabre** (gruesome) is pronounced "mah-*kab*-reh" or "mah-*kahb.*"

- **Niche** (corner) is pronounced "neesh" or "nitch."

- **Obdurate** (hardhearted; unrepentant; stubborn) can be pronounced "*ob*-dur-it" or "*ob*-dyoor-it."

- **Shallot** (small onion; green onion) can be "*shal*-it" or "shuh-*laht.*"

- **Worsted** (yarn) is "*wus*-tid" or "*wur*-stid."

✔ *Ambidextrous* (able to use either hand) has four syllables and is correctly pronounced "am-bi-*deks*-trus." But sometimes speakers add an extra syllable to get "am-bi-*deks*-tree-us" or "am-bi-*deks*-troo-us."

✔ *Chimney* has two syllables: "*chim*-nee." However, people often add a syllable to pronounce the word incorrectly as "*chim*-ah-nee."

✔ *Lightning,* my personal favorite, is correctly pronounced as "*lyt*-ning," but it often gets this added bonus: "*ly*-ten-ing."

✔ *Wondrous,* correctly pronounced "wun-drus," becomes "wun-der-us."

Many other words suffer from an added sound. Table 2-2 lists a few of them (the bolded element is the added syllable):

Table 2-2	Common Mispronunciations from Added Letters	
Word	*Correct Pronunciation*	*Mispronunciation*
athletics	ath-*let*-iks	ath-**e**-let-iks
burglar	*buhr*-gler	buhr-**ger**-ler
encumbrance	en-*kuhm*-brehns	en-kuhm-**ber**-ehns
hindrance	*hin*-drehns	hin-**der**-ehns
jewelry	*joo*-ehl-ree	joo-**ler**-ee
mischievous	*mis*-cheh-vehs	mis-chee-**vi**-uhs
remembrance	ri-*mem*-brehns	ri-mem-**ber**-ehns
schedule	*skeh*-jool	skeh-du-**al**
umbrella	um-brel-uh	um-**ber**-el-uh

Switching letters

Occasionally people switch letters when pronouncing a word. You often hear this kind of mistake when small children try to say the word *spaghetti.* For some reason, it often comes out "pasghetti." Another example, this time from the adult audience, is *abhor* (hate). This word becomes "uh-*bor*" rather than "ab-*hor*." *Cinnamon* (the spice) is another example; it becomes "cimminon." Switching "nuclear" to "nucular" is another classic.

These are understandable mistakes, as are many other mispronunciations that involve switched letters. Unfortunately, these mistakes get in the way of comprehension.

Spoonerisms

Switching the first letters of two or more words and so mispronouncing them is such a common problem that it has a name: a *Spoonerism*. The results are often humorous, as in "blushing crow" for "crushing blow" or "I have a half-warmed fish in my mind" for "I have a half-formed wish in my mind." The term comes from W.A. Spooner (1844-1930), an Englishman noted for such slips of the tongue. He set out to be a bird watcher and ended up being a word botcher!

Garbling sounds

People also have a tendency to run sounds together, making the sounds disappear or become another sound entirely. This kind of mispronunciation is often a regional thing. Folks in different parts of the United States pronounce some words differently. In the North, for example, people say "you all" (*yu all*) — two words. In the South, it's "y'all" (*yahl*) — one word.

Library is another example of garbling. Correctly pronounced it's "*ly*-brer-ee." I often hear the word pronounced "*lie*-berry." Many people also pronounce *sandwich* (*sand*-wich) as "*sam*-wich." Another example is the word *have*. Many native-English speakers tend to pronounce it "haf" when it comes in the middle of a sentence (as in "I *haf* to go to the store"), but pronounce it correctly when it ends the sentence ("Who's seen the movie? I *have*.").

Table 2-3 lists several words that are often garbled. As you read the chart, think about how many of these words you've seen in print but may have been afraid to use because you weren't sure how to pronounce them.

Table 2-3	Commonly Garbled Words	
Word	*Pronunciation*	*Definition*
awry	uh-*ry*	wrong, crooked
banquet	*ban*-kwet	feast; formal dinner for many people
dénouement	day-noo-*mahn*	conclusion
élan	ay-*lan*	impetuous ardor; style
gamut	*gam*-uht	entire range
jocund	*jahk*-und	cheerful
mausoleum	maw-suh-*lee*-um	tomb

Word	Pronunciation	Definition
posthumous	*pahs*-choo-mus	after death
potpourri	poh-poo-*ree*	dried flower petals
quotidian	kwoh-*tid*-ee-un	daily; every day
vehement	*vee*-uh-munt	passionate
wizened	*wiz*-und	shriveled
zealous	*zel*-us	devoted; enthusiastic

Improving your pronunciation

Pronunciation is important to building your vocabulary (not to mention spelling correctly). Following are a few ways you can improve your pronunciation:

- ✔ If you come across a word that you don't know how to pronounce, look it up, and then practice saying it. Keep practicing the word until saying it seems natural. Table 2-4 lists some commonly mispronounced words.

- ✔ As you expand your vocabulary, don't gloss over the dictionary's pronunciation guide. Pay attention and keep practicing.

- ✔ If you're just learning English, consider buying or borrowing a tape that focuses on English pronunciation. You can find such tapes in bookstores and on the Internet.

- ✔ Read aloud. I'm not kidding. Just start reading out loud. You may be surprised how self-conscious you feel when you begin, but with practice you'll get better and feel more at ease. Reading out loud almost always reveals words you may recognize in print but stumble over in speech.

Table 2-4	**Commonly Mispronounced Words**	
Word	*Pronunciation*	*Definition*
aplomb	uh-*plahm*	assurance
apocryphal	uh-*pock*-ruh-ful	of doubtful authenticity
bailiwick	*bay*-luh-wik	person's area of skill or knowledge or control
blasé	blah-*zay*	satiated and bored

(continued)

Table 2-4 *(continued)*

Word	Pronunciation	Definition
cache	kash	hiding place
gecko	*gek*-oh	lizard
khaki	*kak*-ee	light brown; a cotton fabric in that color
larynx	*lar*-inks	voice box
loath	lohth	reluctant
mandible	*man*-duh-bul	bone of lower jaw
quagmire	*kwag*-myre	swamp; difficult position
remuneration	ri-myoo-nuh-*ray*-shun	payment
ribald	*rib*-uhld	vulgar, indecent
vignette	vin-*yeht*	ornamental design; literary illustration or short description; image whose edges fade into the background

Exercising Your New Vocabulary

An expanded vocabulary will do you no good if you don't use it. Here are some ways that you can exercise the words you learn so that they become part of your everyday vocabulary:

- ✔ Use the word as often as you can. Use it in conversation (when it fits, of course), and use it in writing.

- ✔ Make a list of your favorite words. Some words may appeal to you because of the way they sound (I happen to like *leviathan* [leh-*vy*-eh-than]) or because of the way they feel rolling off your tongue: biscuit a la cuillere (bis-*kwee* ah *la* kwee *ayre*) — believe it or not, it's pretty much a sponge cake. You may like other words because of their meaning — *satisfaction* or *accomplishment,* for instance.

Remember to use your new-found word power for good and not for evil. As you expand your vocabulary, you may use words your audience isn't familiar with. Provide the context clues and other aids to determining meaning that I explain in Chapter 3.

Chapter 3

Picking Up Meaning

· ·

In This Chapter

▶ Using context clues to figure out meaning

▶ Understanding the different types of context clues

▶ Deciphering words with multiple meanings

· ·

Walt Worker strolled into the men's room at work and noticed a sign directly above the sink. It had a single word on it: "Think!"

The next day, when he went to the men's room, he noticed a new sign immediately above the soap dispenser that read, "Thoap!"

This joke depends entirely on the setting, or *context*. You understand "thoap" to be a joke on the word "soap" just as "think" is a joke on the word "sink." Without this context, the joke falls flat.

You pick up clues to the meaning of unfamiliar words from the information surrounding the words: the *context*. Using context clues is one of the easiest ways to figure out unfamiliar words. Even if you don't have a clue about what a particular word means, knowing the surrounding words can usually help you get the gist of it. In most cases, that's all you need to understand the speaker or passage. It's quick, easy, and efficient!

Reading Between the Lines

When you're having a conversation, watching a movie, reading a book, or listening to a lecture, you may hear a word you don't know. Sometimes you can look the word up in a dictionary, which is an excellent strategy. Unfortunately, you may not always have a dictionary with you — or be willing to whip one out in the middle of a date, business meeting, or movie. (It can be so hard to read a dictionary in the dark.) The good news is that you can often use the surrounding words to figure out what the unknown word means (and avoid using a dictionary).

When you use context clues, you interpret a word's specific meaning by examining its relationship to the other words in the sentence. To improve your vocabulary, you must understand how a word interacts with other words. Although context can sometimes be as unreliable as your boss or the weather, it can also come through in impressive ways.

Look at the word *epidemic* in the next sentence: "Nearly 40 million Americans are overweight; obesity has become an *epidemic*." An *epidemic* is a rapid, widespread occurrence or growth of a disease. Because the sentence describes the epidemic as affecting "40 million people," odds are good that *epidemic* means "something that happens to a large group of people." So, you may understand that an epidemic indicates a widespread phenomenon, but you may miss the subtle connection between epidemic and disease.

When you pick up only a general sense of meaning from context clues, you risk letting the complete definition slip by. Check a dictionary for an exact definition when you're not sure that you're getting the complete definition from the context.

Combine the information that you get from context clues with the information that you get from the clues offered by a word's root (Chapter 5), prefix (Chapter 6), and suffix (Chapter 7). All of these resources will make your inferences more reliable.

Saying it another way: Restatement clues

Speakers and writers want their words to be understood so that their message will get through. As a result, they often define a difficult word right in the text. You heard me correctly — the definition may be as obvious as the nose on Pinocchio's face.

The following paragraph gives you an example of a context clue where the writer defines the word *levee* right in the passage:

> The Army Corps of Engineers distributed 26 million plastic bags throughout the region. Volunteers filled each bag with 35 pounds of sand and then stacked them to create *levees,* makeshift barriers against the floodwaters.

Right after the word *levee,* you get the definition: "makeshift barriers against the floodwaters."

Each of the following sentences contains a restatement context clue. I put the unfamiliar word, its pronunciation, and its definition on a separate line. As you read, cover the answer and see if you can figure out what each unfamiliar word means.

✔ Fatty deposits on artery walls combine with calcium compounds to cause *arteriosclerosis,* hardening of the arteries.

Arteriosclerosis means "hardening of the arteries."

✔ In many Native American cultures, a *shaman,* or medicine man, acts as a ceremonial priest.

Shaman means "priest or medicine man."

✔ I believe that life is short, so we should enjoy what we eat. As a result, I consume mass quantities of *confectioneries* — candies — and keep my dentist on retainer.

Confectioneries means "candies."

✔ She jumped into the *fray* and enjoyed every minute of the fight.

Fray means "fight."

✔ As with all electric *currents* or discharges, lightning follows the *path of least resistance.* This means that it travels the easiest route.

Current means "discharges."

The path of least resistance means "the easiest route."

✔ Many settlers who lived on the vast American plains in the late 19th century used *sod,* or earth, as a building material for their houses.

Sod means "earth."

✔ To make a living, John Styth Pemberton created so-called *patent medicines,* homemade potions sold without a prescription.

Patent medicines means "homemade potions sold without a prescription."

Talkin' the Talk

Culture vultures Sydney and Stanley are boning up for their proposed trip to the South Seas. They not only want to sink their toes into the sugar-white sand and chug drinks decorated with little umbrellas, they also want to understand a bit of the local lore. They're especially interested in the weather. Settle in for tonight's speaker:

Dr. Mead:	During a tidal wave, a wall of water 25 feet high can rush to shore, pushed by 200-mile-per-hour winds. Called *tsunamis,* these fierce tidal waves strike the shore with tremendous force and cause considerable damage to life and property.
Stanley:	Huh?

Sydney:	Stan, we can figure this out. Think back: The definition followed right after the word. The doctor gave us the definition.
Stanley:	You're right. He said that *tsunamis* (soo-*nah*-mees) are fierce tidal waves.
Sydney:	Fierce tidal waves. . . . Maybe we should consider going to Paris instead?

Context clues after colons and dashes

In addition to restating the word's meaning (see the preceding section), speakers and writers often provide context clues in the form of definitions after colons (:) or dashes (—). The following examples illustrate this type of context clue:

✔ The scientists saw that the drop of water contained *bacteria* — one-celled organisms too small to be seen by the naked eye.

Right after the dash is the definition of *bacteria.* They are "one-celled organisms too small to be seen by the naked eye."

✔ Santa Ana brought with him several objects from home, including a large lump of *chicle:* a gumlike substance made from the sap of the sapodilla tree.

You can tell from the example after the colon that *chicle* is "a gumlike substance made from the sap of the sapodilla tree."

Context clues after transitions

Writers and speakers can also use *transitions* (words or phrases that connect ideas) to signal that more information about an unfamiliar word is coming. The three most common transitions are *for example, that is,* and *in other words.* Consider the examples in the following list:

✔ **For example:** Despite their various forms and subjects, *epics* such as Homer's *The Odyssey,* Milton's *Paradise Lost,* and Spenser's *The Faerie Queen* adhere to the basic epic form; for example, they are all long narrative poems that are presented in an exalted style and focused on the exploits and adventures of great heroes.

The definition of *epic* — "long narrative poems that are presented in an exalted style and focused on the exploits and adventures of great heroes" — comes right after the phrase "for example."

✔ **That is:** Antonio López de Santa Ana, the brave Mexican leader of the attack on the Alamo, later was *exiled*; that is, he was banished from his country. He ended up on Staten Island, New York.

The definition of *exile* — "banishment" — comes right after the phrase "that is."

✔ **In other words:** Sharks are models of efficiency with their boneless skeletons, simple brains, generalized nervous systems, and simple internal structures. Their sleek shapes, razor-sharp replaceable teeth, powerful jaws, and greedy appetites make them excellent *marauders*; in other words, brutal raiders.

The definition of *marauders* (muh-*rawd*-erz) — "brutal raiders" — comes right after the phrase "in other words."

Of course, speakers and writers use more than the preceding three transitions to connect one idea to another. Table 3-1 shows some additional transitions. Note that each transition creates a particular relationship between the linked ideas. By using the transition *as a result*, for example, the speaker is indicating that one thing caused the other: Simon didn't get to the house until 8:30; as a result, we missed the first half of the concert.

Table 3-1	Common Transitions
Relationship	*Transitions*
addition	also, and, besides, further, in addition to, too
example	for example, for instance, thus, namely
time	afterwards, before, next, then, finally, first (second, third, and so on), during, soon, later, meanwhile
contrast	but, nevertheless, however, yet, in contrast, still
comparison	likewise, in comparison, similarly
result	therefore, consequently, as a result, thus, because of this, accordingly
summary	in brief, in conclusion, in short, finally
place	here, there, nearby, in the front, in the back

As you read or listen, search for transitions — a definition often follows them.

Talkin' the Talk

Prudence Patient, who just hasn't felt like herself lately, has finally visited her doctor and had some tests run. When Dr. Overworked calls her to give her the results, this is their conversation:

Dr. Overworked: Prudence, you just have a cold. *Lethargy* — that feeling of passivity and inactivity — is a common symptom.

Prudence Patient: Huh?

Dr. Overworked: Oops. Gotta go. Just got called to surgery.

Prudence Patient: If I call Dr. Overworked back, I'll get charged for another visit, so I'd better figure out what *lethargy* (*leth*-ar-gee) means on my own. The doctor said, 'a feeling of passivity and inactivity.' Therefore, *lethargy* must mean 'a feeling of passivity and inactivity.' That means I'll feel like I'm too pooped to function normally. Yep, that's about right.

Inferential context clues

Sometimes an unfamiliar word is defined right in the text, so you don't have to do any deciphering at all. (See the earlier sections for examples of these types of context clues). Other times, however, you have to *infer* the meaning from what you already know and from details that you have heard or read; in other words, you have to make an educated guess based on the evidence on hand. This takes a bit of detective work.

When you *make an inference*, you combine what you already know with spoken or textual clues to discover the unstated information. You may have heard this referred to as "reading between the lines" or "putting two and two together."

As you read the following passage, use context clues to infer what "maritime" means:

Just before midnight on April 14, 1912, one of the most dramatic and famous of all *maritime* disasters occurred, the sinking of the *Titanic*. The *Titanic* was the most luxurious ship afloat at the time, with its beautifully decorated staterooms, glittering crystal chandeliers, and elaborate food service.

How can you figure out that *maritime* means "related to the sea; nautical"? As Figure 3-1 shows, you can add the context clue to what you already know.

	Context clue	+	What you already know	=	Inference
Figure 3-1: Adding up an inference.	"The Titanic was the most luxurious ship afloat"	+	The Titanic was an ocean liner that hit an iceberg and sank	=	a *maritime* disaster must be a disaster at sea

Each of the following sentences contains a difficult vocabulary word (italicized to stand out). I based all the sentences on the old joke, "Why did the chicken cross the road?" so you can have some fun while you digest some new vocabulary. As you read, cover the answers and see if you can infer the meaning of the unfamiliar word. (***Note:*** These responses are totally fictitious. Karl Marx is dead, Fox Mulder isn't a real person, and Bill Gates, although alive and a real person, doesn't care about chickens crossing the road.)

✔ **Bill Gates (founder of Microsoft):** I have just released e-chicken 02, which will not only cross roads but will lay eggs, file your important documents, and balance your checkbook. The egg-laying program is an *inextricable* part of e-chicken, so they're sold together.

   Context clue: "so they're sold together"

   Definition: *Inextricable* means "cannot be disentangled."

✔ **Karl Marx (19th century philosopher):** This chicken, obviously a member of the *proletariat,* had to cross the road to get to the factory so that he could slave away his life and his energy to further enrich the greedy factory owner.

   Context clue: "to get to the factory so that he could slave away"

   Definition: *Proletariat* means "working class," and as the context makes clear, the proletariat is exploited by the rich.

✔ **Fox Mulder (TV character):** You saw it cross the road with your own eyes. How many more chickens have to cross before you give *credence* to jaywalking poultry and believe what you see?

   Context clue: "and believe what you see"

   Definition: *Credence* means "belief."

Talkin' the Talk

Nilla Wafer and Lance Lotsaluck are trying to find a restaurant for a cozy dinner. Lance is a smart fella who knows a lot . . . except when to shut up. You're sitting in the next booth. We're all shameless, so lean over the booth to listen in.

Lance: Look at this menu. Not a bit of shark meat listed, and this is supposed to be an exotic restaurant. Did you know that shark meat is processed for human consumption all over the world? The British fish-and-chips industry depends on shark meat. The Italians annually consume about 10 million pounds of smooth dogfish shark. The Chinese use shark fins for soup.

Nilla: If all these people are eating shark meat, then 'consumption' must mean *to eat*. Are you saying that people eat shark?

Lance: Certainly they do. So what will it be — crickets? Eel? Grasshoppers?

Nilla: I'll *consume* a salad — without critters.

Bonus words

Here's an opportunity to expand your vocabulary even more. Following is a list of synonyms — that is, words that mean nearly the same thing — for the three words introduced in the "Why did the chicken cross the road" answers (see the section "Inferential context clues").

Word	Part of Speech	Synonyms
credence (*kreed*-ens)	noun	faith assent (uh-*sent*)
inextricable (in-*eks*-trih-kuh-bul)	adj.	connected entangled intricate (*in*-trih-kit)
proletariat (proh-luh-*ter*-ee-uht)	noun	working class lower class

As Nilla discovered, context clues can help you out in the most unexpected places.

Contrasting context clues

You can figure out an unknown word when an opposite or contrasting word or phrase is presented. When you do this, you're making an inference based on what you know. Consider the following sentence:

> Her dress was elegant, in contrast to the flashy styles and gaudy colors she usually wears.

Even if you don't know what *elegant* means, you can infer from this sentence that elegant doesn't mean "flashy" or "gaudy." By the contrasting clue, you can probably figure out that it means "tasteful" and "dignified."

The following words and phrases indicate contrast. Watch for them as you read, or listen for them during conversations:

but	conversely
however	in contrast
on the other hand	still
nevertheless	not
without	yet

For example, you can define *daguerreotype* by finding its contrast in the sentence:

> Keep your hands off that! It's a *daguerreotype* of my great-great-grandmother — not some modern point-and-shoot picture cranked out in a one-hour photo lab!

According to the context in this sentence, a *daguerreotype* (duh-*ger*-oh-type) isn't a regular photograph. Because it's contrasted to a modern photo, you can infer that it's actually an old, and probably valuable, photograph. (A daguerreotype is actually an early photograph, produced on silver plate rather than film.)

Use contrast clues to infer the meaning of *contentious* in the following sentence:

> I was afraid that my mother-in-law would be a *contentious* addition to our family, but she turned out to be a great peacemaker.

Contentious means "quarrelsome." You can infer this from the contrast between "contentious" and "peacemaker."

Being an Armchair Detective

Context is an important tool in helping you define unfamiliar words. In this section, I provide examples where you can apply all the context clues to work for you. See if you can come up with definitions for the italicized words. After each passage, I provide pronunciations and definitions so that you can confirm the meaning you pick up from the context clues.

1. Most natural hazards can be detected before their threat matures. But *seisms* (from the Greek *seismos*, meaning earthquake) have no known *precursors*, so they come without warning, like the *vengeance* of an ancient warrior. For this reason, they continue to kill, in some areas, at a level usually reserved for wars and epidemics — 11,000 people died in an earthquake in northeastern Iran on August 31, 1968, not in the ancient past. Nor is the horror of the *lethal* earthquake completed with the heavy death toll. The homeless are left to cope with fire, looting, *pestilence*, fear, and the burden of rebuilding what the planet so easily shrugs away.

Word	Part of Speech	Definition
seisms (*sy*-zums)	noun	earthquakes
precursors (pree-*kur*-surz)	noun	warnings, forerunners
vengeance (*ven*-juhns)	noun	revenge, retribution
lethal (*lee*-thul)	adj.	deadly
pestilence (*pes*-tuh-luhns)	noun	a deadly widespread disease, like the plague

2. After the success of *The Jazz Singer* in 1927, the film industry *metamorphosed* from silent films to "talkies." Mickey Mouse was one of the few stars who made a smooth *transition* from silent films to talkies with his 1928 cartoon *Steamboat Willie*. Within a year, hundreds of Mickey Mouse clubs had sprung up all across the United States; by 1931, more than a million people belonged to a Mickey Mouse club. The *phenomenon* was not confined to America. In London, Madame Tussaud's *illustrious* wax museum placed a wax figure of Mickey alongside its statues of other *eminent* film stars. In 1933, according to Disney Studios, Mickey received 800,000 fan letters — an average of more than 2,000 letters a day. To date, no "star" has ever received as much fan mail as Mickey Mouse.

Word	Part of Speech	Definition
metamorphosed (met-uh-*mor*-fohzd)	verb	changed
transition (tran-*zish*-un)	noun	change or passage

Word	Part of Speech	Definition
phenomenon (fuh-*nahm*-uh-nuhn)	noun	event, occurrence
illustrious (ih-*lus*-tree-us)	adj.	distinguished, celebrated
eminent (*em*-uh-nuhnt)	adj.	famous

3. A worldwide *economic* depression in the 1930s left many people unemployed. One such person was Charles Darrow of Philadelphia, Pennsylvania, who lost his job as a heating engineer. To try to make a living, Darrow invented a board game that he called "Monopoly." *Initially*, Darrow tried to sell his idea to the leading game manufacturer in America, Parker Brothers. But the company turned the game down because it felt it was too *elaborate*. In *desperation*, Darrow used his own money to have 5,000 games made by a small company. He sold the games himself, and it wasn't long before Monopoly was the latest *craze*. After seeing the success of Monopoly, Parker Brothers changed its mind and paid Darrow for the right to manufacture and distribute the game. In 1975, twice as much Monopoly money was printed in the United States as real money. All told, nearly 100 million Monopoly sets have been sold since 1935.

Word	Part of Speech	Definition
economic (ek-uh-*nahm*-ik)	adj.	relating to money
initially (ih-*nish*-uhl-ee)	adv.	at first
elaborate (ee-*lab*-uh-rit)	adj.	complex
desperation (des-puhr-*ay*-shun)	noun	urgency or despair
craze (krayz)	noun	fad, fashion

TIP

Picking up on context clues can really help you with the reading-passage and fill-in-the-blank questions on standardized tests.

Deciphering Words with Multiple Meanings

Context clues are especially crucial when you encounter words with more than one meaning. The word *favor,* for example, has many different meanings. As a noun, favor can mean "a kind act," "friendly regard," "approval," or "a gift." As a verb, to favor someone can mean that you "support" that person, or are "partial" to him or her; or it may mean that you "resemble" the person.

When you read, you may come across a word that you think you know but that doesn't make sense in the sentence you're reading. That's your clue that the word has more than one meaning. In this case, you must choose the meaning that fits the context.

Follow these three simple steps:

1. **Read the sentence and find the word with multiple meanings.**

2. **Look for context clues that tell you which meaning of the word fits.**

3. **Substitute synonyms for the word until you find the right meaning.**

For example: Luis was *resigned* to working overtime on Friday night.

1. *Resigned* has multiple meanings. *Resigned* means "quit a job." It also means "yielding and uncomplaining."

2. Because Luis is working overtime, he is not quitting his job. Therefore, the second meaning of *resigned* should fit.

3. Replace *resigned* with *agreeable,* its synonym: Luis was *agreeable* to working overtime on Friday night. The sentence makes sense, so you have found the correct meaning for *resigned.*

Table 3-2 lists a few examples of multiple-meaning words.

Table 3-2		Words with More than One Meaning				
Word	*Example*	*Part of Speech*	*Meaning*	*Second Example*	*Part of Speech*	*Second Meaning*
address	home *address*	noun	residence	graduation *address*	noun	speech
game	play a *game*	noun	recreation; amusement	have a *game* leg	adj.	injured
pool	swimming *pool*	noun	place for water	*pool* table	adj.	billiards
rash	have a *rash*	noun	skin problem	*rash* action	adj.	hasty
train	*train* station	adj.	railroad	*train* the dog	verb	teach

There are a ton of English words with multiple meanings. They're called *homonyms.* That means they are spelled the same and pronounced the same, but they have different meanings. (Chapter 9 deals with homonyms in detail.

Head there for a longer list, as well as tips on how you can differentiate between identical words.) Following are a few more examples:

Snake means

A. A long, flexible, coiled-wire rod

B. A legless reptile

C. A sneaky, disloyal person

D. To twist

E. All of the above

Choosing "all of the above" is always the way to go — at least in my book. The word *snake* is a good way to show you how the context helps you determine the meaning of a word. Check out "snake" in each of the following sentences.

✔ The plumber used a *snake* to clear the drain.

(long, bendable metal tool)

✔ The rancher wore heavy leather boots for protection against *snake* attacks.

(legless reptile)

✔ I thought he was my friend, but he turned out to be a *snake*.

(sneaky, disloyal person)

✔ If we *snake* along the ground, the enemy will not see us.

(twist)

Spare means

A. Lean and slender

B. Extra, not in regular use

C. Treat with mercy

D. A small amount, not quite enough

E. All of the above

In the following four examples, the context determines the meaning of "spare."

✔ My uncle is a tall, *spare* man, as thin as a stick.

(lean and slender)

✔ Bring a *spare* pair of socks in case someone forgets to bring any.

(extra, not in regular use)

✔ Sometimes you have to tell a lie to *spare* someone's feelings.

(treat with mercy)

✔ After their *spare* meal, the prisoners were still very hungry.

(small in amount, not quite enough)

You use the same techniques that you use to figure out the meaning of any unfamiliar word. Combine what you already know with what the context reveals. Keep in mind, though, that context clues usually give you a general idea of what a word means. To get the precise definition, you'll probably have to refer to a dictionary or other reference book. Head to Chapter 2 for more information on using dictionaries and reference books.

Chapter 4

Using the Right Word

In This Chapter

▶ Exploring the changing nature of words

▶ Mastering the different levels of diction

▶ Solving the problems that idioms and acronyms can cause

▶ Suiting your words to your audience and purpose

*Y*ou don't use the exact same words every time you open your mouth or type a message, any more than you wear the same clothes every day for every activity. Successful people suit their language to their audiences and circumstances because they know which words are appropriate in each specific situation. Just as people with style know how to select an outfit that makes the right impression, successful people know how to select words to fit their needs.

On the one hand, words can be your best friend when they allow you to express your heart's desire, especially in affairs of the heart. On the other hand, words can be your worst enemy when they stymie your efforts to say what you mean. To keep words on your side, you need to understand them thoroughly.

In this chapter, I give you the tips you need to match the word to the situation.

Choosing Your Words

So many words! So many choices! Which words should you choose to use?

Always choose words that suit your audience and purpose. Although word choice is ultimately a matter of taste and practice, I offer the following hints for making sure that your vocabulary communicates the meaning you intend.

✔ Use words that are *accurate, familiar,* and *suitable.*

- *Accurate* words say what you mean.

- *Familiar* words are words that your audience understands.

- *Suitable* words convey your tone and fit with the other words you use.

✔ **Select the exact word you want.** English is one of the richest languages in the world because it offers many different ways to say the same thing. Select your words carefully to convey the precise meaning that you want. For example, *prosperous, flourishing, auspicious, thriving, triumphant, favorable,* and *exultant* all mean *successful,* but each word has a different shade of meaning. Choose the word that best fits your audience and purpose.

✔ **Don't strain.** When you're mastering new skills, it's natural to try to share what you've discovered. This is admirable if you've just learned how to bake chocolate chip cookies (feel free to send me a box), but it is not as good when it comes to vocabulary. People who *flaunt* (show off) their new words come off as arrogant rather than sophisticated. Here is an example:

> **Show-offy:** "Because of their eccentricities, the members of my family cannot fail to endear themselves to visitors."

> **Better:** "Visitors find my weird family likeable."

✔ **Use specific words rather than general words.** Specific words give your readers a more vivid mental picture than general words. Sometimes simple action verbs such as *run* and *go* will be appropriate to your subject and audience. However, you often need to use words that are more specific in order to make your meaning clear.

For example, did your co-worker *toss* the paper in your direction or *hurl* it? To *toss* something is casual; to *hurl* something is deliberate. *Toss* implies a friendly gesture; *hurl,* in contrast, implies a potentially hostile act.

✔ **Stay on top of current usage to make sure that you use words that fit your purpose and audience.** Language changes with the times; words expand and adapt to suit different situations. Know what your words mean; otherwise, you risk being misunderstood — possibly even embarrassed. (See the sidebar "Mutated meanings" for some examples of word meanings that have changed over time.)

In general, don't sweat your words. The more you master and practice using new words, the more naturally they'll fit into your vocabulary. Sooner than you think, you'll be using just the word to say just what you mean.

LANGUAGE LORE

Mutated meanings

In 1740, Admiral Vernon of the British fleet decided to water down the navy's rum. The sailors weren't too pleased. They started calling Admiral Vernon "Old Grog" after the coats that he wore made of *grogram* — a stiff, wool fabric. The term *grog* soon began to mean the watered-down drink itself. When you were drunk on this grog, you were *groggy,* a word still in use today to describe being muddled, confused, or intoxicated.

Grog isn't the only word that has a past. Many years ago (in the 1500s, to be exact), the word *hussy,* for example, simply meant "the female head of a household" — in other words, "a housewife." Today, the word refers to a woman or girl who acts in a lewd or improper manner. Another example is the word *silly,* which once meant "happy." Now, *silly* means "foolish." And

nice? Well, before 1300, *nice* meant "foolish" or "ignorant." Around 1450, it came to mean "dainty" or "delicate." In the 1500s, it meant "precise" or "careful." By the mid 1700s, it meant "agreeable" or "delightful." *Nice* came to its present day meaning, "kind" or "thoughtful," in the early-to-mid 1800s. In other words, it took about 500 years to transform *nice* from an insult into a compliment.

As these examples illustrate, words are fluid, ever-changing symbols. They change to express the interests and ideas of different times, different cultures, and different situations. Like people, words grow old and decay; they shed old meanings just as we shed old identities and remake ourselves to fit new circumstances.

Digging into Diction

WORDS TO THE WISE

The words you use as you communicate, whether through speech or writing, make up your *diction.* Your diction affects the clarity and impact of your message. The words you want in a specific instance depend on context: your audience and purpose. Your *audience* is the people you're addressing; your *purpose* is your reason for speaking or writing.

Diction can be formal or informal. Yet, just as there are varying degrees of dress, from highly formal (tuxedoes and evening gowns) to very casual (sweat suits and sneakers), there are varying degrees of formal and informal speech:

- **Highly or very formal:** If you must make a presentation to your colleagues about your latest research, give the eulogy at your grandfather's funeral, or say the toast at your best friend's wedding, chances are that you'll use highly formal diction. This type of diction is appropriate at serious or ceremonial events and is marked by words that create an elevated tone.

✔ **Formal** (also referred to as *standard English*): Although meeting your future in-laws over dinner or speaking at your monthly book club meeting are not highly formal situations (usually), they do require a bit more formal language than you use when you're chatting with your buddies over pizza. Formal diction is marked by words that create learned or scholarly, but not elevated, tone.

✔ **Informal** (also called *colloquial*): This type of diction is appropriate if you're getting together with friends to play cards or watch a movie. Informal diction is marked by words (including slang and vernacular) that create a casual tone.

The following sections explain the differences between very formal, formal, and informal diction and help you identify which type of diction to use in various situations.

Speaking and writing formally

Formal diction is the most elevated level of speech and writing. Formal diction has the following characteristics:

✔ A serious tone

✔ A substantial distance between the speaker (or writer) and audience

✔ Few, if any, personal references

✔ Specialized or elevated terms

✔ No contractions

The purpose of formal diction is to convey a serious message in a serious way. Consider this example from the U.S. Declaration of Independence:

When, in the course of human events, it becomes necessary for one people to dissolve the political bands which have connected them with another, and to assume, among the powers of the earth, the separate and equal station to which the laws of nature and of nature's God entitle them, a decent respect to the opinions of mankind requires that they should declare the causes which impel them to the separation.

We hold these truths to be self-evident: that all men are created equal; that they are endowed by their creator with certain unalienable rights; that among these are life, liberty, and the pursuit of happiness; that, to secure these rights, governments are instituted among men, deriving their just powers from the consent of the governed; that whenever any form of government becomes destructive of these ends, it is the right of the people to alter or to abolish it, and to institute new government, laying its foundation on such principles, and organizing its powers in such form, as to them shall seem most likely to effect their safety and happiness.

Table 4-1 shows you some of the characteristics of formal diction found in The Declaration of Independence.

Table 4-1	Characteristics of Formal Diction
Characteristics	*Example*
Serious tone	The subject matter is the justification of the American colonists' rebellion against English rule. The lengthy sentences (notice that there are only two), the structure of the sentences, and the language create a lofty tone.
Distance between speaker and audience	No one talking privately uses phrasing such as: "laying its foundation on such principles, and organizing its powers in such form, as to them shall seem. . . ." This elaborate structure is what you expect from a public speaker addressing many persons whom he or she does not know personally.
Few personal references	There is no "I" or "me" here. The "We" (the second paragraph) refers to the rebelling colonists *en masse* (as a whole).
Specialized or elevated terms	*political bands, impel, endowed, unalienable,* and so on
No contractions	"it is [not *it's*] the right of the people" and "that they are [not *they're*] endowed by their creator"

Another good example of formal diction is Abraham Lincoln's Gettysburg Address (delivered in 1863), which served as both a eulogy of the soldiers who died on the Gettysburg battlefield during the U.S. Civil War and a declaration of the North's commitment to preserve the Union.

Of course, not all formal diction has the same eloquence as that of the Declaration of Independence and the Gettysburg Address. A credit card agreement and a stock prospectus use formal language, but neither is likely to be preserved for hundreds of years because of the beauty of its language or the gravity of its content.

Using standard English

Most businesses and schools use standard written and spoken English. It's the style of writing that you find in magazines such as *The New Yorker, U.S. News & World Report,* and *The Atlantic Monthly.* Standard written and spoken English conforms to the widely established rules of grammar and usage. (In written form, standard English follows established punctuation and spelling rules, as well.) Following are some other characteristics of standard English that differentiate it from formal English:

✔ The sentence structure is usually simpler than that used in formal English.

✔ It has a serious, but not elevated, tone.

✔ It uses familiar, rather than specialized, terms.

If you were to rewrite the second paragraph of the Declaration of Independence (see the preceding section) in standard English, you'd end up with something like the following:

> We believe these things to be true: All people are created equal and have certain God-given rights. Among these rights are life, liberty, and the pursuit of happiness. To secure these rights, people create governments, and these governments get their just powers from the consent of the governed. Any time the government threatens to destroy the lives, liberty, or happiness of its people, the people have the right to change or abolish the government and create a new government that will be most likely to secure their safety and happiness.

The rewritten paragraph contains the characteristics of standard English diction as shown in Table 4-2.

Table 4-2	Characteristics of Informal Diction
Characteristics	*Example*
Simple sentence structure	The sentences follow the traditional subject-verb-direct object structure common to most English sentences. For example, "We [subject] believe [verb] these things [direct object]. . . ." They are also relatively short. As rewritten, this paragraph has four sentences. In its original form, it's just one sentence.
Serious but not elevated tone	By shortening the sentence structure and replacing elevated terms (such as "endowed") with more familiar terms (such as "given"), the tone remains serious but is no longer lofty.
Familiar terms	The paragraph includes "God-given" instead of "endowed by their creator," and "people create governments" instead of "governments are instituted among men."

In most of your speech and writing, you want to use formal diction (or standard English).

Employing everyday English

Informal diction is the kind of diction you use every day, such as when you're talking with co-workers or writing to a friend. Referred to as *colloquial* language, informal diction is straightforward and conversational and has the following characteristics:

- ✔ It uses common terms, as well as slang.

- ✔ It often uses sentence fragments (incomplete sentences) to convey complete meaning.

- ✔ The tone is informal, despite the seriousness of the content.

- ✔ It often uses contractions.

The Before and After examples show the difference between formal diction and colloquial language:

Before

I'm *invigorated.*
I'm *exhausted.*
I *failed* my driving test.

After

I'm *full of energy.*
I'm *beat.*
I *flunked* my driving test.

Two hallmarks of colloquial language are *slang* (coined words and phrases or new meanings for established terms) and vernacular (language peculiar to a region). The following sections explain these in more detail.

Gettin' down with some slang

Slang is fun, informal, and personal — great for casual conversations with friends. It develops just as other levels of language develop. The methods of development include the following:

- ✔ **Words acquire new meanings.** *Cat* becomes a synonym for a cool person.

- ✔ **Meanings become extended.** *Fink* referred only to strikebreakers at first, but it now refers to any betrayer.

> ✔ **Words become abbreviated.** *Hamburger* becomes *burger; neighborhood* becomes *hood.*

> ✔ **Words are created to fill a need.** *Tailgating* describes driving too closely behind another vehicle; *hip-hop* refers to a style of dance and music.

Some fairly recent slang terms are *bozo,* meaning "clown," *dweeb* and *nerd,* which both refer to a social misfit, and *space cadet,* which is a term for someone who doesn't pay attention.

New slang expressions come from a wide range of sources, including teenagers, sports groups, politicians, criminals, and the armed services. Sometimes, with enough exposure, slang expressions will pass into general use. Still, keep the following in mind:

> ✔ Slang doesn't travel well around the country or between generations. As such, you run the very real risk of being misunderstood if you use it indiscriminately.

> ✔ Never use slang in standard written and spoken English. Not only do you run the risk of being misunderstood, but it is also considered inappropriately casual. Therefore, don't use slang in business meetings, job interviews, or formal speeches.

Talkin' the Talk

Joe Cool is going for an interview at the famous Wall Street Stuffy Investment Corporation. Joe is young — only 22 — and smart. He ditched the Ricky Martin haircut, removed his tongue ring, and covered his tattoos with a navy-blue pinstripe suit. He walks the walk . . . but can he talk the talk? Lean a little closer to the door.

Interviewer:	So, why do you think you would be an asset to Stuffy Investment Corporation, Mr. Cool?
Joe Cool:	This is like a totally rad company. Man, it's phat. Like rippin'. I can for sure supersize in a total ten place like this, sir.
Translation:	This is a great company. It's impressive. Very impressive. I can really make a contribution to a great company like this one, sir.
Interviewer:	Well, Mr. Cool, thank you for your time. I shall waste no time reading your resume.
Joe Cool:	Slap me five.

Poor Joe. I bet the interviewer will "waste no time" at all reading Joe's resume before putting it in the circular file — the garbage can. All things being equal, I assume that Joe's rejection is based completely on his language.

Recognizing regional differences

Vernacular, also called "regionalism," is the ordinary language of a particular region. Like colloquial language and slang, vernacular (also referred to as *dialect*) may not be understood by a wide audience. However, as TV and the Internet increase communication between regions, vernacular differences represent fewer and fewer problems and misunderstandings. Table 4-3 lists some common vernacular expressions.

Table 4-3	Common Vernacular Nouns
Vernacular	*Meaning*
gravy, sauce	Italian tomato sauce; marinara
hoagie, hero, grinder, sub	sandwich on a roll
pop, soda, cola	soft drink
flip-flops, thongs, zoris	plastic sandals
lightning bugs, fireflies	Lampyridae beetles
ride	vehicle; transportation

Nonstandard usage is very casual speech where normal grammar rules are ignored or broken. Despite its inclusion in most dictionaries, the verb *ain't* (meaning "am not; are not; have not") is still nonstandard, and you should not use it and other expressions containing double negatives (as in "I don't got no oranges") or subject-verb disagreement ("we was at the movies"), except in the most casual situations when you're absolutely sure that your audience will understand and appreciate your unconventional style.

Bringing Home the Bacon: Idioms

An *idiom* is an expression whose meaning differs from the literal, word-for-word translation. So, if you're the person in your family who "brings home the bacon," you're the one who provides financial and material support for your household — which may or may not include bacon.

Getting your information "straight from the horse's mouth" doesn't mean that you can understand equine speech; it means that you received the news from a knowledgeable, reliable source. Most idioms are nonsense if you take them literally, as Little Willy demonstrates in the following Talkin' the Talk section.

Idioms are easy to understand if you already know them, but very puzzling if you don't. They pose great difficulty for people whose first language isn't English. Table 4-4 lists a few common idioms.

Table 4-4	Common Idioms
Idioms	**Meaning**
a long shot	not likely to happen
a slip of the tongue	verbal mistake
bite the dust	die
dog-eat-dog	fierce competition
get some z's	get some sleep
hit the ceiling	get very angry
lose your marbles	go insane
pack it in	finish working; quit
stack the deck	cheat
toss your cookies	vomit
waltz off with	steal
wipe the slate clean	start fresh

I say turkey, you say turnip

All languages have idioms. For example, Americans say "holy cow;" the French say "holy blue" (sacre bleu). Americans call a bad movie a "turkey;" the French call it a "turnip" (un navel). Americans say, "that's the last straw;" the French say, "that's the last of the string beans." Americans say, "mind your own business," while the French say, "these are not your onions." In French, a short man is "as tall as three apples," but a very short man is "as tall as three sitting apples." Clearly, one country's idiom is not necessarily another's "cup of tea," as they say in England!

Talkin' the Talk

Butch Babysitter is minding Little Willy. Butch, a gentle soul despite his macho name, is planning how they'll spend the day.

Butch: We can't play outside, Little Willy, because it's raining cats and dogs.

Little Willy: Ugh! Are there squished cats and dogs all over the street? That's sooo gross. Can I go look?

Butch: No, Little Willy, 'raining cats and dogs' is just an expression. It means it's raining very hard.

Little Willy: Darn.

Butch: Maybe we'll go to the movies. The new cartoon really caught my eye.

Little Willy: Caught your eye? Does it hurt? (covering his eyes):

Butch: Little Willy, 'caught my eye' is another idiom. It means that something looked very interesting.

Little Willy: Butch, you sure talk funny.

LANGUAGE LORE

Minding your p's and q's while wetting your whistle

Some idioms have interesting histories. For instance, the idiom "mind your p's and q's" hails from English pubs long ago. Back then, ale was ordered by pints and quarts (as it still is in many places in Europe). When customers got unruly, the bartender would yell, "Mind your own pints and quarts and settle down!" Hence the idiom, "mind your p's and q's".

The idiom "wet your whistle" also has a curious past. Many years ago in England, pub regulars had a whistle baked into the rim or handle of their ceramic mugs; they would blow the whistle to get service. "Wet your whistle" was the idiom inspired by this practice.

You can find many more word histories in *Brewer's Dictionary of Phrase and Fable*, 16th Edition, by Ebenezer Cobham Brewer, Adrian Room, and Terry Pratchett (Harpercollins) and *Morris Dictionary of Word and Phrase Origins* by William and Mary Morris (Harpercollins).

When you use idioms, make sure that you get them right. One incorrect word can make the entire idiom sound weird. My sister was talking about trying to maintain her dignity and said, "You know . . . save nose." No one was very dignified as we explained that she meant "save face."

Abbreviating Acronyms

An *acronym* is a word made from the first letters of a series of words. There are no periods between the letters. Table 4-5 lists a handful of the most often used acronyms.

Table 4-5	Common Acronyms
Acronym	*Meaning*
AIDS (aydz)	Acquired Immune Deficiency Syndrome
MADD (mad)	Mothers Against Drunk Driving
NASA (*nas*-uh)	National Aeronautics and Space Administration
NATO (*nay*-toh)	North Atlantic Treaty Organization
scuba (*skoo*-buh)	self-contained underwater breathing apparatus
snafu (sna-*foo*)	situation normal, all fouled up
radar (*ray*-dar)	radio detecting and ranging

Don't confuse acronyms with plain old abbreviations. Abbreviations are said as separate letters, as in MVP (most valuable player), SEC (Securities and Exchange Commission), and NAACP (National Association for the Advancement of Colored People) — you may say "en-double-ay-cee-pee", but you're still pronouncing the letters, not saying them as a word.

Never use an acronym if there is the slightest chance that your listener or reader won't understand what you mean. If you introduce yourself to someone on a cruise ship by saying, "I'm from NASA," your shipmate may think you're from Nassau, the capital city in the Bahamas. Always say the full phrase if you have the slightest reason to think that your audience may not be familiar with a particular acronym.

Part II
Mastering the Basics

The 5th Wave   By Rich Tennant

"I ADVISE COMPANIES WHERE THE USE OF HURTFUL LANGUAGE APPEARS EPIDEMIC. THAT'S RIGHT, YOUR HONOR — I'M AN INSULTANT CONSULTANT."

In this part . . .

To help your vocabulary flourish and grow, you have to nourish it and tend to the basics. The basics of words are roots, prefixes, and suffixes — the core, the element at the beginning, and the element at the end. In a word sandwich, the root is the meat, and the prefix and suffix are the slices of bread.

Of course, vocabulary has lots and lots of open-faced sandwiches — a variety of words with prefixes but not suffixes (and vice versa), plenty of words with just a root, and some with two roots. In these chapters, I assemble a smorgasbord of prefixes, roots, and suffixes, and show you how the same ingredients can create a variety of masterpieces.

Tie your napkin around your neck and get ready for a word feast!

Chapter 5

Getting to the Root of the Matter

In This Chapter

▶ Realizing the importance of roots

▶ Mastering Greek roots

▶ Focusing on Latin roots

*H*ave you ever joined a conversation where people used words you didn't know? It's awful when you can't follow, but who wants to be the one who asks, "What does *that* mean?" You'd just get looks, right? The more words you know, the better able you are to understand what others say and to express what you have to say.

But no one wants to spend hours memorizing lists of words — that's about as appealing as watching paint dry. Instead, by mastering a handful (or two) of word roots, you build a bank of knowledge that you can draw on whenever you encounter a new word.

This chapter gives you fistfuls of the Greek and Latin roots that you may encounter frequently as you expand your vocabulary. When you combine these roots with various prefixes and suffixes (the topics of Chapters 6 and 7, respectively), you have an entire system for puzzling out the meanings of unfamiliar words. This capability is tremendously helpful if you're trying to learn English, preparing for many of the standardized tests given in school, or simply wanting become a more proficient reader or speaker.

Tending to Word Roots

A *root* is the basic element of a word, and it is the foundation on which the meaning of a word is built. Many roots are real words in their own right: *graph* (a diagram) and *term* (a fixed time or date), for example. Although these roots can have other elements, they don't *need* other elements to be complete. Most roots, however, do need other elements. For example, the roots *archy* (government) and *dox* (opinion or belief) need to be combined with other word elements, like prefixes, suffixes, or even other roots:

✔ **dyarchy:** a government with two rulers, from the prefix *dy-* (meaning two) and the root *archy* (meaning government)

✔ **anarchist:** one who rebels against governmental authority, from the prefix *an-* (meaning without or no), the root *archy* (meaning government), and the suffix *-ist* (meaning one who)

✔ **orthodox:** conforming to established doctrines and practices, from the prefix *ortho-* (meaning right or true) and the root *dox* (meaning opinion or belief)

The following sections give you the lowdown on roots and how you can use them to uncover the meaning of words you don't know — yet.

Exploring the basics of roots

In order to use roots to uncover a word's meaning, you need to know a few things about how roots work. Here's a quick rundown:

✔ **Some roots form whole words by themselves.** For example: *Arbor* means "tree"; *vent* means "opening to allow air to enter"; and *audio* means "sound" or "hearing."

Although these roots form words in and of themselves, you can also combine them with other word elements (like prefixes and suffixes) to make new words, as in the following:

Root	Word Element	New Word	Part of Speech	Definition
arbor	eal	arboreal (ar-*bor*-ee-al)	adj.	of or relating to trees
vent	ilate	ventilate (*vent*-il-ayt)	verb	to expose to air
audio	ible	audible (*aw*-dih-bul)	adj.	able to be heard

✔ **Some roots must be combined with other word elements to form words.** Consider the following examples:

Root	Meaning	Word Element	New Word	Part of Speech	Definition
capit	head	al	capital (*kap*-ih-tul)	adj.	most important
carn	flesh	age	carnage (*kar*-nij)	noun	slaughter
chrono	time	logy	chronology (krah-*nahl*-ih-jee)	noun	timeline

➤ **Prefixes and suffixes alter or refine a word's meaning.** For example, the word *audible* means "able to be heard." With the prefix *in-*, the word becomes *inaudible,* which means "unable to be heard."

➤ **A word can contain more than one root.** For example, *matrilineal* contains the roots *matri* (mother) and *lineal* (line). *Matrilineal,* therefore, means "determining descent through the female line."

Whenever you come upon an unfamiliar word, first check to see if you recognize its root. Even if you can't define a word exactly, recognizing the root gives you a general idea of the word's meaning. For example, if you read the word *geocentric*, knowing that the root *geo* means "earth" helps you figure out that *geocentric* has to do with the center ("centric") of the earth, or earth as the center.

Using roots to grow words

Knowing how words are created gives you the key to figuring out the meaning of new words. When you can put together the meaning of a root with the meaning of a prefix and/or a suffix, you can unlock the definitions of words in a snap.

Putting it together

In this sidebar, you can get a little practice at putting elements together to discover meaning. You may already know the definitions of some of the words that follow. Others may be new to you. Your task, if you choose to accept it, is to figure out what each of the following words means.

The Latin root *cide* means "kill" and "cut." Knowing that, you can probably figure out that insecticide means "the killing of insects." As you read the following chart, cover the last column and see how many words you can decode using what you know about the root and its meaning.

Example	Root Meaning	Definition
genocide	people	killing a race of people
homicide	mankind	a person killing a person
matricide	mother	killing your mother
patricide	father	killing your father
fratricide	brother	killing a brother
sororicide	sister	killing a sister
suicide	self	killing yourself
infanticide	baby	killing a baby
ceticide	whales	killing whales

Adding prefixes and suffixes to roots

A *prefix* is a letter or group of letters attached to the beginning of a word that changes the word's meaning. A *suffix* performs the same function at the end of a word. Chapter 6 is devoted to prefixes, and Chapter 7 covers suffixes. In this section, I give you the blueprints to decipher combinations of roots, prefixes, and suffixes.

Examples of adding a prefix to a root:

de + hydrate = dehydrate (to remove the water or moisture from)

anti + depressant = antidepressant (something that combats depression)

Examples of adding a suffix to a root:

zoo + *ology* = zoology (the study of animals)

bronch + *itis* = bronchitis (inflammation of the bronchial tubes)

You can figure out a word's meaning simply by recognizing its root and prefix. Table 5-1 shows several examples of how the combination of prefixes, roots, and suffixes work together to form words.

Table 5-1		Putting Prefixes, Roots, and Suffixes Together					
Prefix	**+**	**Root**	**+**	**Suffix**	**=**	**Word**	**Part of Speech**	**Definition**
ab	+	duct	+	ed	=	abducted	verb	kidnapped
de	+	ter	+	ent	=	deterrent	adj.	impediment
dis	+	pell	+	ed	=	dispelled	verb	scattered
im	+	peril	+	ed	=	imperiled	verb	put in danger
in	+	cred	+	ible	=	incredible	adj.	unbelievable
re	+	puls	+	ion	=	repulsion	noun	strong dislike
re	+	ferr	+	al	=	referral	noun	connection
re	+	tract	+	able	=	retractable	adj.	able to be drawn back

Grafting roots to roots

You may wonder whether a word element is acting as a prefix or as a root when you encounter words formed by combining two roots. The truth is that, although some word elements are always prefixes and others always come at the end of a word, you can find roots in any position. And, to tell you the truth, it really doesn't matter whether the root is at the beginning of a word, in the middle, or at the end, so long as you understand the word's meaning. A few words with two roots are:

- *Cal* (beauty) + *graph* (to write) forms *calligraphy* (kah-*lig*-rih-fee), which means "elegant penmanship."

- *Carn* (meat) + *vor* (to eat) forms *carnivore* (*kar*-nih-vor), which is someone who eats meat.

- *Chron* (time) + *meter* (measure) forms *chronometer* (krah-*nahm*-ih-ter) — an instrument for measuring time.

Being well-versed in roots like the ones in the preceding list can help you immensely in the language portion of standardized tests.

Getting Scientific with Greek Roots

My husband can trace his roots to Greece (I think his family comes from Sparta), but if your ancestors didn't hail from the Greek isles, you can still get in on the great Greek root bonanza. Many of the words we use every day come from Greek roots.

If you're interested in science — whether you're into science as a career, hobby, or consumer — you'll find these Greek roots useful. Many scientific terms use Greek roots.

Measuring roots

Table 5-2 contains the most useful Greek roots for measurements. Notice that several roots mean the same thing. For example, *macro* and *mega* both mean "large." Check out the examples in the table and read the following chart several times, and you can soon get accustomed to the slight variations in spelling.

Table 5-2		Greek Roots for Measurements		
Root	**Meaning**	**Example**	**Part of Speech**	**Definition**
acr/acro	topmost	acrophobia (ak-roh-*foh*-bee-uh)	noun	fear of high places
arch	first	archbishop (arch-*bish*-up)	noun	most important bishop
chromo/ chroma	color	chromosphere (*kroh*-mohs-feer)	noun	glowing, pinkish region around a star
chron	time	chronicle (*krahn*-ih-kul)	noun	historical record
ger	old	geriatric (jer-ee-*at*-trik)	adj.	relating to old age
horo	hour	horoscope (*hor*-ah-skohp)	noun	diagram drawn from planet placements used to foretell the events of a person's life
meter	measure	altimeter (al-*tim*-ih-ter)	noun	device to measure altitude
neo	new	neophyte (*nee*-oh-fyt)	noun	beginner
paleo	old	paleogeology (pay-lee-oh-jee-*ahl*-ah-jee)	noun	the science of earth's history
prot	first	prototype (*proht*-ah-typ)	noun	first of its kind

Table 5-3 gives you some nice, solid roots — roots that give you words you can easily get a handle on.

Table 5-3		Material Nouns with Greek Roots	
Root	*Meaning*	*Example*	*Definition*
anthro	human	anthropology (an-throh-*pahl*-ih-jee)	study of humans
		anthropomorphism (an-thrah-poh-*mor*-fiz-em)	act of attributing human characteristics to non-human beings or inanimate objects
aster/ astro	star	asterisk (*as*-tehr-isk)	star-shaped mark
		astronaut (*as*-trah-nawt)	person who makes flights in outer space
biblio	book	bibliophile (*bib*-lee-ah-fyl)	book lover (as in a book collector)
		bibliography (bib-lee-*ahg*-rah-fee)	a listing of books and their editions,dates, authors, and so on
dem	people	democracy (dih-*mahk*-rah-see)	government by the people
		demagogue (*dem*-uh-gahg)	rabble-rouser
		demographics (dem-ah-*graf*-ix)	statistical data about a population
geo	earth	geography (jee-*ahg*-rah-fee)	science of the earth's formations and life
		geology (jee-*ahl*-ah-jee)	study of the earth's history as revealed through rocks
morph	form	metamorphosis (met-ah-*mor*-feh-sis)	change of form
		morphology (mor-*fahl*-ah-jee)	branch of biology that deals with plant and animal forms
psycho	mind	psychology (sy-*kahl*-ah-jee)	study of the mind
		psychosis (sy-*koh*-sis)	major mental disorder

Table 5-4 lists still more roots. This time, they're a little harder to grab hold of because they deal mostly with concepts.

Table 5-4		Concept Roots with Nouns	
Root	*Meaning*	*Example*	*Definition*
ped	child	pediatrician (pee-dee-ah-*trish*-en)	doctor who treats children
phil	love	philanthropy (fih-*lan*-thrah-pee)	love of humanity
phob	fear	claustrophobia (klos-trah-*foh*-bee-ah)	fear of confined spaces
archy	rule by	monarchy (*mon*-ar-kee)	rule by a single, undisputed leader
nom	rule	autonomy (aw-*tahn*-ah-mee)	self-rule
onym/nym	name	pseudonym (*soo*-dah-nim)	pen name

Describing nature

According to Greek mythology, the ancients were menaced by a hideous nine-headed serpent with breath so bad that it could knock your socks right off. At home in a watery marsh, the monster took its name, *Hydra,* from the Greek root *hydor,* meaning "water." Killing this monster was no easy matter: When you sliced off one head, two grew in its place. Unfortunately for those being menaced, the central head was immortal. Since the ancient Greeks didn't have Arnold Schwarzenegger, Sylvester Stallone, or Steven Seagal, they sent in Hercules to dispatch the many-headed menace. Hercules was triumphant when he burned off the eight peripheral heads and buried the ninth under a huge rock.

Many useful words are formed from the *hydro/hydr* root; Table 5-5 shows some important ones.

Table 5-5		Words Using the Greek Root Hydro
Word	*Part of Speech*	*Definition*
dehydrate (dee-*hy*-drayt)	verb	to remove water from; to dry out
hydrophobia (hy-drah-*foh*-bee-uh)	noun	abnormal fear of water; rabies (thirst is a symptom)
hydroplane (*hy*-droh-playn)	noun	motorboat that can skim the water's surface; airplane boat that can travel on water
hydroponics (hy-drah-*pah*-nix)	noun	science of growing plants in water
hydropower (*hy*-droh-pow-er)	noun	electric power generated from water
hydrate (*hy*-drayt)	verb	to combine with water
hydrangea (hy-*drayn*-jah)	noun	a type of flowering shrub or vine (that needs much water)
hydrotherapy (hy-droh-*ther*-ah-pee)	noun	medical treatment using water
hydrosphere (*hy*-droh-sfeer)	noun	all the water on the earth, including all surface water, underground water, and moisture in the atmosphere

Table 5-6 features some Greek roots, and words formed from them, that describe the natural world. You may find these words useful in both your personal and professional conversation.

Table 5-6		Greek Roots Describing the Natural World		
Root	*Meaning*	*Example*	*Part of Speech*	*Definition*
bio	life	biology (by-*ahl*-ah-jee)	noun	the study of life
gen	race	genetics (jeh-*neh*-tix)	noun	study of heredity
gyn	woman	gynecologist (gy-neh-*kol*-ah-jist)	noun	doctor who specializes in women's health

(continued)

Table 5-6 *(continued)*

Root	Meaning	Example	Part of Speech	Definition
helio	sun	heliotrope (*hee*-lee-ah-trohp)	noun	sunflower (turns to face the sun)
ichthy	fish	ichthyology (ik-thee-al-ah-jee)	noun	study of fish
ornith	bird	ornithology (or-nih-*thahl*-ah-jee)	noun	study of birds
phyt	plant	phytology (fy-*tahl*-ah-jee)	noun	botany
polit	citizen	cosmopolitan (kahz-mah-*pahl*-ih-tan)	noun/adj.	citizen of the world, sophisticated
pyr	fire	pyrogenic (py-rah-*jen*-ik)	adj.	producing heat
soma	body	somatic (soh-*mat*-ik)	adj.	physical
thermo	heat	thermostat (*thur*-mah-stat)	noun	device for regulating heat
zoo	animal	zoology (zoh-*ah*-leh-jee)	noun	study of animals

The Greek meaning of the *pedo/pedi* root is "child" — the word *pediatrician,* meaning "a doctor who treats children," comes from this root. The same root in Latin, however, means "foot." The words *pedal* and *pedestrian* come from the Latin root. This isn't the only instance of a similar root having different meanings to the Greeks and Romans. The root *homo* is another example. The Greek root *homo* means "same." *Homonym* (words that are spelled and pronounced the same but have different meaning) and *homogenous* (alike) use the Greek root. The Latin root *homo/homi,* however, means "man" (as in human). Combine that with the suffix meaning "kill" to get *homicide* (to kill a person).

Greek roots for beliefs and ideas

Several English words use Greek roots for beliefs and ideas. These roots come in handy in the most unexpected situations, like job-hunting. Table 5-7 gives you a few more Greek roots to chew on.

Table 5-7		**Nouns Using Greek Roots for Beliefs and Ideas**	
Root	*Meaning*	*Example*	*Definition*
archy	rule by	monarchy (*mon*-ar-kee)	rule by a single, undisputed leader
cracy	rule by	plutocracy (plew-*tahk*-rih-see)	rule by the wealthy or rich
gam	marriage	polygamy (pah-*lig*-ah-mee)	having more than one spouse at the same time
graph	writing	cardiograph (*kar*-dee-oh-graf)	an instrument that registers the heart's movement
ideo	idea	ideology (aye-dee-*ahl*-ah-jee)	body of knowledge
logy/ ology	branch of knowledge	entomology (en-tah-*mahl*-ah-jee)	study of insects
nom	rule	autonomy (aw-*tahn*-oh-mee)	self-rule
onym/ nym	name	pseudonym (*soo*-dah-nim)	pen name
orama	view	panorama (pan-ah-*ram*-ah)	complete view
path	feeling	sympathy (*sim*-pah-thee)	sharing another's feelings, compassion
psycho	mind	psychology (sy-*kol*-ah-jee)	study of the mind
theo	god	theology (thee-*ah*-leh-jee)	study of God or religious questions
sophy/ soph	wisdom	sophistry (*sahf*-is-tree)	reasoning that seems plausible but is actually misleading; tricky reasoning

Talkin' the Talk

Donna Dimbulb is reading the want ads, looking for a summer job. She's with her best-friend-in-the-whole-wide-world, Candy Coed. Here's what the girls say as their 5-inch-long nail extensions flick the newspaper:

Donna Dimbulb:	'Wanted: music lover to work at the Philharmonic. Responsibilities include filing, answering the telephone, light typing. . . .' *Philharmonic*? I have to fill up harmonicas? I can't play a harmonica. I can't even play the radio.
Candy Coed:	Don-uh, I think the *Philharmonic* is a musical group. *Phil* means love, so the word must mean 'love of music,' like *philosophy* means 'love of wisdom,' and *Philadelphia* means 'city of brotherly love.'
Donna Dimbulb:	Can-deeeee, that's a great idea. Let's get some Philly cheese steaks for lunch. Like totally cool.

Cultivating Latin Roots

If you think the English language has borrowed a lot of roots from the Greeks, wait until you see what it has recycled from Latin. Linguists estimate that 90 percent of all English words can be traced back to classical Greek and Latin roots!

For example, the Latin root *plac* (from the Latin word *placere*) means "pleasure." Words formed from this root include *placid* (smooth or tranquil), *complacent* (unperturbed by surrounding events), *implacable* (not easily soothed or satisfied), and *placate* (to calm someone by giving in). The Latin root *nomin/nomen* (name) has given English a great many words, including the ones in Table 5-8.

Table 5-8		Name Words
Word	*Part of Speech*	*Definition*
ignominious (ig-noh-*min*-ee-us)	adj.	dishonorable or disgraceful to one's name
misnomer (mis-*noh*-mer)	noun	use of the wrong name
nomenclature (*noh*-men-klay-cher)	noun	system of naming things
nominal (*nahm*-ih-nal)	adj.	so-called; in name only
nominate (*nahm*-ih-nayt)	verb	name someone for an office
nominee (*nahm*-ih-*nee*)	noun	person proposed for an office or position

For a dead language, Latin is pretty lively, as attested to by all the English words that use Latin roots.

Making and moving roots

The Romans were the movers and shakers of the ancient Western world. Whereas the Greeks were known for being thinkers, the Romans were known for being people of action. The Roman Empire, during its peak, encompassed all of Eastern and Western Europe (including the British Isles) and extended into Northern Africa and the western parts of Asia. The Roman Empire was known for its strong, centralized government, the 400 years of peace it secured for all the Western world (Pax Romana), and its massive public works (such as the building of roads, irrigation systems, and canals). So it's no wonder that many English words related to making and moving stuff use Latin roots.

For example, the Latin root *dict,* which means "to say," gives the English language words like *dictum* (a formal statement or principle), *dictate* (to command), and *dictator* (one who rules by force; you do what he says). The root *fact,* which means "to make," gives the English language words like *factory* (a place where goods are produced) and *manufacture* (to make for use). Table 5-9 lists other Latin roots that relate to doing something.

Table 5-9		Latin Roots for Making and Moving		
Root	**Meaning**	**Example**	**Part of Speech**	**Definition**
duct	lead	ductile (*duk*-til)	adj.	easily molded
		aqueduct (*ak*-wih-dukt)	noun	canal
fer	carry	transfer (*trans*-fer)	verb	to carry to another place
funct	perform	functional (*funk*-shin-al)	adj.	able to be used, useful
grad	go/step	degrade (dee-*grayd*)	verb	to lower in rank or status; to corrupt
		gradual (*grad*-jew-al)	adj.	going in degrees or phases
ject	throw	reject (ree-*jekt*)	verb	to throw aside; discard
pel/puls	move	impel (im-*pel*)	verb	to urge or propel
scrib	write	scribble (*skrib*-el)	verb	to write quickly and carelessly; scrawl
		inscribe (in-*skryb*)	verb	to write or engrave

Sizing up other Latin roots

You can find several other Latin roots in English words. Consider the following examples:

✔ *Annual* (yearly) uses the Latin root *ann/enn,* which means "year." *Anniversary* (the yearly commemoration of a particular date) uses the same root, as does *biennial* (occurring every two years) and *biannual* (occurring twice in a single year).

✔ The word *annihilate* (uh-*ny*-uh-layt) uses the Latin root *nihil,* which means "nothing." To annihilate something is to do away with it entirely. The word *nihilism* (*nee*-uh-liz-uhm), a belief that life has no meaning or value, also comes from this root.

✔ The word *pendulous* (*pen*-dyoo-luhs), which means "drooping," uses the Latin root *pend,* which means "weigh." The word *pendulum* (*pen*-dyoo-luhm; an object that swings back and forth freely from a fixed point) also uses this root.

Table 5-10 lists other Latin roots, including those that describe size, amount, and location. Study the roots, examples, and definitions. As you read, consider how you would you use some of these words in your daily life.

Table 5-10		Latin Measuring and Other Roots		
Root	*Meaning*	*Example*	*Part of Speech*	*Definition*
alt	high	altitude (*al*-tih-tood)	noun	the height of an object above the earth's surface or above sea level
brev	short	abbreviation (ah-bree-vee-*ay*-shun)	noun	a shortened form of a word or phrase
centr	center	centrist (*sen*-trist)	noun	one who holds a moderate viewpoint
dors	back	dorsal (*dor*-sel)	adj.	situated near or on the back (for example, a dorsal fin is the back fin)
fin	limit	finish (*fin*-ish)	verb	bring to completion
term	final	terminal (*tur*-mih-nal)	adj.	relating to the end or the boundary
magni	large	magnify (*mag*-nih-fy)	verb	to cause to seem larger or more important than is really so
med	middle	median (*mee*-dee-an)	noun	middle; intermediate
multi	many	multiply (*mul*-tih-ply)	verb	to increase or augment
omni	all	omniscient (ahm-*nish*-ent)	adj.	all-knowing
sed/sess	sit	sedate (si-*dayt*)	adj.	calm, quiet, or composed
ten/tin	hold	tenet (*ten*-it)	noun	belief held as true
vid, vis	see	visual (*viz*-yu-al)	adj.	that is or can be seen; visible

Associating with gods and goddesses

The word *panacea* comes from the Greek goddess of healing, Panacea. (A *panacea* is a remedy for all diseases, an answer to all problems and difficulties.) The Greek and Roman gods and goddesses had dominion over various realms, and over the years their names have become tied to their areas of influence. The following list gives you both the Greek and Roman names and their associations. You're probably familiar with a few of them already.

Greek name	Roman name	Domain
Aphrodite	Venus	goddess of love and beauty
Ares	Mars	god of war
Artemis	Diana	goddess of the hunt and childbirth
Athena	Minerva	goddess of wisdom, war, and art
Dionysus	Bacchus	god of wine and madness
Eros	Cupid	god of love
Hera	Juno	goddess of marriage
Hermes	Mercury	god of roads, cunning, commerce, wealth, luck
Hymen	Hymen	god of marriage
Poseidon	Neptune	god of the sea, earthquakes, and horses
Zeus	Jupiter, Jove	supreme ruler; overseer of justice and fate

Chapter 6

Starting Off with Prefixes

. . . .

In This Chapter

▶ Decoding unfamiliar words through prefixes

▶ Getting familiar with a few Greek and Latin prefixes

▶ Discovering the uses of Anglo-Saxon prefixes

▶ Using words that function as prefixes

. . . .

Knowing common prefixes is *very* useful because it enables you to figure out the meaning of many unfamiliar words. In addition, by discovering the building blocks of words, you can easily understand and master thousands of helpful English words. In this chapter, you discover how prefixes can help you improve your vocabulary — without breaking a sweat.

The ancient alchemists wanted to change lead into gold. They didn't succeed, but *you* can by using prefixes to decode unfamiliar words. And that's only the beginning. Knowing just a handful of prefixes can make it easy for you to figure out the definitions of many words — without ever having to use a dictionary.

Going to the Head of the Word

A prefix is a letter or a group of letters that appears at the beginning of a word and changes the meaning of the original word in such a way that you have a different word. For example, if the base word is *make,* "to create, or bring into being," and you attach the prefix *re-,* "do again," to it, you create a different word: *remake,* which means "to make again or anew" as a verb, or "something remade" as a noun. In this case, the prefix alters the word's original meaning.

Sometimes the prefix actually creates a derivative word. You can't remove the prefix, for example, and still have a word that means anything. Take, for example, the word *pseudonym* (*soo*-duh-nim). This English word is derived (or made up of) two Greek elements: the prefix *pseudo-* (false) and the root *onyma* (name). Knowing this, you can figure out that a pseudonym is a false name. Similarly, *anonymous* (uh-*nahn*-uh-mus) comes from the Greek prefix *a-* (without) and the root *onyma* (name). Literally, *anonymous* means "without a name."

The beauty of prefixes — and the reason why knowing a few of the most common ones is important — is that they help you figure out the meaning of a word you may not have seen before. Being able to do that is immeasurably helpful if you're just learning English, or if you find yourself staring down the word *hypaethral* on a college entrance exam.

Just in case you're interested, *hypaethral* (hih-*pee*-thrul) means "open to the sky." The word is made up of the Greek prefix *hypo-,* meaning "below," and the Greek root *aithros* (heaven).

As you become familiar with prefixes, keep the following points in mind:

- ✔ Several prefixes have more than one meaning. For example, the Latin prefix *in-* can mean *in* (as in *inhabit*), but it can also mean *not* (as in *inflexible*). As a result, always use context to help you decode a word. The way the word is used often tells you what it means.

- ✔ It's very common for prefixes to have slight variations in their spelling, such as *syn-/sym-* (together) or *dis-/di-/dif-* (apart). The prefix *ad-* (to or toward) has 11 variations: *a-, ab-, ac-, af-, ag-, al-, an-, ap-, ar-, as-,* and *at-*! Despite these slight variations, the prefix still means the same thing.

The form the prefix takes often depends on what letters follow it in the word. Using the prefix *a-* as an example, you use *ac-* if the letter immediately following it is a *c, k,* or *q* (acculturate, acknowledge, or acquire). You use *af-* if the next letter is an *f* (affirmative), *ag-* if the next letter is a *g* (aggrandize), and so on.

Sometimes you may not even recognize a prefix as a prefix. If that's the case, don't sweat it. You don't have to know it's a prefix. The point of this chapter isn't to force you to remember that *re-* or *pseudo-* — or whatever — is a prefix. The point is to help you understand what these various groups of letters mean so that you can figure out the meaning of whatever word you're stuck on.

Talkin' the Talk

It's Sunday afternoon. The big boys are watching baseball on Ralphie's massive TV. It's a happy time, until star player Shawn Steroid strikes out . . . or does he?

Announcer: The matter will be adjudicated while we break for a commercial.

Ralphie: Huh? What's *adjudicated* mean?

Wally Word: I read in Chapter 6 of *Vocabulary For Dummies* that the prefix *ad-* means 'to,' 'at,' or 'upon.' I know that *judicate* has something to do with judging, therefore, *adjudicate* must mean something like 'to make a judgment upon something.' The umpire will make a decision on the play.

Ralphie: Gee, Wally, you're one smart fella. So why do you keep hogging the Buffalo wings?

Seeing Prefixes Everywhere: De-, Re-, In-, Un-, and Pre-

There are some prefixes in English that are so frequently used that most dictionaries don't even define all the words that are made with them. For example, look up *un-* and you get nearly two pages of nothing but lists of words, without definitions, using that prefix. This lack of definitions isn't a problem, however, because *un-* almost always means "not." Stick *not* in front of the base word, and you have your meaning. *Unbiased* means "not biased;" *unschooled* means "not schooled;" *unsympathetic* means "not sympathetic." Here are some other very common prefixes:

- **De-** means "down," "remove," or "from," as in *delight,* which literally means "from light," and *demented,* which translates to "removed from one's (right) mind."

- **Re-** means "again" as in *renew* (make new again) or *reconnect* (to connect again). It can also mean "back," as in *recall* (call back).

✔ **In-** has several meanings and several forms, including *in-, il-, im-,* and *ir-,* which are Anglo-Saxon prefixes. (See the section "Adding In Anglo-Saxon Prefixes," later in this chapter, for more information on these prefixes.) It is also close cousins with *em-* and *en-.* In all its forms, *in-* can mean "not" (illiterate, immodest) or some form of "in": "within" (inhabit, inherit), "put into" (enthrone), "provide with" (empower), and "surround" (envelope).

✔ **Pre-** means "before" or "prior to" (preteen: before 13 years old; prenatal: taking place prior to birth), or "in front of" (precede: go in front of).

Sometimes it's hard to decide whether you should hyphenate these prefixes. Use a hyphen in the following situations:

✔ When not hyphenating may cause confusion about the word's meaning: *re-creation* (a second creation) versus *recreation* (having fun), or *re-form* (to form again) versus *reform* (to change from bad to good)

✔ When the word following the prefix repeats the letters in the prefix (*re-recover,* for example)

✔ When the second element is a proper noun or starts with a capital letter (such as *un-American* and *re-Christianize*)

The following sections offer a number of examples of words that use these prefixes.

Retooling words

You can do everything from reducing your stress to revitalizing your career by using the two little letters that mean "again" — *re-. Re-* can also mean "back." Table 6-1 lists some verbs that start with *re-.*

Table 6-1	*Re-* Words
Word	*Definition*
reacquaint	meet again
reallocate	distribute again
reattach	fasten or connect again
recertify	issue a license again
recommission	put back into commission
recur	occur a second time
redo	do over; fix

Word	Definition
refer	to send or direct for information or treatment (literally to carry back)
renumber	put in a new order; count or label again
repeat	say again
replace	find a substitute for someone or something that has gone
reschedule	to make a new appointment
revert	go back (literally to turn back)

Deconstructing de-

Like many prefixes, *de-* has several meanings: "reduce," "remove," and "to get off of." Table 6-2 gives you examples of *de-* words. (All the words in the table are verbs.)

Table 6-2	*De-* Words
Word	**Definition**
debone	remove the bones
decertify	remove certification
decommission	take out of commission
decompose	break down
de-emphasize	remove emphasis from
decrease	reduce in size
dethrone	remove from the throne
derail	fall off the rails; throw off course

Notice the hyphen between the two *e*'s in *de-emphasize*. Although personal preference usually dictates whether you include a hyphen after a prefix that ends with the same vowel as the root word starts with, that little hyphen can make things a lot clearer for your readers.

Including in- (and em- and en- and . . .)

The prefix *in-* has a lot of meanings and several variations: *in-, il-, im-, ir-, em-,* and *en-*.

These variations can mean "not," "with," "put into," "provide with," and "surround." To determine the appropriate meaning, look at the context. Table 6-3 lists words using the prefix *in-* (or one of its other forms).

Table 6-3	*In-* Words	
Word	**Part of Speech**	**Definition**
empathize (*em*-puh-thyz)	verb	put yourself in another's place in order to feel what that person feels
enslave (en-*slayv*)	verb	bring into slavery; make a slave of
entomb (en-*toom*)	verb	put into a tomb
illegitimate (il-leh-*jit*-uh-muht)	adj.	not legitimate or legal
immobile (ih-*moh*-bul)	adj.	not movable
imperfect (im-*pur*-fikt)	adj.	not perfect
inactive (in-*ak*-tiv)	adj.	not active
inane (in-*ayn*)	adj.	without substance; shallow or foolish
incessant (in-*ses*-ent)	adj.	without interruption
irrepressible (ir-rih-*pres*-uh-bul)	adj.	impossible to repress

Doing and undoing with un-

The prefix *un-* means "not" or "the opposite of." *Uncharitable* means "the opposite of charitable;" *unhappy* means "the opposite of happy," *uninterested* means "the opposite of interested." The easiest way to deal with *un-* is to simply replace it with *not* when you're figuring out a word's meaning. Table 6-4 lists various *un-* words. Frankly, it's only the tip of the iceberg. (All the words in the table are adjectives.)

Table 6-4	*Un-* Words
Word	**Definition**
unambiguous (un-am-*big*-yoo-us)	not ambiguous; clear
unbuckled (un-*buk*-uld)	not buckled; undone
uncensored (un-*sen*-surd)	not censored; not scanned for objectionable content
unclad (un-*klad*)	not dressed
unjustified (un-*jus*-tuh-fy)	not justified; without good reason
unruly (un-*roo*-lee)	not disciplined; out of control
unswerving (un-*swurv*-ing)	not altering; steady

Previewing pre-

Pre- means "before" or "in front of." Examples of words with the *pre-* prefix include *preview* (view before) and *preamble* (introductory statement to a speech). Table 6-5 lists some more words that use the prefix *pre-*.

Table 6-5	*Pre-* Words	
Word	**Part of Speech**	**Definition**
precede (pree-*seed*)	verb	to go before or come ahead of
precut (pree-*kut*)	adj.	cut before
predestine (pree-*des*-tin)	verb	to ordain beforehand
preface (*pref*-is)	noun	introductory remarks
prehistoric (pree-his-*tor*-ik)	adj.	prior to written history
prelude (*pray*-lood)	noun	introductory performance
premarital (pree-*mair*-uht-ul)	adj.	before marriage
pre-owned (pree-*ohnd*)	adj.	used
premeditated (pree-*med*-uh-tayt)	adj.	planned beforehand
preset (*pree*-set)	verb	set before

The word *prefix* is made up of the Latin prefix *prae*, which means "before," and the root word *fix*, which means "firmly placed." It takes a prefix to describe *prefix!*

Another prefix that means "before" is *ante-. Antebellum,* for example, means "before the war" (*ante-* = before and *bellum* = war). In American history, antebellum refers specifically to the time before the Civil War. To study the antebellum South would be to study the South as it was prior the war between the States. An antebellum mansion is a plantation.

Eyeing Other Common Prefixes

In addition to the most commonly used prefixes (see the preceding section), English words use many other prefixes, also. Examples of these include *anti-* (against) and *con-* (with). Additional prefixes are so basic to English that I include them here, as well. These are the prefixes used to indicate degree, number, and location.

Prefixes meaning "not" and "against": A-, anti-, dis-, and more

Several prefixes mean "not" or "against:" *a-, anti-, dis-,* and *in-* and its variations (see the earlier section "Including *in-* (and *em-* and *en-*)" for details). Table 6-6 lists some examples of these prefixes.

Table 6-6		Prefixes Meaning "Not" and "Against"		
Prefix	**Meaning**	**Word**	**Part of Speech**	**Definition**
a	not, without	atypical (ay-*tip*-ih-kul)	adj.	not typical
		amoral (ay-*mor*-ul)	adj.	without morals; neither moral nor immoral
anti	opposite, against	antipathy (an-*tip*-uh-thee)	noun	hatred

Prefix	Meaning	Word	Part of Speech	Definition
		antihero (*an*-ty-he-roh)	noun	protagonist (or main character) who lacks heroic qualities; opposite of a conventional hero
		anticlimactic (an-ty-kly-*mak*-tik)	adj.	the opposite of a climax; an event that should have been climactic but wasn't
dis	not	discord (*dis*-kord)	noun	not in harmony
		disagree (dis-uh-*gree*)	verb	to not be in agreement
in (il, ir, im, ig)	not or without	inconsiderate (in-kun-*sid*-er-it)	adj.	not sensitive to other's feelings
		illegible (ih-*lej*-uh-buhl)	adj.	not readable
		immodest (im-*mod*-ist)	adj.	indecent (the opposite of modest)
		impeccable (im-*pek*-uh-bul)	adj.	without flaws
		ingrate (*in*-grayt)	noun	ungrateful person
		ignore (ig-*nor*)	verb	refuse to know or notice

Getting it together: Co-, con-, and sym-/syn-

Several prefixes mean "with" or "together." If you express *con*tempt for a *co*-worker and then *com*municate your regret by inviting your *col*league to ac*com*pany you to *con*sume some *con*sommé, you're using many of these prefixes.

In the preceding paragraph, notice the variations of *co-*, including *col-, com-,* and *con-.* They all mean "with." *Sym-* (and its variation *syn-*) also means "with" or "together." Table 6-7 lists more examples of words that use these prefixes.

Table 6-7		Prefixes Meaning "With" or "Together"		
Prefix	**Meaning**	**Word**	**Part of Speech**	**Definition**
co	with, together	co-pay	noun	portion of the total amount due
		cohabit	verb	live together
		co-worker	noun	colleague
com, con, col	with	compress (kom-*pres*)	verb	squeeze; press together
		concave (kon-*kayv*)	adj.	curved like the inside of a bowl
		conjunction (kon-*junk*-shun)	noun	act of joining together
		consort (*kon*-sort)	noun	spouse; group of musicians who play together
		collaborate (kuh-*lab*-uh-rayt)	verb	work together
sym/syn	together	symbiosis (sim-bee-*oh*-sis)	noun	two dissimilar organisms living together
		symmetrical (sih-*meh*-tri-kuhl)	adj.	having parts of equal measure
		synopsis (sih-*nop*-sis)	noun	summary

Homing in on location prefixes

Just as some prefixes show number or degree (as explained in the following two sections), other prefixes — such as *circum-* — indicate location or direction. If you know that *circum-* means "around," then you can figure out that the phrase *circumnavigate the globe* means "to go around the world." Peek at Table 6-8 to see more examples of this and other location/direction prefixes.

Table 6-8		Prefixes That Indicate Location or Direction		
Prefix	**Meaning**	**Word**	**Part of Speech**	**Definition**
a, ad, ap	to, toward	approach	verb	move toward
		address	verb	speak to
cata	down	catacomb (*kat*-uh-kohm)	noun	underground room
		catalogue (*kat*-uh-log)	noun	an extensive list of items
circum	around	circumambulate (sur-kum-*am*-byoo-layt)	verb	walk around
		circumference (sur-*kum*-fur-uhns)	noun	outer boundary of a circle
		circumscribe (*sur*-kum-skryb)	verb	restrict
		circumvent (sur-kum-*vent*)	verb	go around; avoid
hypo	under or below	hypothermia (hy-poh-*thur*-mee-uh)	noun	body temperature below normal
		hypodermic (hy-puh-*dur*-mik)	adj.	beneath the skin
sub	under	subordinate (suh-*bord*-in-it)	adj.	lower than or inferior to
		subterranean (sub-tuh-*ray*-nee-un)	adj.	underground

Words that use location or direction prefixes don't necessarily have to refer to location or direction, although many of them do. *Sub-*, for example, means "under," but *subhuman* doesn't mean "under human." Instead, it means "less than human."

Encompassing prefixes that indicate degree

Certain prefixes indicate the amount of something. Do you love someone a lot or a little? Do you speak many languages or only a few? Are you looking at all of something or only part of it? Table 6-9 lists prefixes that represent indefinite amounts (that is, amounts such as few or many). To find out which prefixes to use to indicate particular numbers, hop to the next section, "Counting on prefixes that show number."

Table 6-9		Prefixes that Indicate Degree		
Prefix	**Meaning**	**Word**	**Part of Speech**	**Definition**
pan	all	Pan-American	adj.	all of the Americas
		pandemic (pan-*dem*-ik)	adj.	widespread disease
poly	many	polyglot (*pahl*-ee-glaht)	adj.	knowing many languages
		polygon (*pahl*-ih-gahn)	noun	figure with many sides
		polynomial (pahl-ee-*noh*-mee-ul)	noun	math expression having two or more terms
super	over, beyond, more than	supercilious (soo-per-*sil*-ee-us)	adj.	arrogant or overly proud
ultra	beyond, excessive	ultramarine	adj.	deep blue
		ultraviolet	adj.	beyond the visible spectrum of light

Counting on prefixes that show number

The symbols used to represent numbers — 1, 2, 3, 4, and so on — come from the Arabians, the first great mathematicians. The words used to speak or write these symbols — one, two, three, four, and so on — come from the

Anglo-Saxons. The prefixes that indicate number come from Greek and Latin. Meet the 10 Greek and Latin prefixes that represent the numbers 1 through 10 (see Table 6-10).

Table 6-10		Number Prefixes		
Prefix	**Meaning**	**Word**	**Part of Speech**	**Definition**
uni (Latin), mono (Greek)	1	unicycle (*yoo*-neh-sy-kul)	noun	vehicle with one wheel
		monologue (*mon*-uh-lawg)	noun	dramatic speech performed by one actor
bi, duo (Latin), di (Greek)	2	bicycle	noun	vehicle with two wheels
		duplex (*doo*-plex)	noun	house with two units
		dichotomy (dy-*kot*-uh-mee)	noun	division into two parts
tri (Latin or Greek)	3	tripod (*try*-pod)	noun	three-legged stand
quad (Latin), tetra (Greek)	4	quadrangle (*kwad*-ran-guhl)	noun	figure with four sides and four angles
		tetrahedron (te-truh-*hee*-dron)	noun	a solid with four sides
penta (Greek)	5	pentagram (*pen*-tuh-gram)	noun	star-shaped figure with five points
hexa (Greek)	6	hexagon (*hek*-suh-gon)	noun	figure with six sides
hepta (Greek)	7	heptagon (*hep*-tuh-gon)	noun	figure with seven sides and seven angles
oct (Latin or Greek)	8	octet (ahk-*tet*)	noun	group of eight
nov (Latin)	9	novena (noh-*vee*-nah)	noun	prayers said on nine consecutive days
deca (Latin or Greek)	10	Decalogue (*dek*-uh-log)	noun	the Ten Commandments

By knowing these prefixes, you can easily figure out how many things are being referred to: How many sides does the Pentagon have? Five (*penta-*). How many tentacles does an octopus have? Eight (*oct-*). How many strings does a heptachord have? Seven (*hepta-*). Easy enough.

Sailing through Greek Prefixes

Many of the most common prefixes in English come from the Greek language. These time-honored prefixes open up a whole new world of words that you may find yourself using a great deal in your daily and professional life.

If you know the meanings of roots and prefixes, you can figure out some commonly used words. Consider these examples:

- *Astronaut* literally means "star sailor." It uses the Greek prefix *astro,* which means "star" and the Greek root *nautes,* which means "sailor." Its English definition is "space traveler."

- *Autonomy* literally means "self-rule." It contains the Greek prefix *auto,* which means "self," and the Greek root *nomos,* which means "law." Its English definition is "self government" or "independence."

- *Synchronize* literally means "timed together." It uses the prefix *syn-* (together) and the root *chronos* (time). If you synchronize watches, you make them agree in time.

Table 6-11 lists some especially useful prefixes that have entered English from Greek. (***Note:*** Some of these prefixes can also function as roots, depending on their placement in the word. For more on roots, turn to Chapter 5.)

Table 6-11		Greek Concept Prefixes		
Prefix	**Meaning**	**Word**	**Part of Speech**	**Definition**
arch	chief	archbishop	noun	chief of the church province
arche/ archae	ancient, original	archetype (*ahr*-kuh-typ)	noun	original pattern or model; perfect example of a type or group
		archaeology (ahr-kee-*ahl*-uh-jee)	noun	study of ancient civilizations

Prefix	Meaning	Word	Part of Speech	Definition
auto	self	automobile	noun	self-propelled vehicle
bio	life	biography (by-*ahg*-ruh-fee)	noun	person's life story
chromo/ chroma	color	chromosphere (*kroh*-mohs-feer)	noun	glowing, pinkish region around a star
chron	time	chronological (kron-uh-*lah*-jih-kuhl)	adj.	in order of time
eu	good	eulogize (*yu*-luh-jyz)	verb	speak well of someone
		euphonious (*yu*-*foh*-nee-us)	adj.	having a pleasing sound
		euphoria (yu-*for*-ee-ah)	noun	feeling of well-being
hyper	overly, above, concerning	hypercritical (hy-pur-*krit*-ih-kul)	adj.	overly critical
		hyperactive (hy-pur-*ak*-tiv)	adj.	excessively active
		hyperbaric (hy-pur-*bair*-ik)	adj.	overly oxygenated
micro	small	microscope (*my*-kruh-skohp)	noun	tool for looking at small objects
		microbe (*my*-krohb)	noun	tiny organism
		microfilm (*my*-kroh-film)	noun	film that reduces images to a very small frame
mis	wrong	misdemeanor (mis-duh-*meen*-ur)	noun	bad behavior
		misspell (mis-*spel*)	verb	spell incorrectly
		mistake (mi-*stayk*)	noun	error
peri	around	perimeter (puh-*rim*-uh-tur)	noun	outer measurement

(continued)

Table 6-11 *(continued)*

Prefix	Meaning	Word	Part of Speech	Definition
phil	love	philanthropy (fuh-*lan*-thruh-pee)	noun	love of humanity
phob	fear	claustrophobia (klos-truh-*foh*-bee-uh)	noun	fear of confined spaces
pseudo	false	pseudoscience (*soo*-doh-sy-uhns)	noun	false science
tele	distance	telephone (*tel*-uh-fohn)	noun	phone (that tramits speech over a distance)
		telecommunication (tel-uh-kuh-myoo-nih-*kay*-shun)	noun	communication across distances
		telepathy (tuh-*lep*-uh-thee)	noun	communication between minds at a distance
theo	God	theology (thee-*ahl*-uh-jee)	noun	study of God or religion

The adjective *cosmopolitan* (kahz-muh-pahl-uh-tun) gets its meaning from *cosmo*, which means "world," and *polit*, which means "state or region." Thus, it means "common to all or many parts of the world" or "not local or national."

WORDS TO THE WISE

Opening the floodgates with cata-

From the Greek language comes the word *katarasso*, meaning "down rushing," as in rain or a river. This word is made up of the Greek prefix *kata-* (or *cata-* in its English derivation), which means "down," and the root *arassein*, which means "to strike or smash."

The earliest evidence of this prefix in English can be found in the Bible, where *cataracts* are the floodgates of heaven to keep back the rain. Today, we use the word *cataract* to mean "a waterfall" or "a deluge." As a medical term, a *cataract* is an opacity that blocks light from entering the lens of the eye. So the word retains its sense of being a floodgate, as well as a flood.

Talkin' the Talk

April Knights is on her first date with Howard Hercules. It's a cheap date: They're parked in an isolated cul-de-sac, admiring the stars from the back seat of Howard's rusty jalopy.

Howard: Look at that starlike body!

April: Mine?

Howard: Uh, no, I was referring to the asteroid, April.

April: One more try, Howie.

Howard: You are my antidote, my arthropod, my automaton.

April: I'm your remedy against poison, your segmented invertebrate, such as a lobster, and your robot?

Howard (weakly):   You are my anemia?

April: No, I'm not your blood deficiency. I sure hope you kiss better than you speak.

Pursuing Prefixes from Latin

Latin — not to be outdone by the Greek language — has also given us some extremely useful prefixes. Several have been mentioned earlier in this chapter: many of the number prefixes (see the section "Counting on prefixes that show number"), and *a-* (to or toward), for example. There are a whole bunch of others; Table 6-12 lists a few of these gems.

It's more accurate to say that these prefixes are derived from Latin words. Whether any particular cluster of letters is a prefix or not depends on whether that cluster appears at the beginning of the word. Some of these prefixes can also be used as roots. See Chapter 5 for more on the root words.

Table 6-12		Latin Prefixes		
Prefix	*Meaning*	*Word*	*Part of Speech*	*Definition*
act, ag	do, act	action	noun	movement
ante	before	anteroom (*an*-tee-room)	noun	outer office
		antecedent (an-tuh-*seed*-ent)	adj.	coming before (in time)
bene	good	beneficial (ben-uh-*fish*-ul)	adj.	favorable
		benefactor (*ben*-uh-fak-tur)	noun	person who gives help
		benediction (ben-uh-*dik*-shun)	noun	good wishes
contra	against, opposite	contraband (*kahn*-truh-band)	noun	substance that is illegally imported or exported
		contrary (*kahn*-trer-ee)	adj.	in opposition
cur	run	current	adj.	up-to-date
e	out	elongate (ee-*lon*-gayt)	verb	stretch out
ex	out	exchange	verb	to transfer or substitute
infra	under	infrared (in-fruh-*red*)	adj.	invisible rays just beyond the red end of the visible spectrum
inter	between	intercom	noun	two-way radio
mal/male	bad; evil	malodorous (mal-*oh*-dur-us)	adj.	smelling bad
		malevolent (muh-*lev*-uh-lunt)	adj.	having evil wishes or intentions
ob	toward	obedient (oh-*bee*-dee-unt)	adj.	obeying; submissive

Prefix	Meaning	Word	Part of Speech	Definition
ob	in the way	obstruction (uhb-*struk*-shun)	noun	something set up in one's way
per	through	perambulate (pur-*am*-byoo-layt)	verb	walk through
post	after	postpone (pohst-*pohn*)	verb	put off until later

Adding In Anglo-Saxon Prefixes

The 100 most often used words in the English language all come from the Anglo-Saxons — as do 83 of the next 100 words in this book. And, of course, the Anglo-Saxons got many of their words from the Romans; so where these prefixes originated is hard to determine. But because they're so often used and share meanings, I grouped the main Anglo-Saxon prefixes in this section.

The most common Anglo-Saxon prefixes — *il-*, *im-*, and *ir-* — all have the same two meanings. *Il-*, *im-*, and *ir-* can mean either "in," "into," or "not." The following list gives you examples of each meaning with each prefix. For more on these prefixes, refer to the earlier section "Seeing Prefixes Everywhere: De-, Re-, In-, Un-, and Pre-."

✔ **In or into:**

- illuminate (bring in light)
- import (bring in from abroad)
- irradiate (let x-rays into)

✔ **Not:**

- illiterate (not able to read)
- immodest (not modest)
- irregular (not regular)

You generally won't have a problem figuring out which meaning these prefixes draw on for any particular word, unless you confuse the adjectives *irrefutable*, which means "cannot be disproved," and *irresolute*, which means "indecisive."

Don't fall into the trap of thinking that because everybody uses it, it must be right. This example shows how wrong "everybody" can be:

Correct: Regardless of the thunderstorm, I'm going swimming.

Incorrect: Irregardless of the thunderstorm, I'm going swimming.

Irregardless isn't a real word — attaching the *ir-* prefix doesn't change that. *Regardless* means "without regard; unmindful," which is what folks who use *irregardless* want to say.

The Anglo-Saxons were Low German folks who settled in England around the fifth century. Robin Hood, as tradition goes, was an Anglo-Saxon, as was the legendary King Arthur. The Anglo-Saxon reign ended with the Norman invasion by William the Conqueror in 1066. Anglo-Saxon English is Old English (think *Beowulf,* the epic Old English poem probably written down in the eighth century — 700–800 A.D.).

Acting Like a Prefix: Words that Do Double Duty

Some words, in their own right, function as prefixes, modifying or altering a given word. Consider the following examples:

✔ *Counter* means "opposed or contrary." When used as a prefix, it retains this meaning and, as a result, essentially negates the meaning of the word it's attached to. Examples of *counter* used as a prefix include *counterintuitive* (not intuitive) and *counterproductive* (not productive).

✔ *Under* means "beneath or below." Examples of *under* used as a prefix include *underage* (not old enough), *underscore* (emphasize, literally by drawing a line under), and *underhanded* (sneaky).

✔ *Over* means "higher than, superior, or excessive." Examples of *over* used as a prefix include *overarching* (dominant), *overreaching* (reaching above or beyond), and *overdrawn* (over your bank balance).

You shouldn't have too much trouble understanding what these dual-purpose words/prefixes mean.

Chapter 7

Ending Well: Suffixes

- -

In This Chapter

▶ Using suffixes to figure out unfamiliar words

▶ Determining a word's part of speech

▶ Enriching your speech and writing by identifying suffixes

- -

*P*refixes and suffixes are called *affixes* — they're affixed (attached) to a root to produce a new word. Knowing common suffixes is a powerful skill because it enables you to figure out the meaning of many unfamiliar words. In addition, by focusing on the caboose of each unfamiliar word, you can easily master thousands of helpful English words.

In the same way that adding a prefix to the front of a word changes a word's meaning, adding a suffix to the end of a word changes a word's meaning, as well. However, suffixes go one step further than prefixes — a suffix can affect how a word functions in a sentence by determining the word's part of speech. By adding a suffix, you can create a verb from a noun, or an adjective or an adverb from a verb, for example. And suffixes can also show amount or quantity. As this chapter shows, these tiny affixes are mighty mites indeed!

Suffixes are often written with a hyphen, like this: *-ment, -ness, -tion.* I'm doing the same thing in this book. Don't be fooled by the hyphen: You drop it when you add a suffix to a word.

Meeting the Most Often Used Suffixes

Some suffixes are used so frequently that you may not even think of them — much less recognize them — as suffixes. These include *-d/-ed,* which are used to indicate tense on a verb, and *-s/-es,* which are used to indicate number. Other suffixes are easy to identify, but you see them so often that they merit mention right up front.

Go to the section "Adding amounts: -s, -es, and others" for more on suffixes used to indicate number, and the section "Changing tense: -d/-ed and -ing" for more on suffixes used to indicate tense.

Admitting my favorites: -ment, -ence/-ance, -able/-ible, and -ion

Who's to say which suffixes are most important? I'm sure some folks support *-ness*, *-ity*, and *-ful*, and certainly *-ate*, *-less*, and *-ly* have their fans. Nonetheless, someone has to draw a line in the sand, and I'm not afraid to be the one. Therefore, I declare that I am especially fond of the suffixes *-ment*, *-ence/-ance*, *-able/-ible*, and *-ion*. I find these suffixes exceedingly useful for deciphering unfamiliar words. Table 7-1 shows what these suffixes mean and gives examples of their use.

Table 7-1	Suffixes *-ment, -ence/-ance, -able/-ible,* and *-ion*			
Suffix	**Meaning**	**Example**	**Part of Speech**	**Definition**
ment	an action, process, or act of a specified kind	encouragement (en-*kur*-ij-ment)	noun	the act of encouraging; helpfulness
		argument (*ahr*-gyoo-ment)	noun	the act of arguing or discussing; a dispute
ence/ance	quality or state; an action or process	conference (*kon*-fur-uhns)	noun	a meeting; the process of conferring
		reverence (*rev*-er-ens)	noun	deep respect mingled with awe; the state of being revered
		clearance (*klear*-uhns)	noun	giving the go-ahead; instance of clearing
able/ible	capable or worthy of, fit for; tending to, causing, given to, or liable to	manageable (*man*-ij-uh-bul)	adj.	submitting to control; capable of being managed
		sustainable (suh-*stayn*-uh-bul)	adj.	tolerable; able to be sustained
		lovable (*luv*-uh-bul)	adj.	worthy of love
		peaceable (*pee*-suh-bul)	adj.	tranquil; given to peace

Suffix	Meaning	Example	Part of Speech	Definition
		collectible (kuh-*lek*-tuh-bul)	adj./noun	desirable; worthy of collecting
		forcible (*for*-suh-bul)	adj.	vigorous; given to force; accomplished by force
ion	act, result of an act, or state or condition	ablution (ab-*loo*-shun)	noun	act of washing
		affirmation (af-er-*may*-shun)	noun	act of agreeing
		rebellion (rih-*bel*-yuhn)	noun	act of resisting
		convocation (kon-voh-*kay*-shun)	noun	act of coming together

The difference between the suffix *-able/-ible* and the other suffixes in the table is that *-able/-ible* creates adjectives. The other suffixes create nouns. Another suffix that creates nouns is *-age,* which means "place of" (*orphanage,* a place of orphans), "an act of" (*breakage,* the act of breaking), and "charge for" (*postage,* charge for post). For more information on suffixes and the parts of speech, head to the section "Figuring out a word's function."

Showing action: -ate, -en, -ite, and -ize

The suffixes *-ate, -en, -ite,* and *-ize* all mean "to make or do." Examples of words using these suffixes include *alienate, liberate, weaken, moisten, unite, ignite, visualize,* and *sanitize.*

As you may have noticed, each of these words is a *verb* (a word that conveys action). For more information about using suffixes to identify parts of speech, head to the section "Figuring out a word's function," later in this chapter.

Like just about every other word element in English, suffixes have multiple meanings and can change the definition of a word. For example, the suffix *-ite,* when it means "to make" or "do," creates verbs. However, *-ite* can also mean "one who." In this case, the suffix creates a noun (socialite, for example). Always examine the word in context, and if you're not sure, consult a dictionary.

Changing tense: -d/-ed and -ing

Suffixes can change a word's *tense* (or time). For example, adding the suffix *-d* or *-ed* to the end of a verb changes it from present tense to past tense. Adding the suffix *-ing* changes a present-tense verb into a present participle, or gerund. Table 7-2 shows the past tense, present participle, and gerund forms of several verbs.

Table 7-2	Suffixes and Verb Tenses	
Word	*Past Tense*	*Present Participle/Gerund*
live	lived	living
fasten	fastened	fastening
run	ran	running
walk	walked	walking

Notice that the past tense of "run" is not formed with *-d* or *-ed*. Many verbs, such as *am/was, buy/bought,* and *sell/sold,* form irregular past tenses. The suffix *-ing*, however, works for all verbs.

Tense is a form of a verb that shows time, action, or state of being. Verbs are the only words in English that can show tense. English verbs have six tenses: *present* (walk), *past* (walked), *future* (will walk), *present perfect* (have walked), *past perfect* (had walked), *future perfect* (will have walked). Adding a suffix to a word to change its tense is called *conjugating* the verb. For four of the six tenses you also add a "helping verb" such as *have* or *will*.

Adding amounts: -s, -es, and others

How many of a certain thing do you have? One? More than one? To indicate number, you use suffixes. In particular, you use the following suffixes: *-s* and *-es*. By attaching these suffixes to a singular noun (*house, tree, boat,* and *box,* for example), you make the noun plural (*houses, trees, boats,* and *boxes*).

Of course, not all English plurals are made by adding a simple *-s* or *-es*. Sometimes the ending of the word is changed in other ways. *Child,* for example, becomes *children. Ox* becomes *oxen.* And then you have the ever-popular Latin words that retain their Latin plurals: *Radius* becomes *radii* (ray-dee-eye), and *alumna* (uh-*lum*-nuh) becomes *alumnae* (uh-*lum*-nee).

Suffixes can show amount or number — something that can come in handy in your daily conversation and writing when you want to explain how many or how much.

Don't forget the suffixes that produce adjectives that show amount in a more subtle fashion: *-ful, -ose/-ous,* and *-y* all mean "full of."

  ✔ *-y* produces *risky* (full of danger) and *wily* (full of sly tricks).

  ✔ *-ful* gives you *healthful* (full of physical well-being) and *cheerful* (full of gladness).

  ✔ *-ose/-ous* leads to *morose* (full of sadness) and *perilous* (full of danger).

Expanding Your Suffix Collection

The English language has a slew of suffixes. In fact, almost every English word can accept at least one (and usually several) suffix. English has descriptive suffixes — those that show states of being — suffixes for comparison, and suffixes that indicate people and what they do.

Showing a state of being: -cy, -dom, -ant, -ness, and more

Socrates said that the unexamined life is not worth living. If that is the case, English speakers must be a pretty thoughtful bunch. What stage of life are we in? What's our lot in life? Are we satisfied with this lot? How do we describe what we see, feel, taste, or encounter? Our awareness of ourselves and our environment is our *state of being.*

Not only do we think about these things, but we also feel the need to describe them to others. How can you tell? Because we have a ton of suffixes that indicate or describe a state of being. These suffixes include *-ant/-ent, -cy, -dom, -hood, -mony, -ness, -sis, -tic, -ship,* and *-ty* (see Table 7-3).

Table 7-3		Suffixes Indicating State of Being		
Suffix	**Meaning**	**Example**	**Part of Speech**	**Definition**
cy	state or quality	infancy (*in*-fun-see)	noun	babyhood
dom	jurisdiction or condition	kingdom (*king*-dum)	noun	realm or domain; government headed by a king

(continued)

Table 7-3 *(continued)*

Suffix	Meaning	Example	Part of Speech	Definition
		freedom (*free*-dum)	noun	independence, right or privilege
ant	being in a particular condition	adamant (*ad*-uh-munt)	noun	unyielding; not giving in
		deviant (*dee*-vee-unt)	noun/adj.	abnormal
ent	doing, behaving, or existing	effluent (*ef*-loo-unt)	noun	something that flows out or forth, as a stream
		diligent (*dil*-uh-junt)	adj.	hard working
hood	state or condition	brotherhood (*bruth*-ur-hood)	noun	a feeling of unity among men or among all people
		neighborhood (*nay*-bur-hood)	noun	community
mony	state or condition	matrimony (*ma*-truh-moh-nee)	noun	state of being married
ness	quality or degree	lightness (*lyt*-nis)	noun	weightlessness; mildness; lack of seriousness
		goodness (*good*-nis)	noun	decency; excellence; kindness
sis	process, action	thesis (*thee*-sis)	noun	proposition defended by an argument, a re-searched opinion
		catharsis (kuh-*thar*-sis)	noun	cleansing, as of the soul
ic	having the character or form of	gigantic (jy-*gan*-tik)	adj.	huge; colossal; immense
ship	state or condition	friendship (*frend*-ship)	noun	state of being a friend

Suffix	Meaning	Example	Part of Speech	Definition
		governorship (*guv*-uh-ner-ship)	noun	condition of being the governor
ty	quality or condition	novelty (*nov*-ul-tee)	noun	quality of being new or fresh
		parity (*pair*-uh-tee)	noun	the state of being the same; equality

Relating to or showing likeness: -ac, -al, -esque, -ish, and others

One of the things that makes the English language so rich (and confusing for nonnative speakers) is that many things are described through a comparison to something else. A tree, for example, can be majestic. *Majestic* relates directly to *majesty,* which means "kingly greatness." So how is a tree like a king? It isn't. But the word *majesty,* in relation to a king, means "imposing and impressive." A tree that is majestic, therefore, has those same qualities, even though it is an entirely different thing.

Many common suffixes indicate similarities: *-esque, -ish, -oid,* and *-wise,* for example. Other common suffixes, like *-ac, -al,* and *-ile,* mean "relating to." All in all, these suffixes enable you to describe your thoughts and feelings, and the things you see and experience. Table 7-4 lists and defines these suffixes (as well as provides examples).

You can't overestimate the power of the suffixes that mean "resembling, like, or of." English has 12 of these handy little guys: *-ac, -al, -an, -esque, -ile, -ine, -ish, -ly, -ory, -oid, -some,* and *-wise.*

Table 7-4		Suffixes Showing Similarities or Comparisons		
Suffix	Meaning	Example	Part of Speech	Definition
ac	relating to	cardiac (*kahr*-dee-ak)	adj.	relating to the heart
al	relating to	pastoral (*pas*-tur-ul)	adj.	relating to nature

(continued)

Table 7-4 *(continued)*

Suffix	Meaning	Example	Part of Speech	Definition
esque	in the style of	Lincolnesque (ling-kun-*esk*)	adj.	in the style of Abraham Lincoln
		arabesque (air-uh-*besk*)	adj.	exhibiting the style of embellished ornamentation
ish	typical of	churlish (*chur*-lish)	adj.	typical of a churl; rude and surly
oid	resembling	ovoid (*oh*-void)	adj.	resembling an egg
wise	in the manner of	likewise	adv.	in a like manner; similarly
an	belonging to	suburban (suh-*bur*-bun)	adj.	belonging to the suburbs; characteristic of outlying districts
ile	relating to	puerile (*pyoo*-er-il)	adj.	immature
ine	made of, relating to	saturnine (*sat*-ur-nine)	adj.	gloomy
ly	like, every	yearly	adj.	taking place every year
ory	relating to, place of	advisory (ad-*vy*-zuh-ree)	adj.	relating to advice
		observatory (uhb-*zurv*-uh-tor-ee)	noun	a place for observing stars; planetarium
some	characterized by	worrisome (*wur*-ee-sum)	adj.	characterized by worry; having a tendency to worry

Talkin' the Talk

Tonya Tomato and Stu Strawberry get along fine — in fact, it's a match made in heaven. They're enjoying a little face time in the gym as they work on their washboard abs. Pretend you're on the treadmill and lean just a little closer.

Tonya Tomato: Ah, Stu, your nose is so Romanesque.

Stu Strawberry: I have a roaming nose? On the contrary, babe, my nose always stays in the same place, right in the center of my face.

Tonya Tomato: Stu, a Romanesque nose is a classic nose, like the famous noses of the ancient Romans.

Stu Strawberry: So you like my schnoz, eh?

Dollarwise, you can't beat this gym. Know that, babe?

Tonya Tomato: You mean they have smart dollars in this gym? I just thought they had a lot of dumbbells.

Stu Strawberry: Babe, *dollarwise* means 'pertaining to money.' The suffix *wise* means 'resembling, like, or of.' I meant that this gym is a great value for the money.

Tonya Tomato: Gee, Stu, we're right on the money.

Focusing on folks

A whole bunch of suffixes relate to people: who they are, what they do, where they live, and what they're like. For example, the suffix *-er* is exceptionally useful because it means "one who does or deals with." This suffix, when added to many nouns, can show occupation. A *worker* is someone who works; a *teacher* is someone who teaches. A *baker* is someone who makes my favorite cookies; a *buyer* is someone who buys items. The suffixes *-or, -ar, -ary, -ian, -ier,* and *-ist* (see Table 7-6) also provide the same function as *-er.*

Table 7-5 lists the suffixes that indicate a person who is something, does something, or deals with something. Because they all refer people, all the words in the table are nouns.

Table 7-5	Suffixes Related to People and Their Positions		
Suffix	**Meaning**	**Example**	**Definition**
ar	being; belonging to	scholar (*skahl*-ur)	student
ary	one connected with	functionary (*funk*-shuh-nehr-ee)	an official
er	one who performs a specific action	hairdresser (*hair*-dres-ur)	beautician
ian	one skilled in	comedian (kuh-*mee*-dee-un)	person who tells jokes, sings funny songs, or otherwise tries to get people to laugh
ier	one engaged in or connected with	furrier (*fur*-ee-ur)	person who works with fur
or	one that does a specific thing	arbitrator (*ahr*-buh-trayt-ur)	mediator

The suffix *-ar* is primarily used in words that end in *le*. To use this suffix, you usually change the *le* to *ul* and then add the *-ar*. Consider the following examples:

> angle → angular
>
> circle → circular
>
> muscle → muscular

Often, words that end with *-ist* describe people engaged in particular hobbies or careers. The *-ite* suffix generally indicates something geographical about a person: A Muscovite, for example, is a person who lives in Moscow. Table 7-6 lists a few examples of nouns that use these suffixes.

Table 7-6	Examples of *-ist* and *-ite*
Word	**Definition**
aborist (*ahr*-bur-ist)	one who manages tree care
entomologist (en-tuh-*mahl*-uh-jist)	one who studies insects
geneticist (juh-*net*-uh-sist)	an expert in the study of genetics
Luddite (*lud*-ite)	one who opposes technological change or advances

Word	Definition
meteorologist (meet-ee-uh-*ral*-uh-jist)	one who studies the weather
numismatist (noo-*miz*-muh-tist)	one deals with or collects coins
philatelist (fuh-*lat*-uh-list)	one who deals with or collects stamps
psychologist (sy-*kahl*-uh-jist)	counselor
socialite (*so*-shuh-lite)	person who socializes on a grand scale

Designating place or condition

The suffixes in Table 7-7 crop up in many of the words and expressions you use every day. As a result, these suffixes are handy to know.

Table 7-7		Suffixes Related to Place or Condition		
Suffix	**Meaning**	**Example**	**Part of Speech**	**Definition**
arium	place	aquarium (uh-*kwehr*-ee-um)	noun	a tank for water animals and plants; a building where such collections are exhibited
		solarium (soh-*lehr*-ee-um)	noun	a glassed in porch
ary	place (*ly*-brehr-ee)	library	noun	a place for keeping a collection of books
		aviary (*ay*-vee-ehr-ee)	noun	a large cage or building for keeping many birds
erly	to, directly	easterly (*ees*-tur-lee)	adj./adv.	to go toward the east
escent	beginning, becoming	pubescent (pyoo-*bes*-unt)	adj.	beginning puberty
		adolescent (ad-uh-*les*-unt)	adj./noun	becoming an adult

(continued)

Table 7-7 *(continued)*

Suffix	Meaning	Example	Part of Speech	Definition
eum	place for	museum (myoo-*zee*-um)	noun	storehouse of exhibits
ferous	bearing	odoriferous (oh-dur-*if*-ur-us)	adj.	smelly
fy	make, form into	magnify (*mag*-nuh-fy)	verb	make larger
		ratify (*rat*-uh-fy)	verb	approve formally; make into a deter- mined thing
ia	condition	anorexia (an-uh-*reks*- ee-uh)	noun	eating disorder
id	inclined to be	florid (*flor*-id)	adj.	highly decorated; gaudy; showy; ornate
ism	a practice	baptism (*bap*-tiz-um)	noun	the practice of baptizing; a reli- gious ceremony
itis	inflammation	sinusitis (sy-nus-*ite*-is)	noun	inflammation of sinuses
ive	inclined to	festive (*fes*-tiv)	adj.	joyful
ment	result of	judgment (*juj*-ment)	noun	result of judging; an opinion
tude	condition	rectitude (*rek*-tuh-tood)	noun	moral virtue
ure	quality	rapture (*rap*-chur)	noun	bliss
ward	to	sideward (*side*-wurd)	adv./adj.	to the side

Putting Suffixes to Work

Knowing suffixes lets you do more than puzzle out the meaning of unfamiliar words. With an understanding of suffixes — what they mean and how they affect the root word — you can figure out the following:

- ✔ **A word's part of speech:** Although not an earth-shattering revelation, knowing the part of speech you're dealing with helps you figure out how to use the word in a sentence.

- ✔ **The number:** Some suffixes indicate number or degree — how many or how much. More than one? More or less? Suffixes can tell you the answer to these questions.

Figuring out a word's function

To figure out how to use a new word, you need to know how a word should function in a sentence. And to know *that,* you need to figure out the word's part of speech. Is it a noun or verb? Or is it an adjective or adverb? (All in all, English has eight parts of speech. See the sidebar "Parsing the parts of speech," later in this chapter, to find out what they are.)

Mudluscious jabberwocky, anyone?

Lewis Carroll and e e cummings weren't the only ones who liked nonsense words. On some standardized tests, the test creators test how well you understand and can manipulate the English language by using made-up words — that is, words that don't exist and don't mean anything. If you know suffixes and the basic structure of English sentences, however, you can decipher these sentences that use made-up words. Consider the following example:

"The woberistic ternonite clored into the vesterminal procrustitude."

The adjective *woberistic* (note the suffix *-ic*) describes the noun *ternonite* (which uses the suffix *-ite*). You know that the ternonite *clored*

(a past tense nonsense verb) into something. That something is a *procrustitude*. You know that *procrustitude* is a noun for the following reasons:

- ✔ Its placement in the sentence.

- ✔ Its use of the suffix *-tude.*

- ✔ The presence of the *the* (nouns always follow articles, which is what *the* is).

- ✔ An adjective (*vesterminal*) modifies it. You know that *vesterminal* is an adjective because of its placement and because it uses the suffix *-al,* which means "relating to" and creates adjectives.

So how do you know what part of speech a word is? Well, you can look up the word in a dictionary to find the part of speech, but that's a lot of trouble. Fortunately, specific suffixes almost always make the new word the same part of speech: Adding a *-y,* for example, makes just about any word an adjective.

The following sections list most of the more common suffixes according to what part of speech they make a word when added to it. If you can remember these basic suffixes and speech parts, you should have little trouble figuring out how to use words formed with these suffixes.

Not every word that ends with a particular suffix is the same part of speech. The suffix *-ly,* for example, is often used to make adverbs (*dutifully, happily, normally,* and so on), but you can find *-ly* at the end of other words that aren't adverbs, such as *rely* (verb), *firefly* (noun), and *ghastly* (adjective).

Suffixes and nouns

Nouns are persons (Joe, mom, the girl), places (Toledo, the house, the garden), things (car, tree, pencil), and concepts or ideas (beauty, honesty, truth). The suffixes that turn words into nouns include the following:

> *-ance, -ful, -ity, -ment, -ness, -sion/-tion, -age*

Whenever you see these suffixes at the end of a word, chances are you're looking at a noun. Here are some example sentences that use nouns created by suffixes:

- ✔ The lack of any other options made her *acceptance* (agreement or approval) of the original plan inevitable.

- ✔ When she told her date that the evening was only slightly more interesting than he was, she said a *mouthful* (comment rich in meaning).

- ✔ The *unity* (state of acting or being as one) of the participants was never in doubt, even though each represented a different region.

- ✔ The administration's policy of *containment* (the act of holding something in check) came too late to stop the spread of the disease.

- ✔ *Happiness* (joy or well-being) means never having to say you're sorry — unless you're caught red-handed.

- ✔ Despite his best efforts, he was unable to hide his *confusion* when asked why he kept his car keys in the mayonnaise jar.

- ✔ The *Canterbury Tales* takes place during a *pilgrimage* (journey to a holy place) to the cathedral in Canterbury.

Suffixes and verbs

A verb is a word that shows action (run, walk, fly, build, has) or that shows a state of being (seem, is, become). By adding the suffixes *-ate, -en, -ite,* and *-ize* to certain root words, you create verbs. Following are a few examples:

activate (to make active)

mutate (to change)

lighten (to make lighter)

fatten (to make fatter)

unite (to bring together)

demonize (to make into a demon)

ritualize (to make a ritual of)

How do you spell that?

Unfortunately, adding a suffix to a word isn't always as simple as sticking the suffix on at the end of the word. If you did that, you'd end up with quite a few spelling mistakes. To help you avoid these mistakes, I've added a couple of spelling tips on adding suffixes: Keep in mind, though, that we're talking about the English language here. There are always exceptions. If you're unsure how to spell a word, crack open a dictionary.

If the word ends in *-y,* change the *y* to an *i* and add the suffix — if it gives you two *i's* in a row, then leave the *y.*

fancy → fanciful, fancied, fancying

happy → happily, happiness

supply → supplying

whimsy → whimsical

Whether you add *-d* or *-ed* to a word depends on the end of the word. If the word ends with an *e,* you generally just add the *d.* If it ends with another vowel, you add *ed* (if the word ends in *y,* remember to change the *y* to an *i*).

candy → candied

charge → charged

halo → haloed

hate → hated

tomato → tomatoed

tree → treed (to force up a tree)

If the word has one syllable and ends in a consonant, you generally repeat the consonant and add the suffix, as in:

bat → batted

if → iffy (uncertain)

wed → wedding

All bets are off for most English words, though. Should you use *-ible* or *-able*? Do you add an *e* or remove an *e* before you attach certain suffixes, like *-ment, -ence,* and *-ity?* When do you use *-tion,* and when should it be *-sion?* When you're stumped — or want to be sure you spelled the word right — head to a dictionary.

Being able to figure out whether a word is a noun, adjective, or verb is a useful skill when you're taking language tests.

Suffixes and adjectives

An *adjective* is any descriptive word that modifies a noun or a pronoun. (Pronouns are words, like *he, she, they, I,* and *them,* that take the place of nouns.) Adjectives can come before the words they modify (the *tall* house), or they can follow the word they modify (the house is *tall*). Certain suffixes, like the following, create adjectives when attached to root words:

- ✔ **-ful:** *thoughtful* (contemplative), *wasteful* (using more than necessary), *purposeful* (aimed at a specific goal), *meaningful* (having significance or purpose), *bountiful* (plentiful)

  As the suffix itself implies, its meaning is essentially "full of." So the words literally mean "full of thought," "full of waste," "full of purpose," "full of meaning," and "full of bounty."

- ✔ **-less:** *armless* (without arms), *bloomless* (without blooms), *boundless* (without end), *loveless* (without love), *meatless* (without meat)

  Basically, the prefix *-less* means "without" or "lacking."

- ✔ **-able/-ible:** *acceptable* (satisfactory or adequate), *negotiable* (open to discussion), *horrible* (terrible or frightful), *convertible* (able to be changed from one form to another), *invincible* (unbeatable), *infallible* (incapable of error), *unalterable* (permanent)

  The suffix *-able/-ible* means "capable of," "able to be," or "causing." Therefore, the literal definitions for the preceding words would be "able to be accepted," "able to be negotiated," "causing horror," "able to be converted," and so on.

- ✔ **-y:** *tricky* (deceitful), *risky* (hazardous), *windy* (characterized or accompanied by wind)

  The suffix *-y* means "having the characteristics of [the noun that precedes it]."

Suffixes and adverbs

Adverbs are words that modify or describe verbs (ran *quickly*), adjectives (*very* warm), or other adverbs (*too* quickly). Adverbs also indicate when an action occurred or will occur (*Tomorrow,* we go to school). Adverbs basically answer the following questions: How? How much? When? The suffix that almost always creates an adverb is *-ly: Smartly, happily, warmly,* and *totally* are all examples of adverbs that use *-ly.*

Suffixes can determine a word's part of speech. For example, adding the suffix *-y* to a verb such as *risk* gives you an adjective, which then needs to modify a noun, as in "risky business."

Parsing the parts of speech

English has eight parts of speech. They are — drum roll please — the following:

✔ **Nouns:** Words that name a person, place, thing, or idea *(sofa, democracy)*

Nouns like *Bob* and *Indianapolis* — proper names of people and places — are capitalized and called *proper nouns.*

✔ **Pronouns:** Words that take the place of a noun or another pronoun *(I, me, you, she, who, they)*

Possessive pronouns, like *my, mine, its* and *yours, theirs,* and *ours* show ownership.

✔ **Verbs:** Words that name an action or describe a state of being *(run, seem)*

✔ **Adverbs:** Words that describe verbs, adjectives, or other adverbs *(yesterday, below, happily, partly)*

✔ **Adjectives:** Words that describe nouns and pronouns *(red, more, second, several)*

✔ **Conjunctions:** Words that connect words or groups of words and show how they are related *(and, or, for, but, after, although, because)*

✔ **Prepositions:** Words that link a noun or pronoun to another word in the sentence *(by, about, behind, above, across, at)*

✔ **Interjections:** Words that show strong emotion *(Oh! Wow!)*

To get more hair-raising details about the parts of speech and how they fit into the wacky world of English grammar, you need an English teacher (they live for this stuff). If you can't find an English teacher, check out *English Grammar For Dummies* by Geraldine Woods (Hungry Minds, Inc.).

Comparing with suffixes

If you have things that you want to rank, you need to be able to show degree. Of these things, which is small, which is smaller, and which is smallest? Or, which is large, which is larger, and which is largest? Although you can use the words *more* and *most* to show degree, doing so often sounds awkward (more large or most large) or just plain wrong (more good and most good, for example). Hence, the comparative suffixes can be helpful:

✔ *-er:* You use *-er* when you're comparing two things. Of your two children, which is the younger and which is the older? Of your two pictures, which is the nicer or which is the prettier?

✔ *-est:* You use *-est* when you're comparing more than two things.

Not all English words lend themselves to these suffixes. Long words, for instance, don't use them (use *more beautiful* instead of beautifuler). Some words, like *good* and *bad,* don't follow the pattern either. The degrees for *bad* are *worse* and *worst;* the degrees of *good* are *better* and *best.* For more tips on using these suffixes, head to Chapter 23.

Part III
Expanding Your Base

The 5th Wave   By Rich Tennant

"I hate the synonyms part of this test. I always get stumped, stymied, puzzled..."

In this part . . .

Words that mean the same thing, words that mean the opposite, words that sound alike, words that are spelled alike, words made from other words, and words that come from other languages — these chapters have them all.

Branching out from the basics of word elements, in these chapters I clue you in to the delightful differences and stunning similarities in the wonderful world of words.

Chapter 8

Shading Meaning: Synonyms, Antonyms, Connotations, Denotations

· ·

In This Chapter

▶ Meaning the same

▶ Meaning the opposite

▶ Understanding connotation and denotation

· ·

*P*eople who speak and write well have the keys to the kingdom. Speaking and writing well helps you get a good job and move up the ladder of success. When you communicate your feelings, ideas, hopes, and fears with confidence, people think you're hot stuff. And you are!

One relatively easy way to expand your vocabulary and your word power is to know piles of synonyms and antonyms. Armed with more words, you can express yourself more confidently and become a more interesting speaker and writer.

This chapter gives you the lowdown on synonyms and antonyms, explains how having a command of them benefits you, and offers lots of examples to give you an idea of how many new words you can encounter and incorporate into your everyday language. Of course, not being one to lead you to a buffet without helping you select the delicacies you crave, I also offer plenty of tips on how you can be sure to pick the word that conveys just the meaning you want.

Distilling Synonym Essentials

Synonyms are words that have the same meaning or nearly the same meaning. Synonyms are useful for the following reasons:

✔ **You can express your precise meaning.** Mark Twain is credited with saying that using the right word and the almost right word is the difference between lightning and the lightning bug. Synonyms help you choose just the right word. Because synonyms never share the *exact* meaning, you can give your message just the shade of meaning that you want.

For example, *meager* and *inadequate* are synonyms. However, if your money is *meager,* you can just stretch it to pay the bills. If your money is *inadequate*, you can't ante up what you need.

✔ **You can add variety to your speaking and writing.** By using synonyms, you can avoid repeating the same word over and over — something listeners and readers find very distracting. English teachers and editors hate it, too. They call it *redundancy.*

✔ **You can substitute words that you *do* know how to pronounce or spell for words that you don't.** Suppose you're speaking about a film you recently saw. You want to use the word *macabre* (muh-*kahb*-ruh or muh-*kah*-bur), but you're unsure how to pronounce it. You can use *gruesome* or *eerie* instead. This ability to switch words also comes in handy when you're taking tests, writing papers, or preparing a report for the boss. Don't know how to spell a word? Use a synonym.

So how do you find the synonyms you need? You can use a print dictionary or thesaurus (or their online versions). High-quality dictionaries explain the differences among synonyms and shed light on the different shades of meaning of each word. And, of course, the reason thesauruses exist is to provide synonyms. Turn to Chapter 2 for full coverage of dictionaries and thesauruses.

Before

This matter is *important* because it can affect *important* decisions you'll be making about *important* situations.

After

This matter is important because it can affect *momentous* decisions you'll be making about *critical* situations.

Sidling up to synonyms

Sidling means "approaching from the side," which is what synonyms do in a way. A synonym never means *exactly* the same thing as the word it replaces.

No word is ever an exact synonym for another word because there is always a slightly different meaning between them. Consider some synonyms for those famous opposites, *love* and *hate:*

- ✔ **Love:** adore, cherish, treasure, adulate, worship, revere, esteem

  Cherish and *treasure* imply that the love object has been raised on a pedestal; *revere* and *worship* show that the person is venerated as a god or goddess. (***Note to fans:*** Feel free to *revere* and *worship* me. You can *venerate* me, too.)

- ✔ **Hate:** abhor, scorn, dislike, shun, abominate, despise, detest

  Even though all these words are synonyms, their meanings are quite different in some cases. For example, *scorn* implies not only hatred but also mockery and even avoidance. When you *scorn* someone, you ridicule them and try to shun their company. Then we have the matter of degree. The words *detest* and *abominate* suggest that the hatred is so strong that the speaker can't even bear to be in the person's presence.

Checking my dictionary, I find that *main, chief, primary,* and *principal* are listed as synonyms, and they're all adjectives. Because they're all adjectives, and they all mean pretty much the same thing, they should be interchangeable, don't you think? And so it appears:

- ✔ The *main* reason for Laurie's migraine was overwork.

- ✔ The *chief* reason for Laurie's migraine was overwork.

- ✔ The *primary* reason for Laurie's migraine was overwork.

- ✔ The *principal* reason for Laurie's migraine was overwork.

You can substitute synonyms for each other, but the following example shows that what you end up with may not be what you want: Roscoe attends *primary* school. If you replace primary with a synonym here, you end up with a sentence that doesn't make sense. Roscoe can't attend *main, chief,* or *principal* school — there is no such thing.

As this example shows, words listed as synonyms in a dictionary (or in *Vocabulary For Dummies!*) can't always stand in for each other. Pay attention to the criteria listed in the following sections when you want to substitute a word.

Context and purpose

Some words are formal; some are colloquial. Some are more scholarly; some are more casual. Make sure that the word you choose matches your message and medium: For example, when was the last time you saw *black hair* referred to as *raven tresses* — outside of a romance novel, that is?

If you're trashing your boss around the water cooler, you may describe the odious toad as despicable, detestable, loathsome, sickening, nauseating, repulsive, obnoxious, execrable, hateful, offensive, and nefarious. But if you're smart and realize that some words are inappropriate in certain contexts, you're more likely to refer to your boss as *formidable, rigorous,* and *challenging.* Context can have a big impact on the words you choose.

Your reason for wanting a synonym

If you're hunting down synonyms to find the right word, great. If you need a synonym to avoid repetition, fine. But if you're loading your speech or prose with synonyms merely to impress folks with the number of words you know, stop. Halt. Cease. Discontinue, end, or terminate the practice. Check and arrest your impulses. Why? Because it's obvious and annoying.

Talkin' the Talk

Herminone is trying to buy a new carpet. She knows that she wants something to jazz up a small room, perhaps a nice bright red. She's trying to explain this to the carpet salesperson, a very knowledgeable man who has just done a complete inventory of all of his carpets.

Herminone (pointing to a lovely plush carpet):	I'd like that carpet, please.
Salesman:	What color, ma'am?
Herminone:	Uh, red.
Salesman (with a sniff):	Ma'am, that carpet comes in crimson, cherry, scarlet, carmine, cerise, ruby, cranberry, maroon, and vermilion. Which *red* would you like?
Herminone:	Maybe blue?
Salesman:	We have it in azure, cerulean, sapphire, blueberry, navy, sea blue, turquoise, teal, cobalt, Prussian, and sky blue. Which *blue* will it be?
Herminone:	Can we start with an aspirin?

This interchange between Herminone and the salesman illustrates one of the joys of English. Because English includes many *synonyms* — words that have the same or nearly the same meaning as another word — it has the ability to distinguish fine shades of meaning.

Substituting synonyms

When you decide that you do need another word, navigating your way through a list of synonyms is only part of the battle. You also have to make sure that you pick an appropriate synonym and use it correctly.

Using the right word

Using the wrong synonym can cause errors and mistakes. People tend to confuse the words *libel* and *slander* because they both mean "to damage a person's reputation." However, there is an important distinction between the two words: *libel* is written defamation, and *slander* is oral vilification. Because synonyms have subtle shades of meaning, you want to use the exact word to suit your audience and intent. Here's a famous example: *Sweat, perspire,* and *glow* are synonyms. However, in polite company, horses sweat, men perspire, and women glow.

Using the word right

You have to pay attention to the mechanics of using one word in place of another:

- **Part of speech:** If the word you want to replace is a noun, for example, make sure that the synonym is a noun too. If the word is an adjective, make sure that your synonym is an adjective.

- **Number and tense:** Make sure that the synonym is the same in tense (if it's a verb) or number (if it's a noun). For example, if you're replacing a verb in past tense, make sure that the synonym is also a verb in past tense. If the noun is plural, make sure that the synonym is plural. (This tip is especially helpful if you're using the thesaurus program in your word processor.)

  Original: We *were walking* through the door just as the sky diver landed.

  Incorrect tense: We *were go* through the door just as the sky diver landed.

  Correct: We *were going* through the door just as the sky diver landed.

  Original: The boat sailed through the rough *waves* (noun) toward the shore.

> **Incorrect part of speech:** The boat sailed through the rough *break* (verb) toward the shore.
>
> **Correct:** The boat sailed through the rough *breakers* (noun) toward the shore.
>
> ✔ **Standard usage rules:** In any language, you use certain words in certain ways. The trick with using synonyms in English is to make sure that you use the word correctly. Here's an example:
>
> **Correct:** Many have died trying to *scale that peak*.
>
> **Incorrect:** Many have died trying to *mount that peak*.
>
> Mountain peaks are *scaled*. They're not *mounted*, even though the words are synonyms.

Analyzing Antonyms

An *antonym* is a word that means the opposite, or nearly the opposite, of another word. Antonyms are just as useful as synonyms. Knowing a wide range of antonyms not only helps you express yourself clearly but helps you remember words and understand their various shades of meaning. Using the same love/hate association I used in the previous section, I offer you these antonyms for the verb forms of these words:

> ✔ **Hate:** adore, adulate, appreciate, cherish, covet, crave, desire, esteem, honor, love, lust after, long for, prize, relish, revere, treasure, worship
>
> ✔ **Love:** abhor, abominate, condemn, curse, despise, detest, dislike, disparage, execrate, flay, loathe, reject, resent, scorn, shun

Notice anything interesting about the words in the examples? The antonyms (or opposites) for *hate* are the synonyms (or like words) for *love*, just as the antonyms for *love* are the synonyms for *hate*. This is more than just a neat little trick. Antonyms of words with opposite meanings are usually synonyms for each other. Because of this, knowing antonyms helps you remember synonyms, too. Think of it as a twofer offer, and check out Table 8-1.

Table 8-1		Synonyms and Antonyms	
Word	*Part of Speech*	*Synonym*	*Antonym*
actively	adv.	vigorously (*vig*-er-us-lee)	passively
commonly	adv.	generally	infrequently

Word	Part of Speech	Synonym	Antonym
depressing	adj.	discouraging	heartening
eliminate	verb	abolish (uh-*bahl*-ish)	retain
gigantic	adj.	immense	tiny
indelible (in-*del*-uh-bul)	adj.	permanent	fleeting
mortified	adj.	humiliated (hyoo-*mil*-ee-ay-tid)	encouraged
positively	adv.	for the better	negatively
pretty	adj.	attractive	repulsive
strengthen	verb	fortify	weaken

Understanding Subtext: Connotation and Denotation

Connotation is a word's understood meaning — its emotional tone or subtext. *Denotation* is a word's dictionary meaning. Every word has a denotation, but only some words have connotations.

Two words may have similar denotations but very different connotations. Consider the denotation and connotation of the words *tumor* and *mass*. Imagine how you would react to your doctor telling you that you have a tumor and may need surgery versus her telling you that you have a mass and could require a procedure. *Tumor* and *mass* mean the same thing, but *tumor* is a scary word; *mass* is less so. *Surgery* and *a procedure* mean the same thing, but *surgery* is a scary word, and *procedure* isn't. *Tumor* and *mass* have the same denotation, "a lump." But *tumor* has a terrifying connotation; *mass* sounds much less frightening.

Here's another example: *Sobbing* and *blubbering* have the same denotation, "crying." However, *sobbing* suggests pitiful crying, while *blubbering* suggests foolish, overwrought crying.

Keeping up with current connotations

A word's denotation can change over time as the word is used in different ways. For example, before computers burst onto the scene, the denotation of the word *mouse* was a small furry rodent — cute in cartoons but not in your kitchen. With the advent of the computer age, however, a *mouse* also came to be known as a palm-sized device used to move the cursor on a computer screen. (*Mouse* can also be used as a verb, meaning "to sneak around.")

Fortunately, you can easily find out whether a word's denotation has changed: Just consult an up-to-date dictionary. A word's connotation, however, can be much more difficult to discern. It depends on the following factors:

- **Time:** In the 1930s, *cat* assumed the connotation of "a person in the know." (The word *cat* was short for "hepcat" — slang for a jazz enthusiast.) Today, that connotation is still used, but it's not as common.

- **Place:** In the same way, place also affects a word's connotation. If you use the word *cool* when you speak to a refrigerator repairman, he may assume that you're discussing a problem that has to do with your frozen peas melting because your fridge is broken. But if you use the word *cool* when you're gyrating in a nightclub admiring someone else's moves, the word's connotation is "sharp" or "attractive" (what people in the 1960s and 1970s called "groovy").

- **Tone:** The speaker's tone also affects a word's connotation. If someone says *great* in an admiring tone, you know that he or she is saying something is "excellent." For instance, if you make your sweetie a favorite food, he or she might say, "Liver and onions? Great!" But if *great* is uttered with a mocking tone, it comes to mean the exact opposite, as in "Liver and onions? Great, I just can't wait."

The connotation of a word sometimes bears no relation to its denotation. A decade ago, *gnarly* took on the connotation "hip or cool." The actual definition is "twisted or contorted."

Deciding between positive and negative connotations

English gives you the power to distinguish fine shades of meaning. But with this great power comes great responsibility: You have to choose words with the exact connotation you need. The word you choose depends on what you mean to say and who you're talking to. Table 8-2 lists examples of positive and negative connotations.

Table 8-2		Positive and Negative Connotations	
Denotation	*Part of Speech*	*Positive Connotation*	*Negative Connotation*
bent	adj.	curved	warped
bright	adj.	dazzling	glaring
civil	adj.	considerate	obsequious (ub-*see*-kwee-us)
collects	verb	preserves	hoards
confused	adj.	puzzled	flustered
courageous	adj.	intrepid (in-*trep*-id)	rash
courteous	adj.	polite	groveling
disorderly	adj.	tousled	unkempt
economical	adj.	thrifty	cheap
elaborate	adj.	ornate	gaudy (*gaw*-dee)
fat	adj.	buxom	obese (oh-*bees*)
flexible	adj.	adaptable	indecisive
horse	noun	steed	nag
inexperienced	adj.	unfamiliar with	naïve (ny-*eev*)
minor	adj.	trivial	petty
offhand	adj.	spontaneous (spahn-*tay*-nee-us)	accidental
old	adj.	venerable (*ven*-ur-uh-bul)	obsolete
packed	adj./verb	filled	glutted
plain	adj.	unpretentious (un-pree-*ten*-shus)	homely
prominent	adj.	outstanding	conspicuous (kun-*spik*-yoo-us)
questioned	verb	inquired	interrogated (in-*ter*-oh-gay-ted)
raw	adj.	unrefined	crude

(continued)

Table 8-2 *(continued)*

Denotation	Part of Speech	Positive Connotation	Negative Connotation
skinny	adj.	slender	emaciated (ee-*may*-shee-ay-tid)
talkative	adj.	chatty	verbose (vur-*bohs*)
told	verb	informed	tattled
uninteresting	adj.	bland	dull
without a friend	adj.	reclusive (ri-*kloo*-siv)	friendless

Connoting colors culturally

Words aren't the only things that have connotations as well as denotations: Colors do, as well. The connotation of a color is very much influenced by cultural context. For example, in Western culture, *white* is the color of purity; in Asian cultures, it's the color of death. In America, it used to be taboo to wear black to a wedding because it symbolizes death; now, wedding guests at formal affairs are asked (sometimes required) to don black. In China, however, black is still out for weddings. Red is the color of celebration in Chinese culture; in the United States, red often has a morally suspect connotation.

Chapter 9

Hear Your Homonyms and Homophones Here

In This Chapter

▶ Understanding the difference between homonyms and homophones

▶ Distinguishing between words with multiple meanings

▶ Creating puns with homonyms and homophones

*W*hether you're a native or nonnative speaker of English, you may have encountered (or may soon encounter) words that sound alike but mean different things. These words, officially referred to as *homonyms* and *homophones,* are just another bane to folks trying to learn or improve their use of the English language.

Teachers who try to get their students enthusiastic about these seemingly inexplicable variations may do their best to convince you that these words are wonderful examples of the beauty, richness, and varied past of the English language. But don't let them fool you. Many teachers still have to rifle through a dictionary to remind themselves of the difference between a homonym and a homophone. Fortunately, you don't have to remember the difference. All you have to know is that English has a lot of words that sound alike (and are sometimes spelled alike) but mean different things. This chapter covers the homonyms and homophones you may come up against most frequently or that may give you the most trouble.

Differentiating Homonyms and Homophones (In Case You're Curious)

The official distinction between homonyms and homophones is described as follows: *Homophones* are simply words that sound alike, regardless of their spelling and meaning. Examples of homophones include:

awl and *all*

piece and *peace*

to, two, and *too*

pie and *pi*

Homonyms are words that are spelled alike and sound alike but have different meanings. Some examples of homonyms are:

ball (the toy) and *ball* (the dance)

fine (as in "Denzel is one fine-looking man") and *fine* (the money you pay when you get a parking ticket)

pool (the game), *pool* (the swimming hole), and *pool* (the verb meaning to gather together)

saw (past tense of see) and *saw* (a blade for cutting)

As you make your way through this chapter, ponder the following nuggets of information about homophones and homonyms. You may find the information to be interesting in a perplexing way:

- ✔ All homonyms are also homophones because they sound alike (and that's what makes a homophone a homophone). But not all homophones are homonyms. To be a homonym, the words have to be spelled alike.

- ✔ Some words fall into both categories: *Course* and *coarse,* for example, are homophones of each other (they sound alike but are spelled differently). *Course* and *coarse* are also homonyms because each spelling has various meanings.

  - *coarse* (rough) and *coarse* (vulgar; crude)

    This fabric is so *coarse* (rough) that it scratches my skin.

    What a *coarse* (obscene) film! We're not showing that at the family reunion!

  - *course* (direction), *course* (series/trend), and *course* (track)

    Which *course* (direction) shall we take?

    The *course* (series) of lectures looks interesting.

    The golf *course* (track) is so crowded we'll never get on the green.

    (*Course* also has some less-often used meanings. You can find them in a dictionary.)

Talkin' the Talk

Pat and Pat are instant messaging each other. Let's drop in on their cyberconversation:

Pat E.:   Hey, what ya doin'?

Pat I.:   Hay back. Just trying to figure out my math lessen for tomorrow.

Pat E.:   Do you mean your *lesson?*

Pat I.:   Yeah. Whatever. I don't understand how this plain thing works.

Pat E.:   Pat, we're studying geometric *planes,* not *plains.* That's geography class.

Pat I.:   LOL. You know what I mean. I just don't get it.

Pat E.:   What don't you get?

Pat I.:   How we're supposed to know what principals to use.

Pat E.:   It's *principles,* Pat. Geometric principles. Look, I have a suggestion.

Pat I.:   What?

Pat E.:   Why don't you study English instead?

Pat I.:   I sea ware your going with this. . . .

Pat E.:   Bye, Pat.

Pat I.:   Buy, Pat.

Dealing with Homonyms and Homophones

Homonyms and homophones are like hurricanes, earthquakes, and other natural calamities. You may get plenty of warning, but you really can't escape them. So how do you deal with homonyms? There are no rules to govern the use of homonyms; there are only a few memory tricks to help you distinguish between them. The few memory tricks that I share here are really only helpful if you're writing and need to know which spelling is correct. For example:

- ✔ *Stationary* has an *a* as in *stay* and means "staying in place;" *stationery* has an *e* as in *letter* and means "letter-writing paper."

- ✔ *Principal* is a person and ends in *pal; principle* is a rule and ends in *le.*

Although this information is helpful as you write (when you need to know how to spell a word), it doesn't help you when you're listening. You need to use context to determine what the person you're listening to is talking about — that's pretty much the strategy you have to use with all homonyms.

So my advice to you is to simply memorize the meanings and spellings of the words. That way, you can instantly recognize the words that are important for helping you say what you mean. If you're unsure about a word's meaning or use, check a dictionary to make sure that you pick the word you want and not its evil twin.

Before

Due ewe no wear eye mite find a sail on stationary sense eye have sew many thank ewe cards too right and male?

After

Do you know where I might find a sale on stationery since I have so many thank you cards to write and mail?

Making a Lo-o-o-ng List

Table 9-1 gives you a long list of the homonyms and homophones that you may come up against often or that are especially troublesome for speakers of English. The table also includes a few helpful tips and examples for words that are especially hard to use or spell. As you use this list, keep a couple of things in mind:

✔ **The list is incomplete.** I'd need another hundred pages or so to include all the homonyms and homophones in the English language. Only the ones I think are the most common or the most problematic are listed in this table.

✔ **If you still have trouble keeping some of these words straight, you're in good company.** No doubt there is a linguist (or two) somewhere who knows all the spellings, meanings, iterations, and derivatives of these words and who never makes a mistake. Everyone else has to look these words up occasionally.

✔ **Some words you may never get.** A lot of people — despite years of trying — still have a hard time with complimentary/complementary and lie/lay, for example. If you have a word that just doesn't stick, don't sweat it. If you don't have access to a dictionary, use another word instead. English, fortunately, is full of synonyms (head to Chapter 8 for a list of those).

Note that in the table, *n* stands for "noun," and *v* stands for "verb." I use the whole word in the rest of the book, but this table is already long enough.

Table 9-1   Common and Problematic Homonyms and Homophones

Word: Meaning	*Examples and Notes*
aid: (v) to help	She offered *aid* to the flood victims.
aide: (n) an assistant	The senator consulted his *aide*.
ail: (v) to suffer from sickness or discomfort	My uncle has been *ailing* for years.
ale: (n) a fermented drink	Although *ale* is popular in England, I prefer beer.
air: (n) atmosphere	The *air* is clear up here.
heir: (n) one who inherits	He married the *heir* to the crown.
err: (v) to make a mistake	Everyone *errs* occasionally.
	Note: Although *err* is properly pronounced as "er," many people pronounce it as "ayr."
allot: (v) divide	*Allot* the candy, donuts, and chips equally among all the children, please.
a lot: (n) many	Question: "I have always wanted to have my family history traced, but I can't afford to spend *a lot* of money to do it. Any suggestions?" Answer: "Yes. Run for public office."

(continued)

Table 9-1 *(continued)*

Word: Meaning	*Examples and Notes*
allowed: (v) gave permission	Despite her concerns, John's mother *allowed* him to go to the concert with his friends.
aloud: (adv) out loud, verbally	Don't say it *aloud*.
all together: (adv) all at one time	We recited the work mantra *all together:* "I owe, I owe, so it's off to work I go."
altogether: (adv) completely or thoroughly	The suit is *altogether* too expensive for my budget.
already: (adv) previously	We've *already* seen that movie; we don't need to see it again.
all ready: (adj) completely prepared	Marissa is *all ready* to head off to college.
altar: (n) consecrated table in a shrine	The bride's father walked her to the *altar*.
alter: (v) change	If you delete a word, you'll *alter* the meaning of the sentence.
arc: (n) part of the circumference of a circle; curved line	He bent the tree limb into an *arc* to form a bow.
ark: (n) a large, flatbed boat, similar to the one the biblical Noah had	People have been searching for the biblical *ark* for years and have yet to prove that it can actually be found.
are: (v) plural of "to be"	There *are* two credit cards for every person in the United States.
our: (possessive pronoun) belonging to us	*Our* emu (like all emus) cannot walk backwards.
	Note: Although there is a subtle pronunciation difference between *are* and *our,* most people pronounce them the same.
ascent: (v) to move up	The *ascent* up the mountain is steep and treacherous.
assent: (n) agree with a statement	The men gave a nod of *assent* to show that they would not challenge the explorer's claim.
ate: (v) past tense of "to eat"	He *ate* the last doughnut.
eight: (n) the number 8	He chose *eight* of the last ten winners.

Word: Meaning	Examples and Notes
bail: (n) money held by the court in order to ensure that a person will appear for trial	The judge refused to reduce the *bail* for the man accused of the heinous crime.
bale: (n) a large bundle	The *bale* of hay toppled from the wagon and landed on the unsuspecting farmer.
bare: (adj) without covering, naked	The tree was *bare*; all of its leaves had fallen earlier in the autumn.
bear: (n) a large, heavy animal with shaggy fur and a short tail; (v) to give birth to; to put up with; to carry or hold	The *bear* sniffed around the campsite, looking for an easy meal. I *bear* no grudges, because I'm too busy trying to decide if I've been insulted. She had to *bear* the indignity of having parents who actually set and enforced a curfew.
base: (n) foundation	The statue's *base* began to crumble, sending Chief Muncee tilting toward the White River.
bass: (n) the lowest singing voice; a musical instrument; a type of fish	Grandfather sang *bass* in the church choir. **Note:** *Bass*, the low singing voice, is pronounced the same as *base,* the foundation. The word *bass,* meaning fish, however, is pronounced "bas" (rhymes with glass).
beau: (n) boyfriend, suitor	The beauty had several *beaus* paying court to her.
bow: (n) a device for shooting arrows; front part of a ship; (v) to bend one's head or body in respect, agreement, worship, recognition, and so on	Hunting with *bows* and arrows is illegal in some states. **Note:** Bow is also a homonym. Pronounced (boh), as a noun, bow refers to the front part of a ship or to looped ribbon. Pronounced (bow, rhymes with cow), it means to bend from the waist, or that movement, or to yield to authority.
berth: (n) a built-in bed or bunk; a ship's place of anchorage	The sailor's *berth* is located in the hold of the ship, near the cargo area.
birth: (n) the beginning of anything; the act of bringing forth offspring	Although the actual dates are not widely celebrated, the *births* of Abraham Lincoln and George Washington are observed on Presidents' Day.

(continued)

Table 9-1 *(continued)*

Word: Meaning	Examples and Notes
bore: (n) tiresome person; (*v*): to drill	Herbert is such a *bore* that people disperse as soon as he comes into a room.
boar: (n) male pig	Wild *boars* are known for their ferociousness when cornered.
board: (n) a thin piece of wood; a group of directors	The *board* of directors decided unanimously to revoke the teacher's license.
bored: (adj) weary and disinterested	The *bored* theatergoer livened things up by yelling "Fire!" in the crowded theater and was promptly thrown into jail.
born: (v) brought forth by birth	George Cohen claims that he was *born* on the Fourth of July.
borne: (v) endured (past participle of "to bear")	Herman had *borne* the inconvenience as long as he could before he decided to get a remote control for his television.
brake: (v) to stop	The new driver *braked* slowly on the ice.
break: (v) to shatter	Mother will have a conniption if you *break* her favorite vase.
bred: (v) developed stock by selective mating (past tense of "breed")	He *bred* his dogs in such a way as to preserve the traits of the breed.
bread: (n) food baked from leavened, kneaded dough made with flour or meal, water, yeast, and so on	Few things smell better than freshly baked *bread*.
	Note: *Bread* is also a homonym. In addition to being food, bread, in slang, also means money: "He always complained about not having enough *bread* to buy what he wanted."
bridal: (adj) relating to weddings	The *bridal* party arrived at the church late.
bridle: (n) horse's rein	It took a while for the horse to get used to its *bridle*.
buy: (v) to purchase	Whenever I shop, I always see so many things that I want to *buy*.
by: (prep) beside or near	Keep the glass of water *by* your bedside in case you get thirsty at night.

Word: Meaning	Examples and Notes
capital: (n) the city or town that is the official seat of government; (adj) punishable by death	Every state has a *capital.* In many U.S. states, premeditated murder is often a *capital* crime, which means that, if you're convicted, you could get the death penalty.
Capitol: (n) the building, in Washington, D.C., where the U.S. Congress meets	When you visit the *Capitol,* you'll likely see senators and representatives from the various states.
carrot: (n) vegetable	Eating *carrots* is supposed to improve your eyesight.
carat: (n) unit of weight in gemstones	She received a one-*carat* diamond ring for her engagement.
caret: (n) proofreading symbol (^) that indicates where to insert material	The *caret* indicates that the missing text should go here.
cell: (n) a small room, as in a prison	The *cell* was small and bare, much as you would expect in a nunnery.
sell: (v) to give up in exchange for money	Plenty of people seem to have velvet paintings of Elvis to *sell.* It's hard to believe that there are enough people to buy them.
complement: (n) a complete set; (v) to make complete	He has an entire *complement* of toy soldiers that were made before 1950.
compliment: (n) something said in admiration or praise	She blushed as she received generous *compliments* from her staff.
	Note: One way to figure out whether you need *compliment* with an *i* or *complement* with an *e* is this little trick: *I* like compl*i*ments; compl*e*ment means *e*ntire.
council: (n) a group of people chosen as an administrative, advisory, or legislative assembly	The city *council* is considering making that land a park.
counsel: (n) advice; (v) to give advice	I rely on my mother's wise *counsel.*
cent: (n) penny	You can't find much one-*cent* candy anymore.
scent: (n) aroma	The *scent* of her perfume lingered long after she left.

(continued)

Table 9-1 *(continued)*

Word: Meaning	Examples and Notes
dear: (n) term of endearment; (adj) much loved or valued	The heirloom was *dear* to me.
deer: (n) animals including white-tailed deer, elk, reindeer, and moose	Recently, we saw a small herd of *deer* grazing in the cornfield.
do: (v) act or make	A decorator's last words: "Either this wallpaper goes or I *do*."
due: (adj) caused by	The poor harvest was *due* to low rainfall.
dye: (n) tint or hue	You can make your own color *dyes,* but doing so is time-consuming and difficult.
die: (v) to cease living	All living things eventually *die*.
discreet: (adj) tactful	Despite knowing the dirt on everyone in the room, the hostess was very *discreet,* refusing to join in on the gossip.
discrete: (adj) separate	The father, when faced with his son's misbehavior, considered his own lifestyle to be a *discrete* issue.
elicit: (v) to draw out	See if you can *elicit* a confession from the suspect.
illicit: (adj) unlawful	The *illicit* behavior landed them in jail for the night.
flee: (v) to run	The hare being chased by the hound tried to *flee* through the meadow.
flea: (n) a small, bloodsucking parasite	The dog had a *flea* infestation and had to be dipped and bathed by the vet.
flew: (v) past tense of "to fly"	The track star *flew* over the hurdles to win the gold medal.
flue: (n) chimney	Make sure the *flue* is open before you start the fire.
fare: (n) the price charged for transporting a passenger	How much is the *fare* to Portland, Oregon, from Portland, Maine?
fair: (adj) not biased; (n) carnival with entertainment and items for sale	That resolution was *fair:* Nobody got what he or she wanted. Children of all ages love going to the *fair* to ride the rides, eat corn dogs, and drink lemon shakeups.

Word: Meaning	Examples and Notes
faze: (v) to stun or perturb	Nothing can *faze* the king of cool.
phase: (n) a stage	During an early *phase* of his life, Richard Nixon worked as a barker for the wheel of chance at the Slippery Gulch Rodeo in Prescott, Arizona.
for: (conj) because	Winston Churchill said, "History will be kind to me, *for* I intend to write it."
four: (n) the number 4	You need *four* people for a Euchre game.
fore: (interj) shouted warning in golf; (adv) at, in, or toward the bow of a ship; (adj) situated in front	The caddy heard "*fore!*" just before the golf ball dropped him to his knees.
forward: (adv) toward the future; ahead	After the stock market crash destroyed his fortune, the investment banker could only look *forward* and hope for the best.
foreword: (n) an introductory statement in a book	The author tried in vain to find a celebrity that was willing to write a *foreword* for her book.
	Note: *Forward* is also a homonym. In addition to other meanings, when used as an adjective, it means "presumptuous."
gamble: (v) to play a game of chance; to take a risk	He *gambled* away his life savings; fortunately, it only amounted to the cash he had in his wallet.
gambol: (v) to frolic	The deer *gamboled* and ran through the meadow.
gilt: (adj) overlaid with gold leaf	Many capital buildings on the east coast have *gilt* domes.
guilt: (n) feeling of self-reproach for wrongdoing	The *guilt* she felt from having deceived her parents took all the fun out of the party that they told her she couldn't go to.
	Note: *Gilt* is also a homonym. As a noun, it means "a young female pig."
gorilla: (n) ape	Question: How many surrealists does it take to screw in a light bulb? Answer: Two. One to hold the *gorilla* firmly and the other to fill the bathtub with brightly colored machine tools.
guerrilla: (n) soldier	The *guerrilla* was armed with a machine gun.

(continued)

Table 9-1 *(continued)*

Word: Meaning	*Examples and Notes*
grate: (v) irritate; reduce to small pieces	Her whiny voice and high-pitched giggle began to *grate* on my nerves.
great: (adj) large; of high importance	The *great* cats are endangered by the encroachment of man into their natural habitats.
	Note: *Great* has a whole slew of definitions and functions as a number of different parts of speech.
hear: (v) to perceive sound	Did you *hear* that loud explosion, Grandpa?
here: (adv) in this place	I left my bag right *here;* now it's not *here.*
heart: (n) the organ that pumps blood; the center of something	She got right to the *heart* of the matter.
hart: (n) a male deer	The lords and ladies went *hart* hunting.
hour: (n) 60-minute period	Some people stayed longer than two *hours.*
our: (possessive pronoun) belonging to us	This is *our* house, not yours.
it's: (contraction) "it is" or "it has."	*It's* lonely at the top, but you eat better there.
its: (pronoun) that or those belonging to it	The dog wagged *its* tail.
	Note: In a contraction, the apostrophe *always* replaces a letter or letters. In *it's,* the apostrophe stands in for the *i* in "is." On the other hand, possessive pronouns, like *its,* don't use apostrophes — think of *his* and *hers,* and *yours, mine,* and *ours.*
imminent: (adj) likely to happen without delay	After the timed explosives go off, the implosion of the building is *imminent.*
eminent: (adj) lofty; remarkable	As a person of *eminent* restraint, the customer decided to wait until after he finished his Super Burger to complain about the service.
	Note: These words have slightly different pronunciations — usually too subtle to distinguish. *Imminent* is pronounced "*im*-uh-nunt;" *eminent* is pronounced "*em*-uh-nunt."

Word: Meaning	Examples and Notes
lesson: (n) something to be learned	She learned her *lesson* the hard way.
lessen: (v) to reduce	He *lessened* the burden on the donkey by walking instead of riding.
lei: (n) a garland of flowers	The tourists were greeted warmly and given *leis.*
lay: (v) to put down; also the past tense of *lie*	*Lay* the book on the desk. When I began to feel sleepy, I *lay* down on the sofa.
	Note: The difference between *lie* and *lay* is that *lay* is an action that you can perform on something else, but *lie* is not. A synonym for *lay* is *put.* A synonym for *lie* is *recline.*
lead: (n) a heavy, bluish-gray metal	A pound of *lead* weighs the same as a pound of feathers.
led: (v) past tense of "to lead"	The guide *led* the travelers through the jungle and to the falls.
	Note: *Lead* is also a verb (pronounced leed), which means "to show the way." Because *lead,* "to show the way," and *lead,* "a heavy, bluish-gray metal," don't sound alike, they are not homonyms or homophones. They just happen to be spelled the same.
load: (n) cargo, a heavy burden; (v) to place as a burden	The wagon was reinforced to withstand the heavy *load.* We *loaded* the piano into the truck.
lode: (n) a vein of valuable metal ore	The prospector hit the mother *lode.*
maid: (n) a (female) servant	According to the wealthy, a good *maid* is hard to come by; according to the *maids,* it's the good employers who are scarce.
made: (v) past tense of "to make"	The mortician *made* the error of assuming his date was as interested in embalming as he was.
mail: (v) to send via the postal system	I must *mail* the package in time for the holidays.
male: (adj) relating to members of the masculine sex	Do you want a *male* or a female dog?

(continued)

Table 9-1 *(continued)*

Word: Meaning	Examples and Notes
mettle: (n) quality of character	The battle tested her *mettle*.
metal: (n) elements such as iron, gold, etc.	Newer cars have little if any actual *metal* on them
medal: (n) a token to commemorate an event or give as an award	He received a *medal* for his valor in the line of duty.
meat: (n) animal flesh	I don't eat *meat;* I'm a vegetarian
meet: (v) encounter	I'd like you to *meet* my parents.
mete: (v) to distribute; to measure	The curmudgeon *meted* out kind words sparingly.
pail: (n) bucket	Jack and Jill went up the hill to fetch a *pail* of water.
pale: (adj) wan, pallid	The color drained from his face, leaving him as *pale* as the ghost he thought he saw.
plait: (n) braid, ribbon; (v) to braid	She *plaited* her thick hair in two braids and pinned it out of the way.
plate: (n) a dish	Because she wanted to get new dishes, she threw every last *plate* she owned down the basement stairs.
peace: (n) calm, quiet, tranquility; a time without war	Give *peace* a chance.
piece: (n) part of a whole	Give me a *piece* of pie.
plain: (adj) not good-looking; obvious (n) an extent of level country	In *Jane Eyre,* the heroine is *plain,* but she captures the heart of the hero nonetheless. The rain in Spain stays mainly on the *plain*.
plane: (n) airplane; a carpenter's tool used to smooth or level a wood surface	After he received his pilot's license, he flew a *plane* whenever he could. You need to smooth that uneven door with a *plane*.
presence: (n) company, closeness	Their *presence* brightened up the dreary afternoon.
presents: (n) gifts	Look at the pile of *presents* under the Christmas tree!

Word: Meaning	*Examples and Notes*
read: (v) to get the meaning of some-thing written by using the eyes (or for Braille, the finger tips) to interpret its characters or signs	Most children learn to *read* in elementary school.
reed: (n) tall, slender grass	She waded through the *reeds* to get to the nearby marsh.
	Note: *Read,* pronounced *red,* is also its own past tense, as in "I read 'The Little Prince' in my high school French class." *Reed* has other definitions, making it a homonym: an arrow, part of a loom, and a musical instrument, for example.
right: (adj) correct	The trouble with doing something *right* the first time is that nobody appreciates how difficult it was.
rite: (n) a ceremonial act or procedure	I celebrate the vernal equinox with a *rite* of Spring.
write: (v) to form words or letters with pencil, chalk, and so on.	Question: What inspires you most to write? Answer: The Internal Revenue Service.
residence: (n) a place where one lives	Her *residence* was the house on the hill.
residents: (n) people who live in a place; doctors serving a period of residency	The *residents* were exhausted from the noise coming from the nearby frat house.
rote: (n) a fixed, mechanical way of doing something	She learned her multiplication tables by *rote*.
wrote: (v) past tense of to write	He *wrote* letters to his idol everyday.
	Note: *Rote* is a homonym that has a couple of other meanings: "a harp-like instrument" and "the sound of the surf beating against the shore."
sail: (v) to travel by water; (n) material used to catch or deflect wind in order to propel and direct a vessel	They *sailed* around the world in a dinghy.
	The wind caught the *sails,* and the boat was off.
sale: (n) the act of selling	The shoes went on *sale* at noon and were gone by 3 p.m.

(continued)

Table 9-1 *(continued)*

Word: Meaning	Examples and Notes
sweet: (adj) tasting like sugar; delightful or good	Caramel is a little too *sweet* for my taste.
suite: (n) a group of connected rooms; a set of matching furniture	We reserved a two-bedroom *suite* for our vacation.
	They bought a living room *suite* for entertaining.
sole: (n) the bottom of a shoe; (adj) alone	He walked so much, he wore through the *soles* of his shoes.
	He was the *sole* occupant in the new housing addition.
soul: (n) spiritual or emotional force	Children often ask where the *soul* goes after the body dies.
seed: (n) any part from which a new plant can grow; the source of something	For their science project, each child got one *seed* to plant and tend as it grew.
cede: (v) to yield	I'll *cede* my place this time, if you'll return the favor later.
sight: (n) vision	Does he have the gift of second *sight*?
cite: (v) to quote	Make sure to *cite* the sources you used for your research paper.
site: (n) location; place	She traveled to the *site* where her ancestors first arrived in America.
there: (adv) in that place	Look over *there*!
their: (possessive pronoun) belonging to them	They decided that their best bet was to return to the restaurant to ask about *their* missing wallet.
they're: (contraction) "they are"	*They're* sure that the wallet fell behind the booth.
throne: (n) king's or queen's chair; sovereignty	After the king's death, his heir assumed the *throne*.
thrown: (v) past participle of "to throw"	The book was *thrown* across the room.

Word: Meaning	Examples and Notes
to: (prep) as far as	I'm going *to* Katmandu next week.
too: (adv) also	I'm traveling there, *too!*
two: (n) the number 2	The main library at Indiana University sinks *two* inches a year because when it was built, engineers failed to take into account the weight of all the books that would occupy the building.
tail: (n) rear appendage on an animal; *(v)* to follow	Every time my iguana wags its *tail*, it knocks over a chair.
	The detective *tailed* the suspect.
tale: (n) story	It's a great *tale* filled with lots of action and humor.
threw: (v) past tense of "to throw"	After we *threw* the ball through the neighbor's window, we spent the summer mowing her lawn to pay for it.
through: (prep) in one side and out the other	My pet beaver chewed *through* the house yesterday.
vial: (n) small bottle for holding liquids	The nurse dropped the medicine *vial*.
vile: (adj) depraved, sinful, offensive	That stew is the most *vile*-tasting concoction he has ever whipped up.
vain: (adj) overly concerned with one's looks; conceited	The rock star was so *vain* that he refused to be seen in public without his hair properly styled.
vane: (n) flat piece of metal set to swing with the wind to show which way it's blowing	After the last heavy storm, the weather *vane* fell off the house.
vein: (n) blood vessel; a streak of color in a substance	To feel your pulse, you have to find a *vein* and apply slight pressure with your fingertips.
waist: (n) part of the body between the ribs and hips	This dress fits perfectly in the hips, but it's a little loose in the *waist*.
waste: (v) to destroy, consume, make weak; (n) excess, unneeded material	The toddler lay *waste* to the toy box in seconds flat.

(continued)

Table 9-1 *(continued)*

Word: Meaning	Examples and Notes
way: (n) a route or course	Do you know the *way* to San Jose?
weigh: (v) to measure the weight of something	During every office visit, the doctors *weigh* the baby to make sure that he is growing as he should.
weak: (adj) without strength	The newborn calf was too *weak* to stand.
week: (n) period of 7 days	A fortnight is a period of two *weeks*.
whether: (conj) if	*Whether* you believe it or not, nothing in the universe travels faster than a bad check.
weather: (n) atmospheric conditions	The *weather* is beautiful — if you're a frog.
whine: (v) to complain or beg in a high-pitched, peevish way	Few things are more aggravating than a child — or an adult for that matter — who *whines*.
wine: (n) fermented grape juice	I'll take a bottle of *wine* with my dinner, please.
whose: (pronoun) belonging to whom	Never go to a doctor *whose* office plants have died.
who's: (contraction) "who is" or "who has"	*Who's* in charge here?
your: (possessive pronoun) belonging to you	Who knew that *your* predictions would come true?
you're: (contraction) "you are"	There is never enough time — unless *you're* serving it.

Having Fun with Homonyms

Homonyms are words that have the same spelling and pronunciation but different meanings. For example, *hearing* refers both to the ability to use your ears and to an airing of issues in a legal setting. For a more complete explanation of what homonyms are, refer to the "Differentiating Homonyms and Homophones (In Case You're Curious)" section earlier in this chapter.

Believe it or not, you can have a lot of fun with homonyms. Because of the way homonyms work, it's easy to create puns with them. A *pun* is a play on words created with a homonym. The joke originates from the word's multiple meanings. Here's an example of the homonym *caliber* used in context:

In the late 1800s, the man who was shot of out the cannon daily at the Barnum and Bailey Circus decided to quit. Circus owner P.T. Barnum hated to lose a good man, so he sent him a message, "I beg you to reconsider — men of your caliber are hard to find."

Caliber has two meanings: "diameter" and "character or abilities." Using context, we can deduce that *caliber* is used in this joke to mean "character or abilities." The humor arises from our understanding of the other meaning.

Another example:

A panda walks into a restaurant and orders a sandwich and a drink. When he is finished eating, he pulls out a pistol and shoots up the place, scaring customers and breaking dishes, glasses, and liquor bottles before turning to leave.

Shocked, the manager says, "Hey, where are you going?"

The panda glances back over his shoulder and says, "I'm a panda — look it up," before disappearing out the door.

The bartender pulls out a dictionary and thumbs through it until he finds an entry for panda. The definition reads, "A tree-dwelling animal of Asian origin characterized by distinct black-and-white markings. Eats shoots and leaves."

The *homonyms* in this joke are *shoots,* which means "fires or blasts," as well as "buds or sprouts," and *leaves,* which means both "departs" and "foliage."

How about a few more favorites:

- How did the piano get out of jail? With its keys!
- How can you tell when a toy is nervous? It's all wound up.
- What is the tallest building in your city? The library — it has the most stories.
- Where is King Solomon's temple? On the side of his head.

You can also use homophones to create puns. The key to creating puns is as follows: If you're *writing* a pun, you want the words to be spelled alike; if you're *saying* a pun, you want the words to sound alike. Otherwise, it appears that you made a mistake, and then the joke's on you.

Chapter 10

Compounding Words

· ·

In This Chapter

▶ Finding out how to define compound words

▶ Discovering closed compounds, hyphenated compounds, and open compounds

▶ Using the parts of compound words to master new words

· ·

*O*ne way to describe something new is to combine two words to form a new word. The combination gives the new word a special meaning that is different from the original meaning of the separate words. For example, you combine "head" and "line" to get "headline." A headline is the title of an article, not a line on your head.

However, you can figure out the meaning of "headline" by looking at the word a little more closely. "Head" is the top of your body. A "headline" is the top of an article. In most cases, we notice a person's head first; in the same way, we notice the headline of an article first. Even though the parts of "headline" didn't seem to add up at first glance, they sure do when you look at them again.

Knowing about compound words can help you quickly and easily decode many unfamiliar words.

Presenting Compound Basics

Compound words are comprised of two or more words written as one word (*hothouse,* for example), a hyphenated word *(comrade-in-arms),* or two or more words that together represent a unique item or idea (such as *commander in chief* or *school bus*).

Because compound words appear in various forms, how can you tell whether a word is truly a compound word or just a compound wannabe? The following list presents two simple guidelines to help you figure out if a word is a true compound:

✔ **Each element must be a complete word.** *Pre-law* is not a compound word because "pre" is not a complete word (even though *law* is). *Goldfish*, however, is a compound word, because "gold" and "fish" are separate words.

✔ **No letters are dropped or added when the compound word is formed.** When a prefix or suffix is added to a word, letters are often dropped or added. Similarly, when two distinct words come together, letters are often dropped or changed in order to join the words. A compound word, however, is formed by just sticking the two words together, without adding or removing any letters to do so:

> **Compound word:** day + light = daylight
>
> **Not a compound word:** holy + day = holiday
>
> **Compound word:** like + able = likeable
>
> **Not a compound word:** justify + able = justifiable

Language is fluid and ever-changing. As language evolves, hyphenated or separate word compounds may become closed compounds. When you are in doubt about the spelling of a compound word, check an up-to-date dictionary.

Gathering up closed compounds

Closed compounds appear as one word with no break between the words used to create it. In addition, no letters are added or removed in order to make the compound; the two words are just put together. As in any compound word, you can use the meanings of the individual words to puzzle out the definition of the compound. As you read the examples in Table 10-1, cover the last column on the right. Knowing each part of the compound word can help you define the new word it forms.

Table 10-1			Combined Compound Nouns
Word	*+ Word*	*= Compound Word*	*Definition*
book	case	bookcase	cabinet for books
cross	road	crossroad	the place where two or more roads intersect; a time in which important decisions must be made
house	fly	housefly	a fly that lives in and around houses
rain	coat	raincoat	a coat that repels rain
steam	boat	steamboat	boat powered by steam

Word	+	Word	=	Compound Word	Definition
window		sill		windowsill	window ledge
with		out		without	not having, lacking
any		one		anyone	any person, anybody

You can form a slew of compound words with the word "super." Most of these words use "super" as a prefix, as in *superabundant* (exceedingly abundant), *superhuman* (more than human), and *supercharge* (charge with an excessive amount). However, a handful of compound words use "super" as a word rather than a prefix. For example, we have *superannuate* (soo-pur-*an*-yoo-ate), which means "to allow to retire on a pension because of age or sickness."

Separating hyphenated compounds

Hyphenated compounds are written as one word — two words joined by a hyphen. As you check out the examples in Table 10-2, try reading only the first two columns, and then see if you can guess the meaning of the compound word.

Table 10-2				Hyphenated Compounds		
Word	+	Word	=	Hyphenated Compound	Part of Speech	Definition
able		bodied		able-bodied	adj.	fit, healthy, robust
bell		like		bell-like	adj.	like a bell
cross		examine		cross-examine	verb	to question, often in court
great		grandfather		great-grandfather	noun	relative
old		fashioned		old-fashioned	adj.	traditional
philosopher		statesman		philosopher-statesman	noun	a politician who combines practical experience with philosophical ideals
secretary		treasurer		secretary-treasurer	noun	one who serves an organization as both secretary and treasurer
well		attended		well-attended	adj.	crowded

Fluttering butterflies

The compound word *butterfly* comes from the Old English words *butere* (butter) and *fleoge* (fly). Although the origin of the word is obscure, it may hark back to the belief that butterflies (or witches in the guise of butterflies) stole butter and milk. As many song writers, poets, and others have noted, switching the initial consonant sounds of the individual words (*butter* and *fly*) gives you *flutter by* — words that describe what butterflies do.

Although many hyphenated compounds are built from two words, as Table 10-2 shows, you can also find a quite a few common three-word compounds: *sister-in-law* (and the other *in-law* words), *five-year-old*, and *show-and-tell*, for example.

TIP

It is often hard to determine whether a word is hyphenated. Sometimes the hyphen depends on what part of speech the word is. For example, *show-off* is hyphenated as a noun but not as a verb (*show off*). To add to the confusion, you can't always rely on similar words being treated the same way. For example, you hyphenate *brother-in-law, mother-in-law,* and the other *in-law* words, but you don't hyphenate *commander in chief.* The following guidelines usually work:

- ✔ **Use a hyphen in compound words beginning with *self*:** *self-satisfied, self-examine,* and so on.

- ✔ **Use a hyphen in compound words that end with *elect*:** *president-elect*, for example.

REMEMBER

When you apply the preceding rules, be sure that you're combining two complete words — not a root and a suffix or prefix that aren't words themselves. For example, *self-examine, self-elect,* and *self-respect* are hyphenated compounds. *Selfishness* and *reelect* aren't compound words and therefore don't use hyphens. (Although, you may choose to hyphenate reelect just to distinguish the double *e*.)

- ✔ **You usually hyphenate compound words that begin with *all* (*all-around* and *all-American*).** Keep in mind, though, that this isn't always the case (*all in one*).

- ✔ **Use an up-to-date dictionary.** If you're not sure whether a word should be hyphenated, look it up.

Making multiword compounds

English contains some compound words that are written as two (or more) separate words. This type of compound word is relatively rare, likely because the two words that make up the compound word get combined into one word for ease of spelling. These two-word compounds are almost always nouns. Table 10-3 lists a few of them.

Table 10-3		Two-Word Compound Nouns	
Word +	*Word* =	*Two-Word Compound*	*Definition*
base	pay	base pay	basic rate of pay for a particular job
base	runner	base runner	any member of the team at bat who has reached base safely (baseball term)
East	Asian	East Asian	nationality
hair	spray	hair spray	a liquid sprayed onto the hair to keep it in place
half	brother	half brother	brother through one parent only
half	gainer	half gainer	type of dive
half	hitch	half hitch	type of knot
half	shell	half shell	half a shell
home	fries	home fries	type of potatoes
home	front	home front	non-combat zones; home
ice	cream	ice cream	frozen dessert
post	office	post office	governmental department in charge of the mails

Dash it all! I want a hyphen!

A hyphen is created by one click of the keyboard. A hyphen looks like this: -. A dash is made with two clicks of the key and looks like this: —. (This two-dash hyphen is called an *em dash* because it is as wide as a capital letter M.) A hyphen and a dash are not the same mark of punctuation. A hyphen is used to join parts of words, while a dash is used to join parts of sentences.

Using Compounds to Build Your Vocabulary

No matter how a compound is written, you can still use the individual words to get an idea of the compound word's definition. Often, the definition of the compound is a sort of combination of the definitions of its individual words. For example, shuffleboard (the game in which you use long cues to shove disks along a smooth surface) is made up of the word *shuffle* (a dragging, sliding movement) and the word *board* (a flat surface, usually of wood).

You can sometimes figure out the definition of a compound word by knowing its history. For example, the compound word *bootlegger* was originally used to describe a person who smuggled outlawed liquor in the tops of his tall boots. From that, the term came to mean anyone who makes, sells, or transports alcoholic beverages illegally. The language also gained the adjective *bootleg*, which describes music and videos copied illegally.

The following suggestions can help you make compound words part of your daily written and spoken vocabulary:

1. **Jot down unfamiliar compound words that you hear or read.**

2. **Look the word up in the dictionary to find out whether it's a closed compound, hyphenated compound, or open compound.**

3. **Group related words.**

    For example, put all the words about the sun together. Doing this makes it easier for you to see how the words are similar.

Because it's easier to remember new words when you group them by theme, I arrange some compound words by related topic in the following sections.

Halving your options with "half"

Of all the words used to build compounds, "half" is probably one of the most common. Many of the compound words formed with *half* are hyphenated. Remembering this quirk makes these compounds easier to use and spell correctly. Table 10-4 lists some compounds made with *half*.

Table 10-4			Compound Words Made with "Half"		
Word	**+ Word**	**=**	**Compound**	**Part of Speech**	**Definition**
half	baked		half-baked	adj.	not fully baked; not completely planned or thought-out
half	cup		half-cup	noun	four ounces
half	filled		half-filled	adj.	partly filled
half	hearted		halfhearted	adj.	lacking enthusiasm
half	hour		half-hour	noun	30 minutes
half	life		half-life	noun	the time required for half the atoms in radio-active material to disintegrate
half	moon		half-moon	noun	the moon in its first or last quarter phase
half	step		half step	noun	short marching step; musical term for the difference in pitch between two adjacent keys on a piano
half	truth		half-truth	noun	a statement intended to deceive

Eating well: Compound words about food

You may get hungry when you read the list of compound words, in Table 10-5, about food! See how many of these compound words you can define from their parts. All of the food-related compound words in the table are nouns.

Table 10-5			Food-Related Compound Words	
Word	**+ Word**	**=**	**Compound**	**Definition**
apple	sauce		applesauce	sauce made from cooked apples
blue	berry		blueberry	small, edible, blue-black berries

(continued)

Table 10-5 *(continued)*

Word +	Word =	Compound	Definition
bread	fruit	breadfruit	starchy fruit that resembles baked bread
cat	fish	catfish	fish with cat-like "whiskers"
cheese	cake	cheesecake	cake made from cottage cheese or cream cheese and other ingredients, usually baked with a bottom crust of crumbs
corn	flakes	cornflakes	breakfast cereal of crisp flakes made from hulled corn
cup	cakes	cupcakes	little cakes baked in cup-shaped molds
head	cheese	headcheese	loaf of jellied, seasoned meat, made from parts of the heads and feet of hogs
honey	dew	honeydew	a sweet fluid, as manna, exuded from various plants; a particularly sweet variety of melon
oat	meal	oatmeal	oats ground into meal; porridge
pan	cake	pancake	thin, flat cake fried on a griddle or in a pan
pea	nut	peanut	a spreading, annual vine of the pea family, with brittle pods that ripen underground and contain edible seeds
pop	corn	popcorn	a variety of corn that, when heated, pops open into white, puffy masses
straw	berry	strawberry	small, red fruit
sword	fish	swordfish	fish with a swordlike protrusion from its upper jawbone
water	melon	watermelon	large, round or oblong edible fruit with a hard, green rind and a sweet, juicy pulp

Here's an interesting compound word about food — *wormwood.* No, it's not wormy wood, even though it sounds that way. Rather, wormwood is the active narcotic ingredient of absinthe, a bitter green liqueur now banned in most Western countries. Originally, the herb was used as a folk remedy for worms in the body — hence the "worm" in its name. Because of the herb's bitter qualities, wormwood's figurative meaning is "something bitter, grievous, or extremely unpleasant."

Getting comfortable with homey compound words

Table 10-6 lists some compound words formed around the word "home." Nearly all are closed compounds. Again, as you look at this list, try to use the two smaller words to define the newly formed compound word.

Table 10-6		Home-Related Compound Words		
Word	+ Word	= Compound	Part of Speech	Definition
home	land	homeland	noun	a person's native country
home	run	home run	noun	safe hit that allows the batter to touch all bases and score a run (baseball term)
home	made	homemade	adj.	made at home
home	plate	home plate	noun	the base that the batter stands beside and over which the pitcher must throw the ball (baseball term)
home	maker	homemaker	noun	person who makes a home; traditionally, a housewife
home	room	homeroom	noun	the room where a class in school meets every day to be checked for attendance, receive school bulletins, and so on
home	sick	homesick	adj.	yearning for home
home	spun	homespun	noun/adj.	fabric made of yarn spun at home; spun or made at home
home	stead	homestead	noun/verb	place where a family makes its home; to build a new home on unimproved land.
home	grown	homegrown	adj.	grown at home
home	body	homebody	noun	person who prefers to stay at home
home	brew	home-brew	noun	alcoholic beverage made at home

(continued)

Table 10-6 (continued)

Word	+ Word	= Compound	Part of Speech	Definition
home	like	homelike	adj.	having qualities associated with home; comfortable
house	wife	housewife	noun	woman whose principal occupation is managing a household
house	work	housework	noun	work involved in housekeeping

LANGUAGE LORE

Few people felt as strongly linked to their area of the country as the Northerners and the Southerners during the Civil War. This is reflected in the language of the period. For example, the compound word *copperhead* was coined by the *New York Tribune* in the early days of the Civil War to refer to a Northerner who sympathized with the South. The term came from the sneaky and poisonous copperhead snake, which strikes without warning.

Sunning yourself: Compound words with "sun"

The hot, bright star that lies at the center of our solar system has sparked many myths, legends, and stories through the ages. According to ancient Egyptian legends, for example, the earth arose as a hill from the featureless ocean Nun. Darkness was dispersed by the sun god Ra, who alit as a phoenix (*fee*-nix) on the hill. His offspring were Shu, the god of air, and Tefnut, the goddess of water. Each day, Nut (depicted as a cow) would give birth to the sun anew. Each dawn, the sun rose as Khepri, a giant scarab beetle, and crossed the sky as Ra in a ship crewed by other gods. Each night the sun sank below the horizon as an old man, then crossed the underworld to begin the cycle again.

In addition to sparking fascinating myths and legends, the word *sun* has been combined with many other words to form important compound words. Try adding the words in Table 10-7 to your vocabulary.

Table 10-7   Compound "Sun" Words

Word	+ Word	= Compound	Part of Speech	Definition
sun	bathe	sunbathe	verb	to bathe in sunlight
sun	beam	sunbeam	noun	ray of sunlight

Word	+	Word	=	Compound	Part of Speech	Definition
sun		burn		sunburn	noun	inflammation of the skin resulting from prolonged exposure to the sun's rays or a sunlamp
sun		down		sundown	noun	sunset
sun		flower		sunflower	noun	plant with large, yellow, daisylike flowers that produce edible seeds
sun		glasses		sunglasses	noun	glasses with tinted lenses to protect the eyes from the sun's glare
sun		lamp		sunlamp	noun	lamp that radiates ultraviolet rays, used for tanning
sun		light		sunlight	noun	light from the sun
sun		rise		sunrise	noun	daily appearance of the sun above the eastern horizon
sun		set		sunset	noun	daily disappearance of the sun below the western horizon
sun		shine		sunshine	noun	shining of the sun; light and heat from the sun
sun		stroke		sunstroke	noun	heatstroke caused by excessive exposure to the sun
sun		up		sunup	noun	sunrise

Eyeing compound words with "eye"

Human eyes are amazingly powerful. Astronauts that have orbited the earth have reported spotting the wakes of oceangoing ships. Many people consider vision to be the team captain of the five senses. Because people get most of their information about a word from their eyes, it's no wonder that English has so many compound words that contain the word "eye." Sometimes these words are used as nouns, but they can also function as verbs (to *eyeball* something, for example).

Adding up the days

English and related Germanic languages (such as German, Dutch, Danish, and Swedish) derive most of their names for the days of the week from Germanic and Norse mythology. French and other Romance languages, such as Italian and Spanish, derive their names for the days of the week from Latin and classical mythology. Here are the origins of the English names for the days of the week:

✔ Sunday: sun day (from Old English *sunnandaeg,* literally "day of the sun")

✔ Monday: moon day (from Old English *mondaeg,* literally "day of the moon")

✔ Tuesday: Tiw's day (from Old English *Tiwesdaeg,* literally "day of Tiu" — the Germanic god identified with Mars)

✔ Wednesday: Woden's day (from Old English *Wodnesdaeg,* literally "day of Woden" — also known as Odin, the chief Norse god)

✔ Thursday: Thor's day (from Old English *Thurresdaeg,* literally "day of Thor" — Norse god of thunder and war)

✔ Friday: Frigg's or Freya's day (from Old English *Frigedaeg,* literally "day of Frigga" — Germanic goddess of heaven and love)

✔ Saturday: Saturn's day (from Old English *Saeternesdaeg,* literally "day of the planet Saturn")

The compound words in Table 10-8 are all formed with the word *eye.* (All the words in the table are nouns.) I bet you can find some old favorites, as well as some newcomers, among these words. As you go over the list, try to use each word in a sentence in order to help you fix the words in your "mind's eye."

Table 10-8			"Eye" Compounds	
Word	**+**	**Word**	**= Compound**	**Definition**
eye		ball	eyeball	the ball-shaped part of the eye
eye		brow	eyebrow	the bony arch over each eye; the arch of hair growing on this
eye		dialect	eye dialect	nonstandard respelling of words to suggest dialectal or informal pronunciation
eye		glasses	eyeglasses	lenses to help correct faulty vision
eye		lash	eyelash	hair on the edge of the eyelid

Word	+	Word	=	Compound	Definition
eye		let		eyelet	small hole for a cord or lace to pass through
eye		lid		eyelid	skin that covers and uncovers the front of the eyeball
eye		opener		eye-opener	surprising piece of news
eye		shade		eyeshade	visorlike shade for the eyes
eye		sore		eyesore	something unpleasant to look at
eye		tooth		eyetooth	canine teeth in upper jaw
eye		witness		eyewitness	person who sees or has seen an event happen

Idioms are phrases and expressions that cannot be taken literally, or word for word. Instead, they are understood in a figurative sense. English has several common idioms that involve the word eye: *to have an eye for* (to appreciate); *to keep an eye on* (to watch); *to see eye to eye with* (to agree with).

Combing through some "hairy" compound words

Hair was a hit musical. Hair is also the silky, curly, or rough stuff that covers your head (and most of the rest of your body). And hair is the basis of many important compound words. Table 10-9 holds some "hairy" compound words that you may find beneficial in conversation and writing. (All the words listed are nouns.)

Table 10-9				Compound Words Using "Hair"	
Word	+	Word	=	Compound	Definition
hair		breadth		hairbreadth	extremely small space or amount
hair		cloth		haircloth	fabric woven from horsehair, camel's hair, and so on, often used for covering furniture
hair		do		hairdo	hair style
hair		dresser		hairdresser	person who styles hair

(continued)

Table 10-9 *(continued)*

Word	+	Word	=	Compound	Definition
hair		line		hairline	the outline of the hair on the forehead; a very thin line; narrow margin or degree of difference
hair		piece		hairpiece	toupee
hair		raiser		hair-raiser	something that is terrifying or shocking
hair		shirt		hair shirt	shirt of haircloth, worn over the skin as penance
hair		space		hair space	thin divider of space used to separate words (printing term)
hair		spring		hairspring	slender, spiral spring used in a watch
hair		trigger		hair trigger	a trigger that allows the firing mechanism in a firearm to be operated by only slight pressure

Chilling compound words with "snow"

Ever hear the saying, "Everybody talks about the weather, but no one does anything about it"? Well, we talk about the weather all the time because it is a powerful force of nature that affects everything we do. As sophisticated as the modern world is, we're still pretty much at the mercy of the weather. We hide in the cellar when a tornado strikes and cancel school when it snows. Speaking of snow, Table 10-10 lists compound words that contain the word "snow." Use the words to describe some of the interesting weather in your neck of the woods!

Table 10-10 Compound Words Using "Snow"

Word	+	Word	=	Compound	Part of Speech	Definition
snow		bank		snowbank	noun	large pile of snow, such as a drift on a hillside
snow		bird		snowbird	noun	bird commonly seen in the winter; slang term for northern tourists who vacation in the South during the winter

Word +	Word =	Compound	Part of Speech	Definition
snow	blind	snow-blind	adj.	blinded temporarily by ultraviolet rays reflected from snow
snow	bound	snowbound	adj.	shut in or blocked off because of snow
snow	drift	snowdrift	noun	snow blown into a pile by the wind
snow	fence	snow fence	noun	fence used to control the drifting of snow
snow	flake	snowflake	noun	single crystal of snow
snow	job	snow job	verb	the attempt to deceive someone through flattery or trickery
snow	mobile	snowmobile	noun	motor vehicle used to travel over snow
snow	plow	snowplow	noun	bulldozerlike device used to clear snow
snow	shoe	snowshoe	noun	racket-shaped frames of wood, fitted with crosspieces and criss-crossed with strips of leather, worn on the feet to prevent sinking in deep snow
snow	storm	snowstorm	noun	storm with a heavy snowfall
snow	tire	snow tire	noun	tires created for travel through snow
snow	white	snow-white	adj.	white as snow

While we're on the topic of weather, the coldest place on earth is Prospect Creek Camp, Alaska, which recorded a temperature of –80 degrees Fahrenheit. The hottest place on earth is Death Valley, California, which recorded a temperature of 134 degrees Fahrenheit. The snowiest month occurred in Tamarack, California, when the city received 390 inches of the cold white stuff.

Fooling around with "play" compound words

You work so hard, why not take a break and play a little? No, it's not time for baseball, football, or even a hacky sack. Rather, it's time for some compound words that all contain the word *play*. Table 10-11 lists a few "play" words that describe different kinds of playing. Use the nouns listed in the table the next time you take a break!

Table 10-11			**Compound Words Using "Play"**
Word +	*Word* =	*Compound*	*Definition*
play	back	playback	reproduction of sounds, images, and so on, from a recorded disc or tape
play	bill	playbill	program of a play, listing the cast, staff, and so on
play	girl/boy	playgirl, playboy	a wealthy man or woman who devotes most of his or her time to pleasure-seeking
play	ground	playground	recreation field
play	house	playhouse	theater for live dramatic productions; a child's toy house or doll house
play	mate	playmate	friend; buddy
play	pen	playpen	enclosure for toddlers
play	off	playoff	game played to decide a championship, as between the top finishers in the divisions of a league
play	room	playroom	recreation room
play	suit	playsuit	woman's or child's outfit for sports or play, consisting usually of shorts or pants and a shirt
play	thing	plaything	toy
play	time	playtime	time for play or recreation
play	writing	playwriting	the art, profession, or work of writing plays

Compounding a Few, Final Words

Airport, bathtub, birthday, boardwalk, corncob, doorway, flowerpot, lemonade, mountaintop, paintbrush, playground, pocketbook, railroad, rainbow, rosebud, seashell, seahorse, seesaw, sliding-glass, spell-binder, teardrop, toothache, tree-house, and wishbone — these are a few of my favorite compound words. The list is completely arbitrary, so feel free to add your own contributions!

Chapter 11

Romancing English: Words from French, Spanish, and Italian

- -

In This Chapter

▶ Using French-born words with panache

▶ Speaking Spanish the English way

▶ Eyeing Italian–American words

- -

*F*rance has one television for every two people in its population, 63 airports, and a ton of perfume. Spain? Over 895,000 metric tons of fish were caught there in 1996. Italy has lip-smacking spaghetti and ice cream so sinfully delicious (and fattening) that it should be illegal. So what do all of these countries have in common? In addition to people, perfume, and pike, they have all given English a huge amount of handy words. They also derived their languages from Latin way back when, and along with Portuguese, Romanian, and a few other Indo-European languages, are called the *Romance languages.*

English has embraced words from a heap of other languages and dialects, near and far, ancient and modern. In fact, three-quarters of all English words are foreign born. English has begged, borrowed, and swiped some of its most useful social words from countries both near and far. These borrowed words pertain to art, architecture, geography, hobbies, music, dance, food, and entertainment.

This chapter covers words that entered English from French, Spanish, and Italian. For words from other countries or regions, head to Chapter 12.

One of the most effective ways to stretch your vocabulary is by exploring a word's origins, or *etymology.* Doing so helps you link related words so that you can figure out the meaning and usage of many commonplace words that have entered English from other languages.

Ooo La La! English Words from French

From the French, the United States has imported some great perfumes, pâté (a meat paste), and words. For example, Americans use many French words to describe people, including their personalities, occupations, and personal habits. Some of these borrowed words are adjectives like *naive* (ny-*eev*), which means "unsophisticated or simple," and petite (peh-*teet*), which means "small and trim of figure." Others are nouns, such as *ingenue* (an-zhuh-*noo*), which means "a frank or artless young woman." You may be surprised by how many English words with French origins you use regularly. The following words, for example, are other ordinary English words that also happen to be French:

- **Avalanche** (*av*-uh-lanch): a sudden rush of snow and/or earth down a mountain
- **Crouton** (*krew*-tahn): a small cube of bread
- **Etiquette** (*et*-i-kit): rules of conduct and behavior
- **Garage** (gah-*rahj*): a building used for housing a car or other vehicle
- **Toile** (twahl): a sheer, airy fabric

An effective way to learn new vocabulary is to expose yourself to words that are used in particular topics: words relating to social situations, for example, or words relating to food and cooking. Giving the words a common frame of reference makes them easier to memorize, recall, and use correctly. For that reason, I arrange the words in the following sections into related groups.

Socializing with French flair

At one time, France in general and the French courts in particular were the center of the western world. Considered the zenith of European culture and refinement, the French courts set the standard of courtly behavior. As a result, from the French came many English words that relate to social interactions and etiquette (itself a French word). Table 11-1 lists a few of these words.

Table 11-1	Twelve French Words for Social Situations	
Word	*Part of Speech*	*Definition*
bon mot (*bohn-moh*)	noun	clever saying
bourgeois (boor-*zhwah*)	adj.	middle class; materialistic
charlatan (*shar*-luh-tuhn)	noun	faker, quack
chic (sheek)	adj.	stylishly sophisticated

Word	Part of Speech	Definition
élan (ay-*lahn*)	noun	spirit or vivacity, liveliness of imagination
faux pas (foh-*pah*)	noun	social blunder
gauche (gohsh)	adj.	socially inept
genteel (jen-*teel*)	adj.	elegant, refined
nonchalance (nahn-shuh-*lahns*)	noun	indifference
raconteur (rak-ahn-*tur*)	noun	expert storyteller
rapport (ra-*por*)	noun	harmony, accord
repartee (rep-ahr-*tee*)	noun	witty reply

Talkin' the Talk

Estelle is having a conversation with her new, very sophisticated acquaintance, Sarah Snooty. They're sitting in a posh French restaurant, thinking about trying the overpriced *escargot* (a fancy-schmancy word for snails in garlic butter — I think they taste like greasy rubber bands, but what do I know?). Let's be shameless and listen in.

Sarah Snooty:	Since I'm so popular, beautiful, and rich, I get along with everyone. I even have a good rapport with the staff here.
Estelle:	Yes, you seem very genteel.
Sarah Snooty:	We'll both order the steak tartar. It's very chic.
Estelle (no longer afraid of making a *faux pas* and fed up with Sarah Snooty's attitude):	No, raw meat with a raw egg is so gauche. I'll have the escargot.

Practice makes perfect, so practice using new words. Who knows, some cutie-pie may walk by, overhear your conversation, and be impressed with your sophistication and polish!

More pig, please

France has almost always been closely — although not always happily — tied to England for several reasons. First, only a short distance separates the two countries (the English Channel is only about 30 miles wide). Second, there were several marriages between the countries' royal families. Third, the countries were politically entangled. Several English kings, for example, claimed to rule parts or all of France, and several French kings claimed to rule all or parts of England.

But perhaps the event that led to the greatest influence of the French on the English was the Norman invasion. In 1066, the Normans (folks from the northern part of France, called Normandy), led by William the Conqueror, invaded Anglo-Saxon England. The victorious William (actually the last person to invade the British Isles successfully) became king, bringing with him French customs and the French language. Of course, the ruling class (the Normans) spoke French; their subjects (the Saxons) spoke English.

An interesting result of the division between the aristocratic French and the conquered Saxons is that the names of meats (a culinary luxury of the wealthy) come from French words: beef, pork, mutton, and venison, for example. The names of animals — cow, pig, lamb, and deer — have English histories. It would seem that the English subjects raised the livestock, and the French invaders ate the meat.

Dining on words

In addition to French words related to social ineptness and style (see the preceding section), the French have also given English a whole slew of words that have to do with food. (Given that French chefs are among the world's most renowned, this is appropriate.) Table 11-2 lists several food-related words that English appropriated from the French.

Table 11-2	French Nouns Related to Food and Cooking
Word	*Definition*
aspic (*as*-pik)	cold jelly of meat juice, tomato juice, and so on, served as a garnish or molded
béchamel (bay-shuh-*mel*)	white sauce made of milk, butter, flour, and, sometimes, cream
bouillon (*bewl*-yahn)	clear broth, usually of beef
casserole (*kas*-uh-rohl)	covered baking dish, or stewlike meal cooked in such a dish
charlotte (*shahr*-luht)	molded dessert consisting of an outer layer of strips of bread, cake, and so on, filled with fruit or custard

Word	Definition
compote (*kahm*-poht)	dish of fruits stewed in a syrup
crêpe (krayp)	small, thin pancake
croquette (kroh-*ket*)	patty of chopped, cooked meat, fish, or vegetables, coated with egg and crumbs and fried
cuisine (kwee-*zeen*)	style of cooking; prepared food
escargot (es-kar-*goh*)	edible variety of snail
fricassee (*frik*-uh-see)	stewed or fried meat served in a sauce of its own gravy
meringue (muh-*rang*)	sweetened whipped egg whites baked until lightly brown
ragout (rah-*goo*)	highly seasoned stew of meat and vegetables
terrine (teh-*reen*)	an earthenware dish or casserole in which meat or vegetable mixtures are cooked and served

The word *crepe,* without the accent on the first *e,* also comes from French and indicates a thin, crinkled fabric. You can spell the thin pancake *crepe* without the accent if you wish, but it's kind of fun to feel French for a moment.

To reinforce your knowledge, try to use each word in a sentence — preferably while you're cooking a delicious French dish.

Entertaining words from French

New York may be the city that never sleeps, but France's capital city, Paris, is the City of Light and, as such, has quite a reputation for being a pretty lively place. France can also lay claim to some of the world's greatest artists (Claude Monet, Édouard Manet, Paul Cézanne, and Georges Seurat, to name just a few). So it seems fitting that the French language has given English several words related to entertainment and the arts. Table 11-3 lists a few of these words.

Table 11-3	French Nouns Related to Entertainment and the Arts
Word	Definition
arabesque (air-uh-*besk*)	fanciful interlaced patterns; ballet position; light, whimsical music composition
bas-relief (bah-rih-*leef*)	sculpture in which the figures project slightly from the background

(continued)

Table 11-3 *(continued)*

Word	Definition
burlesque (buhr-*lesk*)	ludicrous parody
cabaret (kab-uh-*ray*)	dinner show
cotillion (koh-*til*-yuhn)	complex, formal dance; a formal ball
croupier (*krew*-pee-ay/er)	the attendant at a gaming table
marquee (mahr-*kee*)	rooflike awning or sign used over a theater entrance
masque (mask)	masked ball; short, allegorical dramas performed in the courts of the 16th and 17th centuries
pirouette (pir-oo-*et*)	to whirl on one foot
plie (plee-*ay*)	a ballet move in which the knees are bent outward, with the back held straight
pointillism (*pwan*-tuh-liz-em)	the technique of painting with dots or small strokes of color in such a way that, from a distance, the dots blend together to form a recognizable image
roulette (roo-*let*)	game of chance played by rolling a small ball around a shallow bowl with an inner disk revolving in the opposite direction
surrealism (suh-*ree*-uhl-iz-em)	modern movement in art and literature, in which an attempt is made to portray or interpret the workings of the unconscious mind as manifested in dreams
troubadour (*trew*-buh-dohr)	wandering singer
trompe l'oeil (trohnp leh-y)	painting that tricks the eye into believing that the thing depicted is actually real
vaudeville (*vahd*-vil)	stage show consisting of mixed specialty acts

Walking the streets

You have to give the French credit for having a beautiful language. Even French words that represent the more mundane things in life — like streets, buildings, and desks — sound pretty darn good. In fact, you can probably say "I am eating a worm" in French and have the folks around you order up a helping, too.

So, to end this little tour of French words turned English, Table 11-4 has a few of the more ordinary items. Even when you're not talking about culinary delights or artistic expression and technique, French words are still pretty darn cool. You have to admit, after all, that sitting down at an escritoire (es-kri-*twar*) to do your homework sounds a lot cooler than plopping yourself down at a desk.

Table 11-4	Other Nouns from French
Word	*Definition*
avenue (*av*-eh-new)	road or path, often lined with trees
boulevard (*bool*-eh-vard)	broad avenue in a city, often lined with trees or grass
bureau (*byoor*-oh)	office; desk; agency that collects and gives information
canteen (kan-*teen*)	small, portable container used to hold liquid; place where food and refreshments are served
chaise (shayz)	light, open carriage; chair
chateau (sha-*toh*)	castle; large country house and estate
concierge (kahn-see-*erzh*)	doorman; head porter of a hotel
ensemble (ahn-*sahm*-buhl)	all parts of a whole; a person's outfit; the performance of a musical group or theatre production
epergne (ee-*pern*)	ornamental stand for holding fruit or flowers
facade (fuh-*sahd*)	front of a building; front of anything, with implications that an imposing appearance hides something inferior
mansard (*man*-sard)	type of pitched roof where each of four sides has two slopes, the lower one steeper than the upper
salon (sah-*lahn*)	large reception hall or social room; room or gallery for the exhibition of works of art; a shop or business providing a personal service

Talkin' the Talk

Buff Bruce and his arm-candy, Leslie, are shopping for antiques at a trendy shop on the boulevard. Having taken a page from this book, they can now talk the talk and walk the walk. Because they're so attractive, feel free to lean closer and eavesdrop.

Leslie:	Let's get a bas-relief for the living room.
Bruce:	Huh?
Leslie:	There's an attractive bas-relief over there. It would fit right over the fireplace.
Bruce:	Now I know what you mean. And the answer is no.
Leslie:	You're so cheap. Next you're going to tell me that we can't afford that chateau in the Loire Valley.
Bruce:	The Dow tanked, baby. We can't afford a house in France — we'd be lucky to afford a shed in the Loire Valley.

Ole! Words from Spanish

Before the 1500s, English was only lightly flavored with Spanish. Queen Mary's marriage to Philip II of Spain changed all that. Even though the reign of "Bloody Mary" lasted only five years before Queen Elizabeth (the first one, that is) took charge, it was enough time to forge a strong link between the Spanish and English courts. Spanish coins, precious goods, and words were freely traded. Although the money and spices are musty relics, most of the words remain robust nearly 400 years later. In the following sections, you find a listing of some Spanish-born words that have become a part of English. The words are used in everyday English and can become a valuable addition to your daily vocabulary.

WORDS TO THE WISE

Don Quixote the quixotic

In 1605, Spanish writer Miguel de Cervantes created the downtrodden nobleman Don Quixote and his faithful servant Sancho Panza to satirize the valiant knights and faithful servants of previous writers. The elderly Don (a title of respect, almost like "ma'am") was the embodiment of chivalry — gallant, helpful, and polite.

Unfortunately, Don Quixote was blinded by some very strong rose-colored glasses. He was almost pitifully unaware that his efforts to embody and demonstrate the highest principles were directed toward people who had no desire for or appreciation of his usually ineffectual efforts. Today, the word *quixotic* describes lofty but impractical sentiments like those held by Don Quixote.

Spanish words have entered English not only from Spain, but also from the many other Spanish-speaking places around the world, including Mexico, Puerto Rico, Central America, South America, and Cuba.

Eating words

I'm a practical person, so I'm going to cut to the chase and give you the words near-and-dear to my heart: Spanish nouns for foods that have become commonplace in America (see Table 11-5). The words are especially useful when you're ordering delicious dishes in restaurants. (My kitchen is closed until I finish this book . . . and then I'll think of another excuse!)

Table 11-5	Spanish Food Nouns
Word	*Definition*
anchovy (*an*-choh-vee)	small fish
avocado (av-uh-*kah*-doh)	thick-skinned, pear-shaped tropical fruit
chili (*chil*-ee)	spicy pepper
chili con carne (*chil*-ee kon *kar*-nee)	meat, bean, and tomato dish seasoned with chilis
dorado (doh-*rah*-doh)	firm-fleshed fin fish
marinade (mar-uh-*nayd*)	sauce that food is soaked in before cooking
pimento (puh-*men*-toh)	small pepper used as a stuffing for olives
pompano (*pom*-puh-noh)	fish with spiny fins and widely forked tails
tamale (tuh-*mah*-lee)	minced meat and spices in a cornmeal dough, wrapped in corn husks
tortilla (tor-*tee*-uh)	round, flat bread made with cornmeal or flour

Building on Spanish words

Many Americans know that the British and French colonized America, but many do not know that the Spanish colonized America, as well. In fact, until Americans began pushing westward and moving out the folks already there, much of the American southwest was under Spanish and then Mexican control (Mexico gained its independence from Spain in 1821). As a result, many of the names of places in the American southwest — as well as words related to agriculture and architecture in that region — came from Spain. Table 11-6 lists some Spanish words that are used in English to describe places and building materials. Table 11-7 lists Spanish words that are related to ranching — the primary livelihood of the people who settled the American southwest.

Table 11-6	Spanish Nouns Related to Structure
Word	*Definition*
adobe (uh-*doh*-bee)	sun-dried brick; building made of sun-dried bricks
arroyo (uh-*roy*-oh)	dry gully; stream
canyon (*kan*-yun)	long, narrow valley with steep sides
hacienda (hah-see-*en*-duh)	large estate; house on a large estate
patio (*pat*-ee-oh)	courtyard; paved area used for dining and lounging
pueblo (*pweb*-loh)	communal village
rancho (*ran*-cho)	large farm or ranch; hut that shelters ranch workers
sierra (see-*ehr*-uh)	range of hills or mountains

Table 11-7	Spanish Nouns Related to Ranching
Word	*Definition*
bronco (*brahn*-ko)	untamed horse
caballero (kab-uh-*yehr*-oh)	Spanish gentleman; a horseman
chaparral (shap-uh-*ral*)	dense thicket of shrubs or thorny bushes
corral (kah-*ral*)	enclosed pen for horses
lariat (*lar*-ee-uht)	rope used for tethering horses
lasso (*las*-oh)	long rope with a noose, used for catching cattle or horses
mustang (*mus*-tang)	small, wild or half-wild horse
rodeo (*roh*-dee-oh)	public exhibition of cowboy skills
stampede (stam-*peed*)	sudden, frenzied rush of cattle or horses
vaquero (vah-*kehr*-oh)	cowboy or herdsman

Welcome to America!

According to *The New York Times 2001 Almanac,* 21,631,601 Americans are foreign-born. Of these newcomers, over one-third come from Spanish-speaking countries, including Spain, Cuba, Mexico, South America, and Central America. Nearly 40 percent of all Hispanics in the United States are first-generation immigrants.

But Spanish-speaking people have a long and illustrious history in America. In fact, the names of many places in America come from the Spanish language. Some of my favorite Spanish names are Amarillo (yellow), Los Angeles (the angels), Rio Grande (large river), Santa Fe (holy faith), Mesa (table), Las Vegas (fertile plain), Los Alamos (the poplar trees), Sierra Madre (mother mountain range), and Sierra Nevada (snowy mountain range).

You can use some Spanish-flavored words to help spice up your vocabulary. Check out the following:

Before

Tomorrow is that big horsey event. Are you showing the horses?

Let's get the rope and see if we can tie him up. We don't want him running into the trees or frightening the other animals.

After

Tomorrow is the rodeo. Are you showing the mustangs and broncos?

Let's get the lariat and see if we can lasso him. We don't want him running into the chaparral or starting a stampede.

Getting to know you

In Table 11-8, you find words from Spanish that describe people. Many of these words are common English words that just happen to be Spanish (*albino* and *renegade,* for example). But some of the words — *don, doña, duenna,* and *hombre,* for example — are rarely used in general conversations, unless you're speaking colloquially or, in the case of *don* and *doña,* referring to a person who actually uses the title. As the American South and Midwest become more multicultural, however, knowing these words may help you communicate successfully.

Señor, Señora, and Señorita

If you're ever lucky enough to travel in a Spanish-speaking country or be a guest in a Spanish home, you may want to know the traditional terms of address. *Señor* is Spanish for "Mister," *Señora* is Spanish for "Mrs.," and *Señorita* is Spanish for "Miss" or "Ms." (And be sure to ask for second helpings of paella, a delicious chicken and fish dish.)

Table 11-8	Spanish Nouns that Describe People
Word	*Definition*
albino (al-*by*-noh)	person or animal lacking skin pigmentation
bravado (brah-*vah*-doh)	fake courage or defiance
desperado (des-per-*ah*-doh)	bold, reckless criminal
Don (dahn)	Spanish title of respect for a gentleman
Doña (*doh*-nyah)	Spanish title of respect for a lady
duenna (doo-*en*-uh)	chaperone; governess
hombre (*ahm*-bray)	man
renegade (*ren*-uh-gayd)	deserter
toreador (*tor*-ee-uh-dor)	bullfighter

Every word has a *denotation* (its dictionary meaning). In addition, many words also have *connotations* (emotional overtones). For example, *peon* is a word for a day laborer or a person who tends a horse. The word's connotation, however, is negative. The term *peon* is often used to refer to a peasant or a person of a lower class.

Living la Dolce Vita: Words from Italian

Along with Latin and French, Italian has provided the English language with some of its most frequently used foreign words and phrases, from *la dolce vita* (the good life) to *arrivederci* (good-bye). Many imported Italian words relate to areas of art, music, and literature, but other areas are flavored by Italian, as well. Knowing some of these words can help you polish your vocabulary — whether you're with your sweetie, a client, or the kinfolk.

Soothing the savage beast

Attention culture vultures: It's not every day that you get to attend a formal music event, such as a concert, recital, or opera. If you do get the chance to go to an opera, it may be handy to know the lingo. *Allegro* (ah-*ley*-groh), for example, means "a brisk or rapid pace." It's an adverb or adjective that is often used as a musical direction. Table 11-9 lists a group of music-related words that have entered English from Italian — hardly surprising because Italian is the language of opera, and of music in general. The words in this section can help you to articulate your feelings about the selection of music you're enjoying.

Table 11-9	Italian Nouns Related to Music
Word	*Definition*
bravo (*brah*-voh)	well done; good
cantata (kahn-*taht*-uh)	musical composition used as a setting for a story to be sung but not acted
crescendo (krih-*shen*-doh)	a gradual increase in force, volume, or loudness
duet (doo-*et*)	musical composition for two voices or instruments
finale (fih-*nal*-ee)	concluding part of a composition
forte (*for*-tay)	very loud
impresario (im-pruh-*sahr*-ee-oh)	someone who organizes or manages public entertainment
legato (lih-*gaht*-oh)	a piece of music performed in a smooth and connected manner
libretto (li-*bret*-oh)	the text of a musical piece, such as an opera
maestro (*my*-stroh)	composer, conductor, or teacher
mandolin (man-dah-*lin*)	stringed instrument with a pear-shaped body
pianoforte (pee-*an*-oh-for-tay)	an instrument similar to the harpsichord
soprano (seh-*pran*-oh)	the range of the highest singing voice
tarantella (tar-un-*tel*-uh)	rapid, whirling Italian dance

The Italian phrase *prima donna* refers to the principal female singer in an opera or concert company. Literally, the word translates to "first lady." Prima donnas are notorious for their unwillingness to share the spotlight. In modern American usage, prima donna means "a temperamental, vain, or arrogant person."

Talkin' the Talk

Cassandra has dragged Penelope to the opera. The intermission finally comes, giving Cassandra and her friend an opportunity to talk about the performance thus far.

Cassandra:	Didn't I tell you? Opera can be so uplifting.
Penelope:	You're just here because the maestro is good-looking.
Cassandra:	I am not. I liked the soprano's aria.
Penelope:	That wasn't a soprano, and it wasn't an aria. It was the tenor singing a duet with someone in a donkey suit.
Cassandra:	You're just mad because you wanted to see a movie instead.
Penelope:	No, I'm mad because I'm still waiting for the fat lady to sing.

Being an armchair architect

The Leaning Tower of Pisa. The Colosseum. The Sistine Chapel. The Vatican. There's no doubt that Italian architects have given the world some magnificent buildings. Along with these landmark buildings come the words to describe their features. Today, these born-in-Italy words are found in common English currency. No doubt you've heard them used often. Check out the list of architectural terms in Table 11-10 and find the common terms that you might have missed. All the words came from Italian originally, but English-speakers have made them their own.

Table 11-10	Italian Nouns Related to Architecture
Word	*Definition*
arcade (ar-*kayd*)	arched passageway; shops
balcony (*bal*-kuh-nee)	platform projecting from a building and enclosed by a railing; upper row of seats in a theater; gallery
catacomb (*kat*-uh-kohm)	vault or gallery in an underground burial place

Word	Definition
colonnade (kahl-uh-*nayd*)	series of columns
corridor (*kor*-ih-door)	hallway; passageway
frieze (freez)	series of decorations forming a band around a room
grotto (*grah*-toh)	cave, especially an ornamental cave in a formal garden
loggia (*lah*-juh)	gallery projecting from the side of a building
mezzanine (*mez*-ah-neen)	lowest balcony; low-ceilinged story in a building
pedestal (*ped*-es-tuhl)	base or support
piazza (pee-*ahz*-uh)	plaza; covered gallery or arcade
portico (*por*-ti-koh)	porch; a porchlike structure around a formal doorway
rotunda (roh-*tun*-dah)	round building, hall, or room, often with a dome
stucco (*stuk*-oh)	plaster or concrete mixture used for surfacing walls or molding relief ornaments
villa (*vil*-ah)	country house or estate

Don't worry if you confuse *pizza* and *piazza.* If you do, you have plenty of company! To set the record straight, *pizza* is the delicious bread, sauce, and cheese pie; *piazza* is a plaza.

In the Middle Ages, the short, upright columns that supported handrails were made in circles that swelled to a pear shape at the bottom. The handrails looked like the flowers of the wild pomegranate, called *balaustra* in Italian. Because the handrails had this flowerlike appearance, they came to be called *balaustras.* The French took the name and spelled it *balustra,* which became *baluster* in English. Careless speech soon turned the word into the familiar term *banister.*

Invigorating Italian words (and a couple of others)

Italians have a reputation for being a passionate people. Stereotype or not, they have given English speakers a lot of action-packed words. Many of the words listed in Table 11-11 are military terms, while others, like *fracas,* simply refer to an action-filled event.

Table 11-11		Italian Fighting Words
Word	*Part of Speech*	*Definition*
bandit (*ban*-dit)	noun	thief; robber
bandolier/bandoleer (ban-deh-*lir*)	noun	cartridge belt worn over the shoulder and across the chest
barrack (*bar*-ahk)	noun	building for lodging soldiers
battalion (buh-*tal*-yuhn)	noun	large group of soldiers
cavalier (kav-uh-*lir*)	noun	armed horseman; knight; gallant gentleman
citadel (*sit*-uh-del)	noun	fortress
fracas (*fray*-kus)	noun	uproar
gala (*gay*-lah)	noun	big gathering; affair; party
incognito (in-kog-*nee*-toh)	adj./adv.	in disguise
intrigue (in-*treeg*)	verb/noun	to scheme or plot; secret or underhanded plot
parasol (*par*-uh-sol)	noun	umbrella
salvo (*sal*-voh)	noun	round of artillery; burst of cheers
stiletto (stih-*let*-oh)	noun	short dagger with a slender blade; shoe with a tall, narrow heel
valise (vah-*lees*)	noun	bag; suitcase
vendetta (ven-*det*-ah)	noun	bitter quarrel or feud

Okay, so *parasol* and *valise* aren't action-packed words. But have you ever seen a person hit someone with a valise or parasol? It can be pretty intense.

Before

Let's eat outside and watch the group of boats.

After

Shall we eat alfresco and watch the regatta?

Using foreign-born words gives your vocabulary *panache* (pah-*nash*) — a dashing, stylish elegance.

Chapter 12

Borrowing from the Neighbors: Words from Other Languages

In This Chapter

▶ Lifting language from Latin

▶ Drinking in words from the Irish and Scots

▶ Getting expressive with words from Yiddish

▶ Incorporating Arabic words

You can borrow sugar from a neighbor only because English borrowed the word "sugar" from Sanskrit centuries ago. And the borrowing didn't stop there. In fact, many of our most useful everyday words come from other languages, including Latin, Celtic (Irish and Scottish), Arabic, and Yiddish. In case that isn't enough for you, I go through some Indian, West African, and Russian words that English adopted.

To help you discover the variety of English words incorporated from different languages, this chapter explains some of the common — and not-so-common — words English gained from other languages.

If you wonder whether there are any *English* words in the English language, take heart. There are. I just don't have room to include them in this book. Just kidding. Actually, all of these words *are* English words. But knowing where they came from can help you remember what they mean. It can also help you understand why some words (like Latin nouns) behave oddly.

Liking Latin

Latin is considered a "dead" language, but that hasn't prevented it from having a major impact on today's English. Many of English's most common words have Latin roots, prefixes, and suffixes (see Part II for more on word parts, particularly the ones that came from Latin). But the impact of this ancient culture on English extended far beyond mere word parts. English took piles, stacks — even truckloads — of actual Latin words, also.

Using Latin every day

Would you believe that the words *major* and *minor* are actually Latin words? They are. *Major* means "greater or larger;" *minor* means "lesser." Ursa Major is the Big Bear (the constellation we call the Big Dipper); Ursa Minor is the Small Bear (the Little Dipper). You can find more Latin words that came intact into English in the following list. Some of these words are probably familiar to you. Others you may have heard or read and wondered what they meant.

- **decorum** (deh-*koh*-rum/*kor*-um): This word is a noun that means "propriety and good taste in behavior and dress." Example: The maid of honor's lack of *decorum* at the wedding caused a rift in the family.

- **gratis** (*grat*-is): *Gratis* is an adverb that means "without charge or payment" or "free." Example: The lawyer provided her services *gratis*. Many people say something is "free and gratis," but that's redundant. It's like saying its free and free.

- **in toto** (in *toh*-toh): *In toto* is an adverb that means "in the whole" or "as a whole." Example: The editor decided to print the book *in toto*, not just selected passages.

You often hear the French word *en masse* used instead of *in toto*. *En masse* means essentially the same thing as *in toto*, but it is usually used in reference to people: The crowd moved *en masse* to the gates to greet the arriving starlet. See Chapter 11 for other French words English has usurped.

- **odium** (*oh*-dee-um): This noun means "intense hatred of a person or thing regarded as loathsome." Example: I feel only *odium* for that toad. The adjective form of *odium (odious)* is more common. That *odious* toad got pond slime all over my garage floor.

- **per se** (pur *say*): The adverb *per se* means "by or in itself." Example: He is not a lover of fine art, *per se,* just someone who appreciates looking at pretty pictures.

- **pro tempore** (proh-*tem*-puh-ree): This adjective means "for the time being" or "temporarily." Nowadays, people usually shorten this term to *pro tem*, as in "The president *pro tem* is the senator who presides over the Senate when the vice president is absent."

- **status quo** (stat-us *kwoh*): This noun means "the existing state of affairs." Example: Politicians are generally skeptical of new policies and block legislation in order to preserve the *status quo*.

> ✔ **terra firma** (*ter*-uh *fur*-muh): This noun means "dry land" or "solid ground." Although it is not an everyday term, you usually hear *terra firma* used when someone has finally touched ground after a prolonged or harrowing journey either at sea or in the air. Example: The ship's crew, after months in rough and stormy seas, was glad to be back on *terra firma*.

The following sections offer other Latin words that have come into English pretty much unscathed.

Paying attention to problematic plurals

To form most English plurals, you simply add *-s* or *-es* to a noun: boxes (box), houses (house), and cats (cat). Of course, not all nouns fall quietly into line: knives (knife), children (child) and mice (mouse), for example. Some of the most baffling irregular plurals come from Latin. Why? Because many Latin words don't follow the English rule for making plurals (add *-s* or *-es*). Nor do they fall nicely into line with the other English irregular nouns. Instead, Latin words insist on using the Latin rule for making plurals. And the Latin rule is to change the last letters of a word to *-a, -ae,* or *-i.* Table 12-1 lists several examples of irregular plurals from Latin and Greek.

Embracing the British Invasion

The British have given us a lot more than rock bands. (Okay, so there's also fish and chips.) You guessed it: I'm going to steer the conversation around to some British English words. Many terms used by the British seem to be the same as American English words, but you may be surprised at how differently the terms are used. Most Americans know that a *bobby* is a police officer in Britain. But did you know that a *jitney* is a bus or that a *mackintosh* is a raincoat? Check out these other examples:

✔ In the United States, *bonnet* is used to describe a hat. In England, *bonnet* means the hood of an automobile. The trunk is the *boot.*

✔ When Americans want something to dip into the onion dip, they ask for *potato chips.* The British ask for *crisps.*

✔ Americans wait on the *curb* before crossing the street. The British wait at the *kerb.*

✔ In America, *French fries* are a popular side dish. In England, this same side dish is known as *chips.*

✔ At the license branch, Americans line up. The British get in a *queue.*

I know what you're thinking: "I'll never go to England. The weather stinks, and the beer's warm." Ah, you may be right about your vacation plans, but keep in mind that British English — not American English — is taught, spoken, and used in India, the Caribbean, Africa, and many other places around the world. So when you meet English speakers who have come to America from around the world, you'll have the words you need to understand what on earth they're talking about!

Table 12-1	Examples of Irregular Plurals	
Singular	*Rule*	*Plural*
medium, datum, curriculum	change -um to -a	media, data, curricula
phenomenon, criterion	change -on to -a	phenomena, criteria
alumna	change -a to -ae	alumnae
radius, focus, alumnus	change -us to -i	radii, foci, alumni

Some English words (hippopotamus, thesaurus) can be made plural the Latin way (hippopotami, thesauri) or the English way (hippopotamuses, thesauruses). To complicate matters even more, some Latin words, because of common usage, can take the English plural: mediums, curriculums, and phenomenons, for example. If you're not sure how to make a word plural or which is the preferred form, look the word up in the dictionary.

Talkin' the Talk

Sam Shark has just picked up an important British client, Ms. Thornberry-Smyth-Throckmorton-Blain, at the airport. A slick cookie, Sam Shark is trying to impress Ms. T-S-T-B with his smooth lines.

Sam Shark: I'll just fill 'er up with gas, and then we can catch a flick.

Ms. T-S-T-B: Pardon?

Sam Shark: I'll just fill up with petrol, and we can go to the cinema.

Ms. T-S-T-B: Cheeky bloke, aren't you?

Sam Shark: Shall we stop at the hotel bar before we unload your luggage — or after?

Ms. T-S-T-B: You're quite the bold boy. But I have a better idea. Drop me at the kerb. There's a cab rank; I'll get on the queue. You can take yourself to the pub.

Talking Blarney: Words from the Irish and Scots

Another fertile source of English words is *Celtic* (pronounced with either a hard or soft "c"), the language spoken by the Irish, Scottish, and Welsh. America's Celtic immigrants have added great richness to the English language. The following list contains a few of the more common Irish words:

✔ **blarney** (*blar*-nee): *Blarney* is a noun that means "smooth talk used in flattery and coaxing." In other words, a sweet-talker who convinces you to do something against your better judgment by telling you how intelligent/beautiful/handsome/charming/intriguing you are is using blarney.

The origin of the word *blarney* comes from the Blarney Stone, a stone in Blarney Castle near Cork, Ireland. According to legend, anyone who kisses the Blarney stone receives the talent for eloquent cajolery.

✔ **brogue** (brohg): A *brogue* is an Irish accent or pronunciation — the lilt that folks from Ireland have when they speak English. (While the Irish have a *brogue*, the Scottish speak with a *burr*, characterized by a rolled "r" sound.)

✔ **galore** (guh-*lor*): *Galore* is an adjective that means "in abundance." You use *galore* after the word it modifies. For example, you may say "My favorite restaurant has desserts *galore*."

✔ **plaid** (plad): *Plaid* is a fabric with stripes or bars of various colors and widths that cross at right angles.

A plaid whose design represents a particular Scottish clan is called a *tartan*. Scots wear *plaids* over their left shoulders as part of their national costume.

✔ **shamrock** (*sham*-rok): A *shamrock* is a type of clover with three leaves. In the United States, you often see this emblem of Ireland around St. Patrick's Day, when just about everyone drinks green beer, wears buttons proclaiming "Kiss me, I'm Irish," and pretends to know who Brian Boru was.

Table 12-2 lists more useful everyday words that have come into English from Irish and Scottish immigrants. All of the words in the table describe objects that you likely know and use — or have wondered about for years!

Table 12-2	English-Irish Nouns
Word	**Definition**
banshee (*ban*-shee)	a female spirit who warns of approaching death by wailing unseen under the windows of the house a night or two before the death she foresees
clan (klan)	group of families claiming descent from a common ancestor, having the same family name, and following the same chieftain; informally, a group of people related by ancestry or marriage
colleen (kol-*leen*)	a girl
crag (krag)	steep, rugged rock that rises above others
leprechaun (*lep*-reh-kahn)	in Irish folklore, a fairy in the form of a little old man who reveals the location of a buried pot of gold to anyone who catches him
loch (lahk)	lake
ptarmigan (*tar*-mi-gen)	type of bird
quay (kway)	a wharf used for loading and unloading ships

If you're ever lucky enough to visit Ireland, the superlatives are *grand, gorgeous,* and *brilliant,* as in "Ah, but it's a *grand* potato, a *gorgeous* loaf of brown bread, and a *brilliant* pint of lager."

Oy Vey! English Words from Yiddish

Some people claim that Yiddish is a dying language. If that's so, why have so many Yiddish words become commonplace in the daily usage of English? Yiddish words appear in books, on television, and in conversation. The word *bagel,* for example — also called "a donut with a college education" and an "alligator teething ring" by comedians — has become ubiquitous throughout America, thanks to mass marketing.

Table 12-3 lists some Yiddish words that pertain to food. (All the words in the list are nouns.) How many of these Jewish-American foods would you like to add to *your* shopping list?

Table 12-3	Yiddish Words for Various Foods
Word	*Definition*
blintz (blintz)	pancake folded around a cheese or fruit filling
borscht (borsh)	beet soup served either hot or cold, usually with sour cream
challah (*kha*-lah)	braided or twisted rich, white bread, eaten by Jews on the Sabbath and holidays
gefilte fish (guh-*fil*-tuh fish)	chopped fish mixed with chopped onion, egg, seasoning, and so on, and boiled, usually served cold in the form of balls or cakes
knish (kuh-*nish*)	potato or meat filled dumpling
kreplach (*krep*-lakh)	small casings of dough filled with ground meat or cheese, and so on, boiled, and served usually in soup
latke (*laht*-keh)	pancake, usually made from grated potatoes
lox (lox)	variety of salty smoked salmon
matzo (*maht*-suh)	thin, crisp unleavened bread

Talkin' the Talk

Happy Guest is at a *bar mitzvah.* The solemn ceremony is over, and the 13-year-old Jewish boy has officially become an adult member of the Jewish community. (The female version is called a *bat mitzvah* or *bas mitzvah.*) The reception has started, and it's a lavish spread indeed.

Happy Guest (first trip to the buffet table): Ah! Blueberry blintzes — so nice with a dollop of sour cream. But aren't they fried in butter to get that crispy golden shell?

Glowing Hostess: How many times a year do you get blintzes? Splurge a little.

Happy Guest (second trip to the buffet table): A slice of lox on a bagel would be perfect.

Glowing Hostess: Don't forget a schmeer [spread] of cream cheese and a slice of onion.

Happy Guest (third trip to the buffet table): The rabbi [Jewish religious leader] is cutting the challah. It looks tasty, but I don't think I should. I already have borscht.

Glowing Hostess: Look at you, you're so thin. What's a little more? And how about a nice fat oval of gefilte fish, with a dab of the aspic it's nestled in.

Happy Guest (fourth trip to the buffet table): Time for dessert. Let's see, there's rugelach (pastries filled with jam) — prune-filled, raspberry-filled, apricot-filled. So many choices!

Glowing Hostess: What, you'd insult the cook? Take a little of each.

Dressing Up with Words from Arabic

Many Arabic words filtered through French or Spanish during the seven centuries that the Arabs ruled Spain, and later, as words passed from trader to trader along the spice routes that linked the Eastern world of the Orient with the Western world of Europe. Much later, these words passed into English. As a result, English is flavored with words from northern Africa, especially the Arabian states. Arabic words adopted into English include everyday words like *cotton* (thread or fabric made from seed hairs of certain plants), *bandana* (large, colored handkerchief), *sequin* (small, shiny spangle sewn as decoration to clothing), *henna* (a dye used to dye hair or skin auburn), *lute* (stringed instrument similar to a guitar), and *sherbet* (a frozen fruit dessert).

Trading words along with goods

Because of its access to seas and proximity to both the Eastern and Western worlds, Northern Africa was a key hub along the ancient and not-so-ancient trade routes. Not surprisingly, most of the words the English language received from Arabic identify items traded in the Middle East, as Table 12-4 shows.

Table 12-4	Nouns from Arabic
Word	**Definition**
albacore (*al*-bah-kor)	type of tuna, an important game and food fish in areas with warm seas
amber (*am*-ber)	translucent yellow or brownish-yellow fossilized resin used in jewelry
camphor (*kam*-for)	strong-smelling chemical compound used to protect fabric from moths
carafe (kah-*raf*)	glass bottle for serving wine, water, or coffee
civet (*siv*-it)	yellowish, fatty substance with a musklike scent, secreted by a gland near the genitals of the civet cat and used in making some perfumes
elixir (ih-*lix*-er)	a supposed remedy for all ailments; a panacea
ottoman (*aht*-uh-mahn)	a low, cushioned seat or footstool
marabou (*mar*-ah-boo)	bare-headed, large-billed African stork; soft feathers from the wing coverts and tail of the marabou
tamarind (*tam*-ah-rind)	tropical tree, with yellow flowers and brown pods with an acid pulp; fruit of the tamarind tree, used in beverages and foods
tarragon (*tar*-ah-gon)	a plant of the wormwood family whose leaves are used for seasoning

As you may expect, the words listed in Table 12-4 are especially useful for shopping, home decorating, and communicating with people who trace their heritage to the Middle East.

Changing words to gold

As the study of chemistry developed in Europe in the late Middle Ages, much knowledge came from the work of Arabian alchemists who had preserved and developed scientific scholarship during the Dark Ages. The following list describes just a few examples. (Table 12-5 lists other useful English-Arabic words. All of the words in the table are nouns.)

✔ The word *chemistry* (the study of the properties of substances and reactions) comes from the mystical science of alchemy.

✔ The word *alchemy* comes from the Arabic *al-kimiya* ("philosopher's stone"), which may have derived from an Arabian name for Egypt — *Kemia.* An early form of chemistry with philosophic and magical associations, alchemy's chief aims were to turn base metals into gold and to discover the elixir of perpetual youth.

✔ Other chemical terms, such as *alkali* (a water-soluble chemical containing hydroxide) and *alcohol* (a pungent chemical combination), derive from Arabic words.

The prefix *al-* is simply the Arabic word for "the."

Table 12-5 lists several nouns that come to English by way of Arabic.

Table 12-5	Useful English-Arabic Words
Word	*Definition*
alcove (*al*-kove)	recessed section of a room, as a breakfast nook
algebra (*al*-juh-bruh)	a branch of mathematics
hazard (*haz*-ard)	early game of chance played with dice; chance or chance occurrence; risk
minaret (min-eh-*ret*)	high, slender tower attached to a mosque from which the muezzin, or crier, calls the people to prayer
monsoon (mon-*soon*)	a seasonal wind of the Indian Ocean and South Asia, blowing from the southwest from April to October, and from the northeast during the rest of the year
mosque (mahsk)	a Muslim temple or place of worship

An *almanac* (*ahl*-muh-nak) is a book published every year that contains a wealth of information on such topics as countries, states, nature, and culture. Nobody knows where the word comes from, but linguists conjecture that it's an Arabic derivation.

Pursuing English-Arabic words about people

The useful words listed in Table 12-6 entered English from Arabic. All of the words are nouns and describe people. You probably use some of these words every day. Now that you know their origins, you may be able to link them to the words on the list that you have not encountered before.

Table 12-6	English-Arabic Words that Describe People
Word	**Definition**
admiral (*ad*-muh-rul)	commanding officer of a navy or fleet
Bedouin (*bed*-oo-in)	Arab of any of the nomadic desert peoples of Arabia, Syria, or North Africa
dervish (*duhr*-vish)	a Muslim devoted to a life of poverty and chastity: some practice whirling or chanting as a religious act
fakir (fuh-*kir*)	member of a Muslim holy sect who lives by begging; any Muslim or Hindu itinerant beggar, often one reputed to perform marvels
harem (*hair*-em)	part of a Muslim household in which the women live
sheik (sheek/shayk)	chief of an Arab family, tribe, or village
sultan (*sul*-tan)	a Muslim ruler; the former monarch of Turkey

Today, Arabians still use the language of the prophet Mohammed more than 1,300 years after his death. Modern written Arabic — and the spoken language of educated Arabians — is not significantly different from classical Arabic, the language in which the Koran was written down soon after Muhammad died. Modern colloquial Arabic, however, has diverged from the written language. The numerous dialects are as different from each other as Dutch is from English. So, although today Mohammed would be able to speak to educated Arabians, he would probably need an interpreter to talk with Arabians who speak colloquially.

Talkin' the Talk

Amber and her husband Ted have each spent a busy day preparing for their move to a new house. Amber's been shopping for last-minute things. Ted cleaned out the attic of their current home. They meet at a restaurant for dinner.

Amber: What's that smell? Is it you?

Ted: What smell?

Amber: That overpowering odor. What have you been doing?

Ted:	Oh, it must be the camphor oil I put on. Being in the attic all day really made me congested.
Waiter:	Are you ready to order?
Amber:	Yes, thank you. I'll have the albacore.
Waiter:	And you, sir?
Ted:	I'll take the same thing. We'd also like to go ahead and order sherbet for dessert.
(Turning to Amber)	So what did you do today?
Amber:	I found the perfect ottoman for the family room. It goes with our sofa and will look wonderful in the alcove.
Ted:	How much did it cost?
Amber:	I got it on sale.
Ted:	How much?
Amber:	You don't want to know.
Ted (to Waiter):	Could you bring us a carafe of wine?
Waiter:	How many glasses, sir?
Ted:	One.

1, 2, 3, 4, can I have a little more?

The numeral system used almost universally today was probably invented by the Hindus (the inhabitants of India). This numbering system simplified calculations by making the value of a number depend on its position, as well as on the number itself. In fact, a synonym for Arabic numerals (1, 2, 3, 4, 5, and so on) is Hindu numerals.

The Hindu system, which included a zero, was adopted by the Arabians and may have reached Europe as early as the 10th century (although it was some time before it replaced Roman numerals). English appropriated two useful mathematical words from the Arabians: *algebra,* a branch of mathematics, and *algorithm,* a set of rules for solving a problem.

Lapping Up Words from Other Lands

In addition to the languages mentioned so far, scores of other languages have contributed to our word-hoard. For example, from West Africa, we get *cameroon,* a game of chance played with five dice. From various Indian dialects, we get *shampoo, loot,* and *pal,* as well as the following:

- ✔ **chutney** (*chut*-nee): sweet and sour sauce

- ✔ **ginger** (*jin*-jer): a spice

- ✔ **darjeeling** (dar-*jee*-ling): a fine variety of tea grown especially in the mountainous districts of northern India

- ✔ **nabob** (*nay*-bob): wealthy, powerful person

- ✔ **thug** (thug): a hoodlum, gangster and so on

From Russia, English absorbed *babushka* (a folded kerchief worn over the head and tied under the chin), *shaman* (a priest or medicine man reputedly able to heal the sick and foretell the future), and *tundra* (vast, treeless plains of the arctic regions). Table 12-7 lists other words that came into English from the Russian language.

Table 12-7	English Nouns from Russian
Word	*Definition*
Bolshevik (*bohl*-shuh-vik)	member of the Russian Social Democratic Workers' Party, which formed the Communist Party after seizing power in the 1917 Russian Revolution
Cossack (*kahs*-ak)	member of any of several groups of peasants of mostly Russian and Polish descent that lived in autonomous communal settlements, especially in the Ukraine, until the late 19th century
dacha (*dak*-ah)	in Russia, a country house or cottage used as a vacation retreat
pogrom (poh-*grohm*)	organized massacre and persecution of a minority group, usually at the prompting of officials
Tsar (zar)	emperor or king who has absolute authority: title of any of the former emperors of Russia and the sovereigns of other Slavic nations
vodka (*vahd*-kuh)	a colorless alcoholic liquor distilled from rye, wheat, and so on

Guess how much I love you

The Taj Mahal in Agra, India, is a mausoleum of pure white marble, built by the Mogul emperor Shah Jahan to house the body of his beloved second wife, Mumtaz Mahal ("The Chosen of the Palace"). She bore him 14 children and died during childbirth in 1630 at the age of 39.

Originally, Shah Jahan had planned to build a matching mausoleum in black marble on the opposite bank of the river to house his own body. The project was never completed. Instead, he was buried (in 1658) beside his wife in the shrine that he had built for her.

Part IV

Getting Savvy with Vocabulary

In this part . . .

You can pick and choose among these chapters for the specific type of words you want. Your choices include words related to business, money (and how to spend it on food and clothing), law, and healthcare.

I devote a chapter to pointing out ways to use vocabulary basics on standardized tests. I fill you in on some of the words added to the language within recent memory (at least my recent memory), and I tell you about people and places whose names have become words in their own right.

Read them all or just dip into the chapters that interest you. Either way, you can increase your vocabulary savvy.

Chapter 13

Trying Your Skills on Standardized Tests

In This Chapter

▶ Knowing which vocabulary skills can help you on standardized tests

▶ Understanding the different types of test questions that require vocab knowledge

▶ Preparing for a test

Humans have invented many cruel kinds of torture — stiletto heel shoes, the Department of Motor Vehicles, automated dialing systems, and standardized tests. SAT, LSAT, GRE, GMAT, and ACT are some of the better-known tests, but you don't have to be heading to college, law school, or graduate school to face a standardized test. Many states require that students get an acceptable score on one (or several) standardized tests before moving on to the next education level.

A broad vocabulary can help you when you take standardized tests: After all, the more words you know, the better you do on the verbal portions of the tests. But the ugly fact is that you're not going to know every word — and in some cases, most of the words — you come up against. Instead of panicking, you can use a few vocabulary skills to increase your chances of getting a better score.

For more in-depth help on preparing for standardized tests, check out one of the many Hungry Minds books devoted to test preparation, such as *The GMAT For Dummies, The ACT For Dummies, CliffsTestPrep SAT I/PSAT,* or *CliffsTestPrep LSAT.*

Assembling the Skills You Need

Some portions of standardized tests are specifically designed to test your vocabulary. The test questions are generally multiple choice, and you select the best answer from the options provided. One example is antonym questions, in which you have to indicate which word means the opposite of a given word. Other sections of standardized tests (like the dreaded analogy sections) try to determine how good you are at understanding implied relationships between words. Still other sections — like the sentence completion or fill-in-the blank sections — test how good you are at completing an idea based on context clues. In addition to these types of questions, standardized tests often include sections that test your reading comprehension (how well you understand written material) and your writing ability (how well you express yourself).

In each case, vocabulary plays a large part, regardless of whether vocabulary skills are being tested directly (as in the analogies or sentence completion portion of the tests) or indirectly (as in the reading comprehension and essay portions of the test). Following are a few language skills that can help you with standardized tests.

Knowing roots, prefixes, and suffixes

One of the handiest vocabulary skills to have is being able to define each of the elements in a given word. Many English words are built from *root* (or base) words, and they often include prefixes and suffixes that alter or narrow that root's definition. For example, if you dissect the word *transmutable,* you see that it's made up of the following parts:

- ✔ ***trans-*** (prefix): *Trans-* is a Latin prefix that means "beyond, across, or through," as in *transatlantic* (across the Atlantic) and *transform* (to change shape).

- ✔ ***mut*** (root): *Mut* comes from the Latin word *mutare,* which means "to change." You see this root in words like *mutation* (a major change) and *immutable* (unable to change).

- ✔ ***-able*** (suffix): The suffix *-able* means "capable or worthy of," and it appears in a host of words, including *abominable* (worthy of abomination) and *portable* (able to be carried).

If you put these definitions together, you get "able to change through or across." Now this doesn't give you the precise definition of *transmutable* (capable of being altered into another form or substance), but it does give you an idea of the definition, and sometimes that's all you need to make an educated guess.

Many English prefixes, roots, and suffixes come from Greek and Latin. One of the best ways to prepare for any standardized exam that tests your verbal skills is to know as many of these as you can. The chapters in Part II of this book cover prefixes, roots, and suffixes.

Using context clues

If you come across an unfamiliar word and can't decode it by breaking the word into its prefix, root, and suffix, as explained in the preceding section, you can sometimes get an idea of the word's meaning by looking for context clues. When you use context clues, you look in the surrounding sentence or paragraph for embedded information about the word. Sometimes this context information is as obvious as a definition (the italicized word is the one I'm focusing on):

> The *fuselage,* the body of the airplane, sustained little damage during the emergency landing.

Other times, the context clues are less obvious:

> The fire chief, suspecting arson, searched for the *incendiary agent,* only to discover later that faulty electrical wiring was to blame.

In the first example, the definition of *fuselage* is given in the sentence. In the second example, you have to use the clues to figure out what an *incendiary agent* is (a substance that causes a fire).

Being able to comprehend a word's meaning by the information around it can help you in the reading comprehension and sentence completion portions of standardized tests. Chapter 3 offers more detail in using context clues to define unfamiliar words.

Understanding the relationship between words

Understanding the relationship between words means knowing whether the terms are synonyms (have similar meaning) or antonyms (have opposite meaning). This skill is vital for scoring well on the analogy section of a test. A typical question in an analogy section gives you three words in the following format: "chatty : talkative :: unhappy :___." Turned into words, this reads: "chatty is to talkative as unhappy is to ___." Your job is to find the word that is in the same relationship to "unhappy" that "talkative" is in to "chatty." Because chatty and talkative are synonyms, you want to choose the word that is the best synonym for "unhappy": "sad." In addition to synonyms and antonyms, you also need to be able to identify more complex relationships and the order of the relationship. For example, if the first pair of words are synonyms that go from lesser to greater, the second pair must have the same relationship and structure. For example,

hill : mountain :: pond : lake

is a valid analogy, whereas

tadpole : frog :: horse : colt

isn't. In the first example the word pairs go from smaller to larger; in the second, the younger to older relationship of the first pair is reversed in the second pair.

Understanding the word's *connotation* (or implied meaning) is also important because the connotation becomes part of the relationship. A word with a negative connotation followed by a word with a positive connotation is, in a sense, a type of order, from negative to positive. For details on using connotation and denotation to understand words, head to Chapter 8.

Getting Familiar with the Types of Test Questions

Vocabulary skills won't help you much on the math portion of standardized tests — unless, of course, you're left wondering what an equilateral triangle is (a triangle with equal sides) or how many sides a hexagon has (six). Language skills can help you, however, in the verbal sections — especially in the following types of sections:

- **Vocabulary:** Depending on the test you're taking, this part may simply ask you to indicate a word's definition or, in some cases, a word's *antonym* (a word that means the opposite).

- **Analogies:** To correctly answer an analogy question, you not only have to be familiar with the given words, you also have to be able to see the relationship between pairs of words.

- **Sentence completion:** This type of question offers a sentence with blanks you have to fill in. To do your best here, you need to have at least a passing familiarity with the possible answers. You also need to be good at recognizing and using context clues.

- **Reading comprehension:** In this portion of a test, you answer questions about a passage you read. Sometimes you're asked a simple question of fact. Other times you have to draw conclusions or make inferences about the passage. Having a broad vocabulary is a big plus when you're working on reading comprehension questions. If the vocabulary in the passage gives you problems, however, you can use context clues to get a better idea of the material's meaning.

The following sections explain, in more detail, the different types of questions and how you can put your vocabulary skills to use when you answer them. If you're actually preparing for a particular standardized test, such as the SAT or the ACT, check out the test-prep books that Hungry Minds has for you. You can search by the test name at www.dummies.com to find a book that can help you prepare for the particular test you're facing.

Analogies

Analogies contain two pairs of words. Analogies are presented in the form of a mathematical equation, in which a colon (:) stands for *is to* and a double-colon (::) stands for *as.* For example, *big : small :: large : tiny* is read as "big *is to* small *as* large *is to* tiny." Your task is to recognize the relationship between the first pair of words and then identify which of the answer choices has the same relationship. When you find the second pair that duplicates the relationship shown in the first pair, you have a winner. Check out the following example:

stallion : rooster :: mare : hen

Stallion is to rooster as mare is to hen. A stallion is a male horse; a rooster is a male chicken. In the second pair, a mare is a female horse; a hen is a female chicken.

Generally, you match the grammatical form of every item in an analogy. For instance, if the first word in the analogy is a noun, the other three words must be nouns.

Analogies can show many different relationships. The most common analogy relationships you may encounter on standardized tests are explained in the following sections.

Figuring out the type of analogy you're looking at can help you answer the questions correctly. Unfortunately, the folks who make the tests don't just out-and-out tell you. You have to determine the correct answers for yourself.

Synonym analogies

Synonyms are words that have essentially the same meaning. Because the first pair of words in synonym analogies are synonyms, you want the second pair to be synonyms, too.

gumption : spunk :: verve : vitality

Gumption and *spunk* both mean courage and initiative. As such, the two words are synonyms. *Verve* means "vigor and energy," as does *vitality.* So they're synonyms, too. Each pair of words relates to characteristics that a person may have.

Sometimes the words are not synonyms, but merely similar.

> skiff : dinghy :: hansom : calash

A *skiff* and a *dingy* are both small boats. A *hansom* and a *calash* are both small, lightweight carriages. All four words refer to a means of transportation.

Antonym analogies

An *antonym* is a word that means the opposite of another word. As **always**, the relationship that is formed between the first pair of words must also be found between the second pair of words.

> naiveté : maturity :: gullibility : sophistication

Naiveté (nah-eev-*tay*) and *gullibility* (gul-ih-*bil*-ih-tee) both mean "innocence," while *maturity* and *sophistication* both mean "experience." *Naiveté* is an antonym for *maturity*; *gullibility* is an antonym for *sophistication*.

Remember that the relationship shown in the second pair of words must be the same as the relationship shown in the first pair of words.

Make sure to match the part of speech of the first word to every item in the analogy. For instance, if the first word in the analogy is a noun, the other three words must be nouns, too. You can find more about parts of speech in Chapter 7.

"Type Of" analogies

In this form of analogy, you're asked to show that an object belongs to a class of objects. For instance, a *smirk* is a type of smile, a *squall* is a type of storm, and a *panda* is a type of bear. Follow this example:

> cranial : nerve :: ulna : bone

Here, *cranial* (*kray*-nee-al) is a type of nerve; *ulna* (*ul*-nah) is a type of bone.

"Part to Whole" analogies

In this type of analogy, the first word in the sample pair is a part of the whole category represented by the second word. For example, a *note* is part of a song, a *letter* is part of a word, and a *brim* is part of a hat.

The relationship must always flow in the same direction for an analogy to be valid. For example, consider this analogy and the two choices:

> couplet : poem
>
> A. paragraph : sentence
>
> B. sentence : paragraph

A couplet (*kup*-lit) is two lines that rhyme. Therefore, it is a small part of a poem. A sentence is a small part of a paragraph (choice B). However, a paragraph is not a small part of a sentence, so choice A is not valid. To be valid, the relationship must be presented in the same order.

The following example shows another "part to whole" analogy:

> coda : symphony :: epilogue : novel

A coda (*koh*-dah) is a part of a symphony. An epilogue (*ep*-ih-log) is part of a novel. The relationship is even closer, however. A coda is the last part of a symphony, and an epilogue is the last part of a novel. Finally, both a coda and an epilogue are optional: You can have a symphony without a coda, just as you can have a novel without an epilogue.

A key to solving more complex analogies is to consider the relationship between the sample pair of words in as much detail as possible so that you look for that exact relationship in the answer choices. If you precisely define the relationship between coda and symphony, for example, you can skip right over answer choices such as *introduction : novel* or *chapter : novel* because those relationships are not the same as the one between coda and symphony.

"Object to Function" analogies

This type of analogy tests whether you can determine the function of a specific tool or item.

> ax : chop :: pliers : grip

The function of an *ax* is to chop something, while the function of *pliers* is to grip something. Both an ax and pliers are tools. Therefore, the analogy is valid.

Because the "object to function" relationship is a fairly easy one to recognize, test writers often include some tricky vocabulary to make the analogies more challenging.

"Lack of Something" analogies

In this type of analogy, one word in each pair lacks some quality. The other pair must reflect the same relationship, in the same order. For example, a *coward* lacks courage and a *pauper* (*paw*-per) lacks money. The following examples illustrate this type of analogy:

> hermit : friends :: mendicant : money

A *hermit* is someone who hides away alone, so he or she lacks friends (much like a *recluse* [*rek*-loos]). A *mendicant* (*men*-dih-kent) is a beggar, so he or she lacks money.

"Place For" analogies

In these analogies, you figure out where something takes place or where someone belongs. For example, an *actor* belongs on the stage, a *pilot* belongs in an airplane, and *ore* belongs in a mine. The following example illustrates this type of analogy:

> horse : stable :: pig : sty

A *horse* is usually kept and fed in a *stable* in the same way that a *pig* is cared for in a *sty.* This particular relationship is easy to see, but the word *sty* might present problems if it's unfamiliar to you.

Tips for analogies

When you're working on analogies, make the relationship between the words in the test analogy as precise as you can. Don't go for the simplest relationship; add enough detail to make the relationship distinctive. As you work your way through analogies on standardized tests, follow these steps:

✔ Start by fitting the words into one of the seven relationships explained in the preceding sections.

✔ See which relationship works best.

✔ Use context clues to figure out any words with more than one meaning.

✔ If none of the choices make sense or you have too many answers that seem to be correct, make the relationship more precise.

To find the relationship between word pairs, you have to think creatively. But when you think creatively, be sure not to overthink. When you overthink, you analyze your answers so deeply that you create relationships that don't really exist. You might get hopelessly lost, too.

If you're not sure which pair is the right answer, go for the most logical and obvious choice. If that doesn't fit, dig more deeply into the question and look for an answer that matches your line of thought.

Talkin' the Talk

Larry and Mary finished their SATs at the same time and bumped into each other in the hall.

Mary:	How'd you do on the analogy section?
Larry:	I thought I was doing fine until I got to the *act : play* question. I did what my test prep books said: I made a sentence showing relationship out of it, but it didn't help me.

Mary:	What was your sentence?
Larry:	'An act is a part of a play.' But with that sentence, each of the other pairs made sense, too. A note is a part of music. A line is a part of a poem. A page is a part of a novel. And a chapter is a part of a book.
Mary:	I see your problem. Your sentence wasn't precise enough. An act is a major part of a play. So the right answer was *chapter : book* because a chapter is a major part of a book. Even though a *line* is part of music and a *page* is part of a novel, neither are large parts, so they're not the answer.
Larry:	Well, a lot of good that does me now.
Mary:	You can always take it again.
Larry:	Yeah, but who'd want to?
Mary:	Here's another analogy for you: *joker is to clown as quitter is to* . . . You fill in the blank.
Larry:	Very funny.
Mary:	Want me to explain it to you?
Larry:	No, I get it.

Antonym questions

Several standardized tests, particularly those given in junior high and high school, have vocabulary sections. In some sections, the task is as simple as picking the right definition (simple, that is, if you know what the word means). In other sections, your task is to pick a synonym (a word that means nearly the same thing) or antonym (a word that means the opposite). The Graduate Records Exam (GRE) — the test that people take to get into graduate programs — uses the antonym twist.

Choose an antonym in this example:

ENCOMIUM:

A. panegyric

B. invective

C. tribute

The answer is *B*. An *encomium* is a formal expression of high praise, such as a eulogy. A *panegyric* and a *tribute* are essentially the same thing as each other and as *encomium*. Because you're looking for the opposite, you know that they can't be the answer. *Invective,* which is a verbal attack, is the opposite of encomium.

For more information about antonyms, head to Chapter 8.

Sentence completion

Sentence completion questions include a sentence with one or two words omitted. One-blank sentence completion questions are generally easier than two-blank sentence completions. Regardless of what type of sentence completion you're answering, if you don't know the vocabulary involved, these questions can be more brutal than an IRS tax audit or an afternoon at the Department of Motor Vehicles.

One-blank sentence completion

The next question is an example that has one blank that you must fill with the correct answer:

> By working a great deal of overtime, Ramon gave the boss a(n) _____ reason to give him a raise.
>
> A. autocratic (aw-tih-*kra*-tik)
>
> B. despotic (des-*pah*-tik)
>
> C. compelling (kum-*pel*-ing)
>
> D. dogged (*daw*-gid)
>
> E. intrepid (in-*trep*-id)

The answer is *C:* By working a great deal of overtime, Ramon gave the boss a *compelling* reason to give him a raise. *Compelling* means "forceful; urgently demanding attention." Definitions of the other choices show you why they're not good choices:

> A. *autocratic* means "tyrannical"
>
> B. *despotic* means "dictatorial, oppressive"
>
> D. *dogged* means "stubbornly persevering"
>
> E. *intrepid* means "courageous, fearless"

Two-blank sentence completion

The following item has two blanks:

The critic neither _____ nor _____ the director's latest film: She evaluated the film's strengths and weaknesses carefully and fairly.

> A. aggrandized (uh-*gran*-dyzd) . . . favored
>
> B. maligned (mah-*lynd*) . . . criticized
>
> C. celebrated . . . adapted
>
> D. lauded (*law*-did) . . . derided (deh-*ry*-did)
>
> E. disregarded (dis-ree-*gar*-did) . . . showcased

In this case, you can use context clues to help you arrive at the correct answer. The first sentence tells you what the critic didn't do: She didn't *blank* or *blank* the film. The second sentence tells you what she did do: She gave an unbiased appraisal of the film. From these clues, you know that you're looking for verbs that indicate bias. Finally, the "neither . . . nor" structure of the first sentence lets you know that you're probably looking for opposites.

The answer is *D:* The critic neither *lauded* nor *derided* the director's latest film. She evaluated the film's strengths and weaknesses carefully and fairly. *Lauded* means "praised;" *derided* means "ridiculed." Both words express bias: one positive, one negative. The other choices spelled out are:

> A. *aggrandized* means "increased, expanded;" *favored* means "preferred"
>
> B. *maligned* means "disparaged, defamed;" *criticized* means "condemned, denounced"
>
> C. *celebrated* means "honored;" *adapted* means "fashioned to one's own needs"
>
> E. d*isregarded* means "ignored;" *showcased* means "set off for display."

Tips for solving sentence completion questions

To solve one-blank sentence completion test items, follow these five steps:

1. Cover the answers. Read the sentence and substitute the word *blank* for the blank space.

2. Look for links in ideas and clues in the sentence that show how the sentence makes sense when complete.

3. Predict the best answer without looking at the choices.

4. Read the possible answers and choose the one that best matches your choice. Use the process of elimination to narrow the field.

5. Check your answer by reading the entire sentence. Rereading the answer you've chosen can help you decide if the sentence makes sense. If it doesn't, revise your answer.

To solve a two-blank sentence completion test item, follow these steps:

1. Cover the answers, read the sentence, and focus on the blank that you think is the easiest to complete. Look for hints that point out the word needed to fill in the easier blank.

2. Provide your own answer without looking at the choices.

3. Look at the answers, pick the one that best matches your word, and fill in the easier blank.

4. Follow the same process for the second blank.

5. Be sure to use process of elimination. As you read the answer choices, cross out the ones that are obviously incorrect.

Plugging in every answer choice in a completion question is just as dangerous as plugging in every appliance in your home: You overload your circuits and cause problems for yourself. The folks who devise test questions *try* to confuse you by making every answer sound reasonable. You're much better off coming up with a word on your own and looking for a synonym to it in the answer choices.

Reading comprehension

Being an involved reader can greatly increase your grasp of the writer's point, as well as the subtle elements of his or her style. These two things are important when you're working on reading comprehension questions.

By picking up details, you can make *inferences* (unstated conclusions). When you make an inference, you combine story clues with what you already know to "read between the lines."

Of course, reading between the lines is hard when you don't know some of the words in the passage. In that case, use your knowledge of prefixes, roots, and suffixes, and context clues, to puzzle out a word's meaning. Ask yourself the following questions:

✔ What does this unfamiliar word mean? How can I use prefixes, roots, and suffixes to define the word? How can I use context clues?

✔ Am I confused because the word has multiple meanings? If so, which meaning is being used here?

✔ What point is the author making in this passage? Where is the topic sentence or main idea?

✔ What is the author's purpose? Is it to tell a story? To explain or inform? To persuade? To describe?

✔ How is this passage organized? How is the text organization linked to the author's purpose?

The answers to these questions may not only help you divine the meaning of the word that's tripping you up, but it also may help you identify the main points and the main purpose of the passage — information you need to know.

Paying attention to organization

Identifying the structure of a reading selection can also help you increase your comprehension. Fiction is structured according to *chronological* (krahn-ih-*lahj*-ih-kul) order, the order of time. Events are arranged from first to last, as on a timeline. Fiction writers often use dates to show the order of events. In addition, writers can use time-order words to show when events happen. Time-order words include: *after, at length, before, currently, during, eventually, first, second, third* (and so on), *finally, immediately, in the future, later, meanwhile, next, now, soon, subsequently, then,* and *today.*

Nonfiction articles are often arranged in one of three ways: *chronological order, cause and effect order,* or *comparison and contrast order.*

✔ Cause and effect order shows the reason why something happened (the cause) and the results (the effect). Signal words include: *as a result, because, consequently, due to, for, for this (that) reason, if . . . then, nevertheless, since, so, so that, therefore, thus,* and *this (that) is how.*

✔ Comparison and contrast order shows how two people, places, or things are the same (comparison) and different (contrast). Signal words include: *like, just as, in the same way, likewise, similarly, unlike, but, however, on the other hand,* and *by contrast.*

Alphabet soup for the test taker's soul

You're not in this alone! This section offers a couple of effective reading strategies that can help you boost your reading comprehension. At first glance, these techniques may look like a bowl of alphabet soup. But don't let that put you off. They're easy and effective ways to boost your level of reading comprehension.

Use SQ3R

To use SQ3R, follow these steps:

1. **Survey:** Preview the text by reading the title, headings, illustrations, and captions. Based on your survey, make predictions about the contents, and then skim the passage to get its overall meaning.

2. **Question:** As you survey and skim, ask questions about the material and what you find. Start by turning the title into a question. As you read, look for the answer to this question.

3. **Read:** Read the passage and make predictions. Revise the predictions as you need to. Try to find the main idea by looking at the topic sentence and details in each paragraph.

4. **Recite:** After you finish reading, look back over the passage. Focus on the title, headings, and topic sentences. Summarize the material in your head, reducing what you read to a few sentences. Then say your summary aloud.

5. **Review:** Look back to your predictions. Were they on target? If so, find the details you used to make them. If not, figure out where and why you guessed incorrectly.

Use SMRR

To use SMRR:

1. **Skim:** Preview the passage by scanning the title, heading, art, and captions. Then read the passage as quickly as you can.

2. **Mark:** Using a highlighter, pencil, or pen, mark the topic sentence and key details. Of course, never mark a text that doesn't belong to you!

3. **Read:** Read the text slowly and carefully, checking that you correctly identified the main idea and important points.

4. **Reread:** Go back over the text, checking that you understand the main idea.

Incorporating General Test Prep Tips

Standardized tests are similar to classroom tests in many ways, but they have a few significant differences. These differences change the strategies you use:

✔ **The test items on standardized tests are often arranged from easier to more difficult.** As you work through the test, the questions will get more and more challenging. Therefore, you have to budget your time differently. Spend less time on the first questions and more time on the last questions.

✔ **Be prepared not to know everything you're asked on a standardized test.** You can (and do!) study for a classroom test. As a result, you may be able to ace the test because you know the material and test-taking strategies. This is not true with most standardized tests. You can prepare by learning the types of information you can expect, but you can't study the specific material because the content isn't released beforehand. As a result, there will most likely be questions you can't answer. Don't be upset; this is the way the test is designed.

Following are some suggestions for maximizing your time and avoiding panic.

Make a plan of attack

Here are some suggestions for taking standardized tests:

- Answer the easy questions first and then go back and work on the harder questions. This strategy benefits you in many ways:

  You use your time well by getting some correct answers down in a quick manner.

  You build confidence as you write down the correct answers.

  You often think of clues that help you answer the more difficult questions.

  You may find that clues to difficult questions are revealed in other test questions.

  You build momentum, which gets your mind into the test mode.

  You leave time for the harder questions.

- If you don't know the answer to a question, eliminate any choices that you can. Narrow down your choices to two or three items (out of five) and choose the most likely answer from among the remaining choices. The odds are in your favor.

- If the test that you're taking doesn't penalize you for wrong answers (and some don't), answer every single question, even if you have to guess.

If you decide to work from the beginning of the test to the end, put a checkmark next to any question you skip. Write in pencil so that you can erase the checkmarks (in case you're not allowed to write on the test). When you get to the end of the test, go back to the beginning and start answering the questions you skipped.

Don't panic

Panic is a natural reaction to a pressure situation. Nonetheless, panic can prevent you from doing your best on tests, so reduce or banish it. Here are some don'ts that can help you deal with panic:

- **Don't panic if some questions seem much harder than others.** They probably are! That's the way the test was designed. This is especially true on standardized tests. Accept this, and do the best you can. On standardized tests, you don't have to answer each question to do well. That's because you're not being marked against yourself; rather, you're being judged against all other test takers. They're feeling the same way you are.

✔ **Don't panic if you can't get an answer.** Just skip the question and move on. If you have enough time, you can return to the question later. If you run out of time before you can return to it, you were better off answering more questions than wasting time on a question you didn't know.

✔ **Don't panic if you blow the test all out of proportion.** It is true that some tests are more important than others — especially standardized college admission tests. But tests are only one factor in your overall education. Remind yourself that you have been working hard in class and keeping up with all your homework. Keep in mind that how you do on one test will not affect your entire academic career.

✔ **Don't panic if you freeze and just can't go on.** If this happens, remind yourself that you have studied and are therefore well-prepared. Remember that every question you have answered is worth points. Reassure yourself that you're doing just fine. After all, you are! Stop working and close your eyes. Take two or three deep breaths. Breathe in and out to the count of five. Then go on with the test.

A minor case of nerves can actually help you do well on a standardized test because it keeps you alert and focused.

Chapter 14

Taking Care of Business Vocabulary

· ·

In This Chapter

▶ Discovering vital words common to all businesses

▶ Exploring words specific to individual professions

▶ Making workplace words a part of your everyday vocabulary

· ·

Computer geeks discuss *bits* and *bytes;* the aeronautics industry demands *BAFO* (the best and final offer). Doctors order things to move *stat* (fast); teachers require an *authentic assessment* (a type of evaluation). All careers and occupations have their unique words. In addition to these specialized terms, the world of work shares a core vocabulary — the essential words that all job seekers, employees, and employers need to know.

The bottom line is that business has a language all its own, filled with traditional words, new words, and traditional words with new meanings. It's essential for people who currently occupy the corner office — as well as those who aspire to it — to master the vocabulary of business.

To that end, this chapter provides you with a solid overview of the essential words of many businesses. In addition, because each profession has its own jargon, I give you a list of the specific terms you need to know to be comfortable talking to people from different professions.

Talking on Company Time

Regardless of what business you're in, how you communicate is important. Whether you're speaking with customers or writing reports for bosses, you want to sound like you know what you're talking about. Use the following tips:

> ✔ Know the specialized language of your profession. No one is comforted by a surgeon who calls a *scalpel* a *thingamajig,* or a gourmet chef who

doesn't know the difference between a *terrine* (a casserole dish) and a *tureen* (a giant soup pot).

✔ Be familiar with general business terms. If the project leader puts you in charge of preparing a flow chart (a chart showing each step in a process), you don't want to prepare a report on how things are going instead.

Writing in professional terms

If you didn't like high school English class, you probably convinced yourself that, because you were going to be a computer programmer/mathematician/sales representative (pick a profession), you'd never be forced to put pen to paper again. Or maybe you were going to be your own boss or inherit the family business and have other people write for you. As you have probably discovered by now, you miscalculated.

Although this book can't help you with *how* you write (get *English Grammar For Dummies* for that), it can help you with *what* you write. Table 14-1 lists common business reports that require certain types of information. Because the words are all *tangible* (they can be touched), they're all nouns.

Table 14-1	Business Reports
Word	*Definition*
abstract (*ab*-strakt)	summary of a report (In the general usage, abstract means "hypothetical; not concrete." For other words that have double meanings, see the section "Doing double duty: Words with two meanings," later in this chapter.)
annual report	a report, distributed to stockholders, that summarizes the firm's financial performance and achievement during the year
feedback	receiver's response to a message
flow chart	diagram, often using geometric symbols, showing steps in a sequence of operations
glossary (*glos*-ah-ree)	list of terms and definitions, listed in the back of a book, report, and so on
internal reports	reports written by employees for use only in their organization
memo	informal written communication, such as a note sent from one department to another in an office (*Memo* is short for memorandum.)

In addition to the different types of communication, you may also (or may have already) run across terms that describe a report's *format* — its style, organization, and arrangement. In addition, how the document is presented (is it given to everyone, is it in electronic format, and so on) can be important, too. Table 14-2 lists some common formatting terms. (All the terms in the table are nouns.)

Table 14-2	Formatting Terms
Word	*Definition*
bullets	solid dots used at the beginning of each item in a list
blind copy	copy sent to recipients not listed in the original letter or memo
hard copy	printed version of an electronic document
boilerplate	any of the standard clauses or sections of a document
font (font)	complete assortment of type in one size and style
PowerPoint	Microsoft software presentation package that can be used to produce presentations, slides, handouts, speaker's notes, outlines, and so on
salutation (sal-yoo-*tay*-shun)	form of words serving as a greeting or opening of a letter (like "Dear Dr. Rozakis")
sans-serif (san *ser*-if)	style of printing type with no serifs
serif	fine line projecting from a main stroke of a letter in common styles of type
typeface	full selection of type of a particular design (In general usage, *typeface* and *font* are often used interchangeably.)
white space	portions of a printed page that lack text, illustrations, and so on, and are therefore blank

Keeping current with modern business lingo

Language — especially the English language, it seems — is changing all the time. Not only do old words take on new meanings, but new words and terms are created to describe modern workplace concepts and processes, as well. Consider the following examples:

✔ The latest hot business term for a take-charge person is *proactive* (assuming an active role). Be sure to use it properly, as an adjective:

> **Correct:** "I'm a proactive manager." (adj.)

> **Incorrect:** "I'm getting some proactive in today." (noun)

✔ *Face time* is today's trendy term, meaning "meeting someone in person." It's a noun, so use it like this:

> **Correct:** "I got ten minutes of face time with the boss on Tuesday."

> **Incorrect:** "I face-timed with the boss on Tuesday."

✔ The *grapevine* is the informal informational network in an organization, which carries gossip and rumors, as well as accurate information.

✔ *Office politics* is the term for the strategies that people use in both public and private organizations to gain or maintain a competitive advantage in their careers.

The nouns listed in Table 14-3 describe aspects of today's workaday world. Knowing these terms can help you do your job better and get ahead in your career.

Table 14-3	Words for the Modern Workplace
Word	*Definition*
burnout	state of emotional exhaustion caused by work stresses
business casual	casual style of business dress: a change from the traditional suit-and-tie/stockings-and-pumps dress code
chartjunk	irrelevant decorations on graphics
culture (*kul*-chur)	a company's history, traditions, values, and management style
glass ceiling	unofficial policy imposed on women and minorities that prevents them from being promoted (called "silicon ceiling" in Silicon Valley)
GOOD job	acronym for "get out of debt" job; refers to a job taken in order to pay off debts and then resigned from when the debts are cleared
M.O.	abbreviation for *modus operandi* (*moh*-dus ahp-uh-*ran*-dye); way of doing or accomplishing something
favoritism (*fay*-vur-uh-tiz-um)	unfair partiality
flight risk	employees who are suspected of planning to leave a department or company soon

Word	Definition
performance review	an assessment of a worker's accomplishments, including such factors as leadership, project management, and expense control
sexual harassment	inappropriate, unwelcome, and, typically, persistent behavior, as by an employer or co-worker, that is sexual in nature, specifically when actionable under federal or state statutes
Silicon Valley (*sil*-ih-kahn *val*-ee)	area southeast of San Francisco, California, which is a center of high-technology activities, especially those involving microelectronics
vested interest	established right; emotional stake

To *procrastinate* (proh-*kras*-tih-nayt) is to "put off doing something unpleasant or burdensome until a future time." Not surprisingly, the root of *procrastination* is a Latin word meaning "belonging to tomorrow." We've all worked with people who promise more than they can deliver. I know that you'll put the pedal to the metal and your nose to the grindstone, apply some elbow grease, and master the words you need to get the job you desire — and deserve.

Before

I keep calling the boss and missing her. We keep leaving messages for each other. I want to find out what standards the company is using to judge my qualifications. Maybe there's a job I don't even know about available at the company.

After

I keep playing *phone tag* with the boss. I want to find out what *criteria* (kry-*teer*-ee-ah) the company is using to judge my qualifications. I know there's a *hidden job market* — jobs that are never advertised but may be available or may be created for the right candidate. I need to tap into it.

Talkin' the Talk

Junior is visiting Uncle Tony. Junior found a good job with the law firm Cheatum and Run, and is getting some advice from his uncle.

Uncle Tony: Junior, you need a *rabbi* [*rab*-eye].

Junior: Uh, Uncle Tony, last time I checked, we were Catholic. A *rabbi* is a Jewish religious leader.

Uncle Tony:	Junior, *rabbi* is a slang term for a business *mentor* — a person who shows you the ropes, who teaches you the basics of the job. You don't have to convert to have a rabbi.
Junior:	Can't I climb the ladder of success on my own?
Uncle Tony (as heplayfully smacks Junior's cheeks):	We all have to *network* by using personal contacts to help us in business.

Doing double duty: Words with two meanings

When English speakers need a word, they beg, borrow, or steal one. On the upside, the casual attitude toward word formation enriches the language and makes it easier for you to express yourself. On the downside, English words often get pressed into service to do double duty, which can make it tough to figure out which meaning is being used.

Table 14-4 shows common words that have uncommon business meanings. When you encounter words like these, you simply have to use context clues to figure out which meaning is the right one. Chances are, if the guy in the next cubicle says, "I need the most recent minutes," he isn't talking about time.

Table 14-4		Multiple-Meaning Business Terms	
Word	**Part of Speech**	**Everyday Meaning**	**Business Meaning**
desktop	noun	work surface	computer
figure	noun	form; design	any graphic that is not a table
gutter	noun	drainage ditch	the white space formed by the inner margins of two facing pages in a book
minutes	noun	units of time	record of a meeting
justify	verb	to make an excuse for; to explain	to line up margins
PC	adj.	acronym for politically correct	acronym for personal computer
table	noun	piece of furniture with a flat top	chart of information arranged in rows and columns

Getting the ax

How come there are so many ways to say someone lost a job and only a few ways to say, "I got the job!"? I'm just a writer, not a sociologist, so I don't know the answer to that. I do know, and share, some of the ways former co-workers describe a colleague who is no longer with the company.

	derecruited	canned	
	fired	laid off	
	terminated	excessed	
	discharged	sent packing	
	got the ax	made redundant	
retrenched	uninstalled		
downsized	rightsized		

No matter what you call it, the poor schlub is outta there.

Mastering Jargon

Each profession has its own special words, or *jargon* — the specialized terminology for a particular field. For example, you call a mistake in a computer program a "bug." You know that a computer "bug" is not the same as the insect you swatted yesterday. That's because the computer term "bug," as with many specialized terms, has become a part of everyday vocabulary. Educated people, like you, know how important it is to keep informed so that you can keep pace with a fast-changing world.

You already know that mastering the jargon of your business is essential if you want to understand what people are saying and respond intelligently. However, knowing other business jargon can be almost as important. Being familiar with the jargon in a few areas can be a real asset. For example, I earned my Ph.D. in literature but find myself doing more and more technical writing — which has little to do with my original training in deconstructing fiction and drama.

The following sections list the jargon you're likely to encounter in the areas of computers, engineering, and publishing. See Chapters 14, 15, and 16 for language that pertains specifically to finances, law, and medicine.

Speaking of software (and hardware, too)

Most offices use computers; many have access to the Internet. In fact, the business world is abuzz today with electrical currents hooking workers up with each other and the outside world. Whether you love computers or hate them, chances are you have to deal with them. Table 14-5 lists computer and software terms you should know. Many of the terms are acronyms, and you pronounce them by saying their letters, as in CPU. Only when this is not the case did I provide pronunciation guidelines in Table 14-5. So just say the letters unless you see a different pronunciation.

Table 14-5		Computer Terms
Word	*Part of Speech*	*Definition*
application (ap-lih-*kay*-shun)	noun	computer program
CD-ROM (see-dee rahm)	noun	compact disc-read only memory; a device that stores data
CD-RW	noun	rewritable compact disc
CPU	noun	central processing unit
database program (*dayt*-uh-base *proh*-gram)	noun	computer program, such as Access or dBase, that enables you to organize and access a collection of information
download	verb	to copy files from a distant computer via modem
DVD	noun	digital versatile disc; a sophisticated data storage device
hard drive	noun	a memory storage device, usually built-in to the computer
IS	noun	information services: often the group of folks who care for and maintain a business's computers
ISP	noun	Internet Service Provider: company that, for a fee, provides access to the Internet
mail merge	noun	process by which names and addresses in a database are combined with a form letter to create personalized form letters
modem (*moh*-dum)	noun	device that enables one computer to access a distant computer through phone or cable lines

Word	Part of Speech	Definition
multimedia (mul-ty-*mee*-dee-uh)	noun	combination of text, data, pictures, sound, video, and so on, as on a CD-ROM compact disc, for interactive access through computers
patch	noun	instructions added to a program that has already been translated into machine language, so as to correct an error
RAM	noun	random-access memory; temporary storage space in your computer
ROM (rahm)	noun	read-only memory; memory the computer user can't alter
spreadsheet program	noun	computer program that organizes numerical data into rows and columns for computing desired calculations and making overall adjustments based on new data
virus	noun	an unauthorized, disruptive set of instructions in a computer program that leaves copies of itself in other programs or disks
word processor	noun	computer program that lets you write, edit, and print documents

A computer term you don't ever want to forget is *backup*. Essentially it means to save your heinie by making sure that you have recent copies of important work and information.

Engineering jargon

Table 14-6 lists ten engineering terms that well-educated people should know. (All the terms listed in the table are nouns.) As you read the chart, see how many of these terms you have heard in conversation or on television.

Table 14-6	Ten Engineering Terms
Word	*Definition*
benchmark	reference point in measuring or judging quality, value, and so on
conductor (kun-*duk*-ter)	substance or thing that conducts electricity, heat, sound, and so on
equilibrium (ee-kwih-*lib*-ree-um)	state of balance or equality between opposing forces
fabrication (fab-rih-*kay*-shun)	construction; manufacture
kinetic (kih-*neh*-tik)	of or caused by motion
operational (ah-per-*ay*-shuh-nul)	ready to be used
pulse	any beat, signal, vibration, and so on, that is regular or rhythmical; a brief surge of voltage or current
quality control	system for maintaining desired standards in a product or process
transformer	device that transfers alternating-current energy
transistor (tran-*zis*-ter)	device that controls the flow of electrical current

Some of the instruments that engineers use are important in your daily life, as well. Below are five terms that describe measurement devices. As you read Table 14-7, cover the last column to see if you can figure out what each instrument measures. (For clues, head to Chapters 5 and 6, which list common Greek and Latin roots.)

Table 14-7	Five Measurement Tools
Word	*Definition*
altimeter (al-*tim*-ah-ter)	instrument for measuring altitude
barometer (buh-*rahm*-ah-ter)	instrument for measuring atmospheric pressure
hydrometer (hy-*drahm*-eh-ter)	instrument for measuring the specific gravity of liquids
pedometer (peh-*dahm*-eh-ter)	instrument for measuring the approximate distance covered in walking
thermometer (thur-*mahm*-eh-ter)	instrument for measuring temperatures

Stop the presses: Publishing and printing jargon

Publishing is another industry that has a lot of jargon. Consider, for example, what a *blanket* is. If you're a printer, it's the rubber sheet in a printing press that transfers the image from the plate to the paper. A *slush pile* isn't something you avoid when the snowdrifts melt; rather, it's the pile of unsolicited manuscripts that pour into publishers. Following are other publishing terms that you may find interesting:

- When doctors use the term *bleeding,* it's rarely a good sign for the patient. But when printers and publishers talk about something *bleeding,* they're referring to illustrations or printing that extends beyond the *trim size* (finished size) of the page. If a bleed is the effect they're seeking, it's just dandy.

- To a printer, a *dummy* isn't a blockhead; rather, it's a laid-out copy of a manuscript used to check *pagination* (the numbers on the page).

- *Live art?* It's the actual art being used in a publication — not the placeholder, which is often labeled "FPO" (for placement only).

- And when printers or publishers ask for the *proof,* they're looking for a sample impression of composed type that they can use to check for errors.

Newspaper and magazine folk also talk about *putting the issue to bed,* which means finishing it. I'm now putting this chapter to bed. Sleep well!

Chapter 15

Mutterings on Money Matters

In This Chapter

▶ Discovering the vocabulary of money management

▶ Exploring words for investments and the financial world

▶ Forming tax-related words

*I*t's been called *moolah, cash, bread, lettuce, clams, scratch, bucks,* and *greenbacks.* No matter what you call it, you know what we mean — money. The word *money* comes from the Latin *moneta,* meaning "a mint." Since ancient times, money has fascinated people like few other tangibles.

I'll be the first to assert that money *isn't* everything, but having the vocabulary to discuss money knowledgeably does make it easier to manage the green stuff. This chapter gives you the words you need to talk about financial matters, understand the basics of money management, and give intelligent consideration to investments.

Managing Your Money Day to Day

The eccentric American billionaire Howard Hughes once made half a billion dollars in one day. A recluse (*rek*-looz) who never left his home in his later years, Hughes received a bank check in 1966 for $546,549,171 in return for his 75 percent holding in TWA airlines.

Table 15-1 can help you manage *your* millions. It presents essential words for dealing with financial issues.

Table 15-1	Terms for Managing Your Money	
Word	*Part of Speech*	*Definition*
assets (*as*-ehts)	noun	total resources of a person or business
ATM	noun	automated teller machine
balance	noun/verb	the excess of credits over debits or of debits over credits / to find any difference that may exist between the debit and credit sides of an account
bankrupt (*bank*-rupt)	noun	person or other entity legally declared unable to pay his or her debts
bounce	verb	to be returned to the payee by a bank as a worthless check, because of insufficient funds in the drawer's account (slang)
budget (*buj*-it)	noun/verb	a plan or schedule adjusting expenses during a certain period to the estimated or fixed income for that period / to plan according to a budget
credit	noun	money made available by a bank, on which a specified person or firm may draw
debit card (*deb*-it kard)	noun	a kind of bank card that allows the cost of purchases to be automatically debited, or deducted, from the cardholder's bank account
interest charge (*in*-trest charj)	noun	fee paid for the privilege of using money or credit (also called *finance charge*)

Both checks and credit cards are essentially promises to pay, backed by the person signing the card and guaranteed within limits by a bank or credit card company. Increasingly, electronic banking has begun to replace paper money and coins completely, leaving no trace of metal or paper.

Talkin' the Talk

Lorna Doone's life would be wonderful if only she could get a credit card. Because she's a smart cookie, Lorna talks the matter over with her friendly neighborhood banker, George Bailey. Hurry up and listen in because the bank closes promptly at 3 p.m.

Lorna Doone: George, what's a *credit limit*?

George Bailey: A credit limit is the maximum amount a person can borrow under a credit account agreement. Your credit limit will be about $500, for now.

Lorna Doone: How much will I pay in *interest*?

George Bailey: Your card's *APR* (annual percentage rate) is used to determine your daily periodic rate. The higher your card's APR, the more interest you may pay. *Variable rate* cards are based on *inflation* and are guided by the *financial index* (such as the prime rate). When the index goes down, so does the interest rate on your card. *Fixed rate* cards keep the same rate of interest, regardless of inflation.

Lorna Doone: In other words, if I get a variable rate card, the rate keeps climbing?

George Bailey: We *cap* the rate by limiting how much the interest rate can increase or decrease during a set length of time.

Lorna Doone: George, you're an angel.

George Bailey: Actually, that's my friend Clarence. . . .

Folding money

The use of paper money is believed to have started in China sometime between the 7th and 9th centuries A.D. to overcome a shortage of coins. In medieval Europe, letters of credit (amounting to personal checks) were exchanged between tradespeople who knew and trusted each other. Later, goldsmiths started giving receipts for gold left in their keeping. These receipts could then be exchanged for money — basically, the first gold standard.

During the 18th and 19th centuries, private bankers, and eventually central banks, took over this role. They issued notes with a "promise to pay" — words that still appear on many bank notes. Until the 1930s, when many countries went off the gold standard, the holders of these bank notes were entitled to redeem the notes for gold.

Investigating Investment Terms

Warren Buffett, chairman of Berkshire Hathaway, is likely the greatest investor of all time. If you had invested $10,000 in Berkshire Hathaway when Buffett took over in 1965, you would have more than $20 million today. Buffett's investment record is strong evidence that it's possible to consistently outperform the market.

Of course nowadays you don't have to be a Warren Buffet — or a Warren Buffet wannabe — to invest money. Table 15-2 describes some basic terms for investors in the stock and bond markets. (All terms in the table are nouns.) If you've been investing for a while, and you read the finance section of your newspaper, you're probably already familiar with these words. If you're new to investing (or if you aren't particularly interested yourself but find that the folks in your carpool are), you may find that knowing these terms can be helpful.

Table 15-2	Terms for Investors
Word	*Definition*
annuity (ah-*noo*-ih-tee)	investment yielding periodic payments during the owner's lifetime, for a stated number of years, or in perpetuity
beneficiary (ben-uh-*fish*-ee-ehr-ee)	person named to receive the income or inheritance from a will, insurance policy, trust, and so on
bond	interest-bearing certificate issued by a government or business, promising to pay the holder a specified sum on a specified date

Word	Definition
capital (*kap*-uh-tul)	money or property owned or used in business by a person, corporation, and so on; net worth of a business; amount by which the assets exceed the liabilities
certificate (sur-*tif*-ih-kit)	document certifying ownership, a promise to pay, and so on
interest (*in*-trest)	fee paid for the use of money
heir (ehr)	individual who inherits or is legally entitled to inherit another's property or title upon the other's death
liability (ly-uh-*bil*-ih-tee)	debt of a person or business, as a note payable or a long-term debenture
mutual funds (*myoo*-choo-uhl fundz)	funds consisting of a number of diversified securities that are owned jointly by those who have purchased shares in them as an investment
stock	capital invested in a company through buying shares

Lucky Lucinda has just come into a *windfall* (an unexpected gain or piece of good fortune). She's standing in the bank trying to decide how to invest her money. After she learns the vocabulary of investment, Lucinda can pick the investment vehicles that suit her needs.

Before

Ms. Banker, I need to invest this money in different stuff.

After

Ms. Banker, I need to diversify my portfolio. Perhaps I'll put some of the money in *certificates of deposit* (federally insured investments offered by banks) and the rest in *money-market funds* (short-term investments that are typically safe and easy to redeem).

Talking about Markets

Bull market is the term for a prolonged period of rising prices, usually by 20 percent or more. A *bear market* is the opposite — a prolonged period of falling prices, usually by 20 percent or more, accompanied by widespread pessimism.

Are you *bearish* (pessimistic about the market) or *bullish* (optimistic about the market)? In either case, knowing the inside lingo of the stock and bond markets can help you increase your assets and minimize your liabilities.

Table 15-3 lists essential words for anyone who wants to invest in the stock and bond markets. And *who* doesn't want to make money?

Table 15-3		Market Terms
Word	*Part of Speech*	*Definition*
accrue (uh-*kroo*)	verb	to grow
acquisition (ak-wuh-*zish*-un)	noun	the act of gaining something
balloon loan	noun	a long-term loan, often a mortgage, with level payments due during a long-term schedule and the remaining balance due upon maturity (also called *balloon note* or *bullet loan*)
day trader	noun	active stock trader who holds positions for a very short time and makes several trades each day
market	noun	place where stocks and bonds are regularly bought and sold
NASDAQ	noun	National Association of Securities Dealers Automated Quotations
negotiable (nih-*goh*-sheh-bul)	adj.	legally transferable to another person by endorsement or by proper delivery
nest egg	noun	assets set aside as a reserve or to establish a fund
NYSE	noun	New York Stock Exchange
paper loss	noun	loss that has occurred but has not yet been realized through a transaction, such as a stock that has fallen in value but is still being held (also called *unrealized loss*)
paper profit	noun	profit that has been made but not yet realized through a transaction, such as a stock that has risen in value but is still being held (also called *unrealized gain, unrealized profit,* or *unrealized paper*)

Saying it with money

Check out this list of common expressions that contain the word *money*. Use these sayings in your conversation and writing to express yourself with more precision and style.

- **blood money:** fee paid to a hired assassin

- **conscience money:** money paid, sometimes anonymously, by someone who hopes to atone for previous wrongdoing

- **even money:** equal stakes, with no odds, given or offered in a wager

- **front money:** money paid in advance, especially to start a project

- **hush money:** money paid as a bribe to keep a person from revealing something, such as a scandalous or criminal act

- **mad money:** bit of money set aside for emergency use or for frivolous purchases

- **pin money:** small sum of money, as for incidental expenses

- **pocket money:** cash for small expenses; small change

- **seed money:** money provided to begin the financing of, or to attract additional funds for, a project

Inflation grew to dizzying heights in Germany after World War I. The government printed money frantically as the value of the mark (the German monetary unit at the time) plunged. People needed wheelbarrows of paper money to buy everyday necessities. In 1921, the German rate of exchange was 81 marks to 1 U.S. dollar; two years later, the U.S. dollar was worth 100 million German marks.

Taxing Terms

According to American humorist Will Rogers, the income tax has made liars out of more Americans than golf. Liars or not, all working Americans have to deal with taxes. If you can grasp a few common tax terms, making your way through the tax forms will be much easier (not more pleasant, mind you, just easier). Table 15-4 lists some of these nouns.

Table 15-4	Tax Terms
Word	*Definition*
deduction (dee-*duk*-shun)	expense you can subtract from your income to help lower your taxable income

(continued)

Table 15-4 *(continued)*

Word	Definition
dependent (dee-*pen*-dent)	person you support that you can claim on your taxes as an exemption
exemption (eg-*zemp*-shun)	personal deduction amount you are allowed to deduct for yourself and each dependent
gross income	total taxable income before deductions are subtracted
net income	amount of income left after expenses and deductions

Here are two words you don't want to hear, especially together — *audit* and *fraud*. During an audit, someone from the IRS (the Internal Revenue Service) examines your tax form to verify that it's accurate and that you're being honest. If you commit fraud, you knowingly and willing lie to pull a fast one on ol' Uncle Sam. And he doesn't take kindly to that, which can lead to two more particularly unpleasant terms — *penalty* and *jail time*.

All that glitters isn't necessarily gold

Many early prospectors in the American west and northwest mistook chunks of pyrite — a gold-colored iron ore — for gold. The ore became known as "fool's gold" and was considered worthless. However, the golden phrases in the following list are valuable, as you'll discover when you mine them for your speech and writing.

- **gold bond:** bond backed by gold, often issued by gold mining companies

- **gold bug:** one who buys gold as protection against an anticipated collapse in the value of currency, stocks, and so on

- **gold fixing:** twice-daily setting of the price of gold, based on supply and demand, by specialists in London, Paris, and Zurich

- **Gold Pool:** representatives of seven countries who seek to stabilize the price of gold

- **gold standard:** monetary system that backs its currency with a reserve of gold and allows currency holders to convert their currency into gold (The U.S. went off the gold standard in 1971.)

- **goldbrick:** anything worthless passed off as genuine or valuable; a lazy person

- **golden handcuffs:** rewards and penalties designed to discourage key employees from leaving a company

- **golden handshake:** financial incentive for a worker to retire early

- **golden parachute:** large payment made by a company to a senior executive upon termination of employment

- **goldilocks economy:** term used to describe the U.S. economy of the mid- and late-1990s as not too hot, not too cold, but just right

So who are the people you love to hate? The folks at the *Internal Revenue Service* (IRS), the federal agency responsible for administering and enforcing the U.S. tax laws. They're the ones who assess and collect taxes, determine pension plan qualification, and do other stuff that generally ticks people off.

Talkin' the Talk

Laurie is meeting with her tax preparer, her long-suffering husband Bob. Because Laurie works well with words, and Bob works well with numbers, their annual tax conferences are rarely pretty. However, the meetings are always instructive, as well as amusing. The walls are thin and their voices loud, so listening in is a snap.

Laurie:	Dear husband, I have so many *deductions* this year.
Bob:	Remember that a *deduction* is an allowable reduction of income. Deductions come off your *gross* income [total assets or earning], not your *net* income [the amount remaining after certain adjustments have been made for debts, deductions, or expenses]."
Laurie:	Gotcha. . . . I want to deduct the lawn because it would die without me.
Bob:	No lawn deduction.
Laurie:	Can we take exemptions for the kids? That would make them deductions.
Bob:	Yes, because the kids are still dependents. They rely on us for support.
Laurie:	Goody. Remember that we have 25 kids.
Bob:	Last time I looked, we had two kids. Let's follow the Internal Revenue Code, so if we are called for an audit and our income tax return is checked, the IRS won't fine you for fraud.
Laurie:	No lawn deduction?
Bob:	No lawn deduction. Besides, the lawn is dead.

Chapter 16

Speaking Legalese

· ·

In This Chapter

▶ Discovering words related to the law

▶ Exploring terms used in government

▶ Making legal terms a part of your daily vocabulary

· ·

*I*t's almost too easy to find a good lawyer joke, but it's no joke that we all have to know the language of the law. In addition to helping you deal with everyday legal business — leases, credit, mortgages, wills, and so on — legal language also helps you understand the finer points of government and politics. That's what this chapter is all about.

Mastering Legal Terms

Americans like courtroom drama. Whether it's fiction (think *Perry Mason, L.A. Law,* or *Law & Order*) or reality TV, like *Court TV, The People's Court,* or the televised O.J. Simpson trial, Americans are fascinated by the idea that the truth will come out, and justice will be served.

Even if you don't care about anybody's legal business but your own, you still need to know a few general legal terms. You may encounter legal terms as you take care of your own legal matters or as you read the newspaper.

E is such a small letter that it can't have much impact on your legal rights . . . or can it? Actually, that little *e* matters a whole lot when it comes to cases and cakes. To a lawyer, a *tort* is a civil wrong for which the injured party is entitled to compensation. To a baker, a *torte* is a rich cake, especially one that contains little or no flour. Both words are pronounced the same way. The only change is that itty-bitty *e.* Small, but powerful.

Bellying up to the bar: General legal terms and your rights

Knowing your legal rights not only helps you protect yourself against possible legal problems but also enables you to avoid potentially disastrous misunderstandings. You can't fully understand your legal rights until you know commonplace legal terms. Table 16-1 shows general legal terms, some of which concern individual rights under American law. Here's your chance to bone up on the language of the law so that you can become a real legal beagle!

Table 16-1	General Legal Terms	
Word	**Part of Speech**	**Definition**
acquit (ah-*kwit*)	verb	to free from blame
alias (*ay*-lee-us)	noun	an assumed name
appeal (ah-*peel*)	noun/verb	the transference of a case to a higher court for rehearing or review; to make a request to a higher court for the rehearing or review of a lower court's decision
attorney (ah-*tur*-nee)	noun	person trained in the law and legally allowed to advise and represent other people in legal proceedings (also called an *attorney-at-law* or *lawyer*)
bail (bayl)	noun	money or property deposited with the court to bring about the temporary release of a person from legal custody on assurance that the person will obey the court's orders and appear for trial
citation (sy-*tay*-shun)	noun	written order for an offender to appear in court
culprit (*kul*-prit)	noun	criminal; a person guilty of an offense
custody (*kus*-tuh-dee)	noun	detention; in a divorce case, the right of one parent to keep the children under her or his care
defense (deh-*fens*)	noun	arguments in behalf of the defendant in a case; the defendant and his or her lawyer or lawyers, collectively
extradite (*ex*-trah-dyt)	verb	to give up a fugitive to another nation or authority

Word	Part of Speech	Definition
litigation (lit-ih-*gay*-shun)	noun	act of carrying out a lawsuit
subpoena (suh-*pee*-nuh)	noun/verb	written order commanding a person to testify in court; to summon a person to court
waive (wayv)	verb	to give up a right
warrant (*war*-ent)	noun	a written directive to a law officer to perform a specified act, such as an arrest, seizure, or search
witness (*wit*-nis)	noun	person who testifies about his or her relevant observations, or one who has expert knowledge of a relevant topic
writ (rit)	noun	legal document ordering or forbidding the performance of a specified act

Courting legal myths and facts

The judicial system in the United States is subject to perhaps more than its fair share of misinformation. The following list debunks a few common myths:

✔ **Myth:** America has too many lawyers — more than any other country.

Fact: The United States has 9.4 percent of the world's lawyers and ranks 35th in number of lawyers on a per capita basis. Among those ranked ahead of the United States are Japan, France, and Italy.

✔ **Myth:** The jury system is a uniquely American institution.

Fact: The origins of the jury system have been traced to ancient Egypt (circa 2000 B.C.). The right to trial by jury was guaranteed to English citizens by the Magna Carta, signed by King John at Runnymede in 1215.

✔ **Myth:** The unemployed and illiterate make up juries. Therefore, juries are not a true representation of the American population.

Fact: Juries are typically chosen from voter and driver lists, which provide a fair representation of the population. A recent study indicates that the average prospective juror is educated, employed, middle-aged, and married.

✔ **Myth:** People dislike serving on juries.

Fact: A National Center for State Courts survey revealed that 81 percent of those who served on juries had a favorable attitude toward jury service.

An *appeal* is a request to a higher court for the review of the decision of a lower court. Knowing what appeal means can help you decode related words. For instance, an *appellant* is a person who makes the appeal or the person on whose behalf the appeal is made. The *appellate court* reviews the judgments of other courts. As you may expect, the appellate court has *appellate jurisdiction,* the legal authority to review a decision made by a lower court.

Many legal terms are built on similar roots, so knowing just a handful of legal words can help you figure out many more.

Talkin' the Talk

The neighborhood is discussing the delicious news about their neighbor's recent arrest. The neighborhood folks aren't really mean-spirited; they just enjoy some good gossip — especially when it's about Mr. Big, who seems to have more than his share of goodies. Pull up a fence post chair and join the gossip.

Eleanor:	So now we know how Mr. Big was able to afford a tennis court, an in-ground pool, and a private jet — he committed *credit card fraud.*
Ben:	You heard that he used credit cards to get things he had no intention of paying for? I heard he was a *cyber-criminal.*
Brianna:	Computer crimes? Naw, he committed *arson.*
Arturo:	Setting buildings on fire? I don't think so. Harry down the street heard that he's guilty of *embezzlement* and *extortion.*
Eleanor:	I can buy that. Mr. Big seems like the kind of criminal to misappropriate money and use threats to do it.
Brianna:	Well, we all know for sure that he's a *felon.* Such a criminal!

Punishing words about crime

Basically, there are two classes of crimes: A *misdemeanor* (mis-duh-*meen*-ur) is a minor crime, one for which you pay a fine or spend a limited time in jail. A felony (*fel*-uh-nee), on the other hand, is a major crime (like murder or arson) and generally results in greater punishment than a misdemeanor.

Within these two classes, however, are a lot of different types of crimes. Consider the following examples:

- *Assault* (ah-*salt*) means "to threaten or attempt to do violence to another person."

- *Battery* (*bat*-er-ee) — often paired with assault for *assault and battery* — is a physical attack on another person, from mere touching to more severe violence.

- *Aggravated assault* (*ag*-ruh-vay-ted ah-*salt*) means "to cause serious injury to someone else, with or without a weapon."

Table 16-2 lists more words describing crime. By becoming familiar with these words, you can more easily understand what you read in the paper or see on the evening news.

Table 16-2		Words about Crime
Word	*Part of Speech*	*Definition*
bias crime	noun	crime in which the target is a group of people, represented by the victim (as when a member of a particular race is attacked only because the attacker holds a hatred toward that race); hate crime
burglary (*bur*-gla-ree)	noun	act of entering a house or building unlawfully to commit theft
capital offense (*kap*-ih-tal ah-*fens*)	noun	criminal act punishable by death or life imprisonment
collusion (kuh-*loo*-zhun)	noun	conspiracy; a secret agreement for fraudulent purposes
fraud	noun	deceit; trickery
larceny (*lar*-seh-nee)	noun	theft; robbery
libel (*ly*-bul)	noun/verb	false and malicious written statements about another person / to give an unflattering or damaging picture of another person
manslaughter (*man*-*slot*-er)	noun	killing of another human being, especially such without malice
perjury (*pur*-jeh-ree)	noun	making false statements while under oath in court

(continued)

Table 16-2 *(continued)*

Word	Part of Speech	Definition
slander (*slan*-der)	noun	false and malicious oral statements
swindle (*swin*-dul)	verb	to cheat out of money or property
terrorism (*tehr*-er-iz-em)	noun	use of force or threats to demoralize or intimidate in order to gain a political objective
treason (*tree*-zun)	noun/verb	betrayal of one's country / to betray one's country
vandalism (*van*-da-liz-um)	noun	intentional destruction or damage of property
white-collar crime	noun	nonviolent crime for financial gain committed by people who use their technical and professional knowledge for deception

Judging the law: Words related to "judge"

When reading or writing English words related to the legal system, you can't help but run up against the Latin root *jus/jur*, which means "right" or "law." It's the root used in the English words *judge* (a public officer authorized to hear and determine cases in a court of law), *justice* (the use of authority and power to uphold what is right, just, or lawful), and *jury* (the group of people who hear the evidence and decide guilt or innocence). Table 16-3 lists some words that contain the *jus/jur* root.

Table 16-3 Terms Using the Latin Root *Jus/Jur*

Word	Part of Speech	Definition
adjudicator (ah-*joo*-dih-kay-ter)	noun	person who acts as a judge and sits in judgment
judge advocate (juj *ad*-veh-kit)	noun	military legal officer designated to act as a court-martial prosecutor
judicial (joo-*dish*-el)	adj.	pertaining to the justice system
jurisdiction (joor-is-*dik*-shun)	noun	legal power to hear and decide cases
jurisprudence (joor-is-*proo*-denz)	noun	philosophy of law

Word	Part of Speech	Definition
jurist (*joor*-ist)	noun	person who is an expert in law
jus sanguinis (jus *san*-gwih-nis)	noun	the legal principle that says a child's country of citizenship is the same as his or her parent's country of citizenship

Not all terms that contain the word *jury* pertain to the legal system. The following example shows just such a boo-boo:

Correct: The jury-rigged television antenna worked well until last night's storm.

Incorrect: I'm going to serve on the jury-rig tomorrow.

The adjective *jury-rigged* describes setting something up to work for temporary or emergency use. It has nothing to do with the law.

Talkin' the Talk

The judge has *impaneled* a jury by selecting people to hear evidence and make a ruling. The jury's deliberations of the evidence presented during the trial are dragging on and on, however. The lawyers have their ears to the jury-room door. Feel free to listen as a couple members of the jury vent their frustrations.

Elsie: Jury *tampering*, jury shampering . . . is it our fault that two members of the jury took bribes to spill their guts to the press?

Elmer: I hear you. Being *sequestered* is a royal pain.

Elsie: Being sequestered makes me feel like a prisoner. We're not allowed to talk to anyone outside the jury, we're not allowed to read the newspapers, we're not allowed to watch TV.

Elmer: And we're a *blue-ribbon* jury, which means that we all have a lot of education and a higher-than-average income. We're prominent citizens.

Elsie: Fat lot of good that did us.

Courting courtroom terms

Notice the two *courts* in the heading just above: As a verb, *court* means "to woo or entice," but as a noun, *court* refers to "a physical space," "a group of judges," or "a specific judicial region." Table 16-4 lists essential words about trials and courtrooms. Every educated American, and anyone who wants to understand the judicial process and what goes on in a courtroom, should know these words.

Table 16-4		Words about Courtrooms
Word	*Part of Speech*	*Definition*
appearance (ah-*peer*-ens)	noun	the act of coming into a court and submitting to the court's authority
arraign (ah-*rain*)	verb	to bring before court to hear and answer charges
bailiff (*bay*-lif)	noun	court officer who keeps order in the courtroom, ministers to the jury, and so on
circumstantial evidence (sur-kum-*stan*-shul *ev*-ih-dens)	noun	indirect evidence or evidence that requires interpretation
contempt (kun-*tempt*) of court	noun	intentionally obstructing a court, reducing its dignity, or failing to obey its orders
defendant (dee-*fen*-dant)	noun	the person being accused or sued
deposition (dep-ih-*zi*-shun)	noun	testimony under oath taken down in writing
hearsay (*heer*-say)	noun	something that was heard but not known to be true
indict (in-*dyt*)	verb	to accuse or charge with a crime
malfeasance (mal-*fee*-zuns)	noun	wrongdoing or misconduct by a public official; the commission of an act that is positively unlawful
plaintiff (*playn*-tif)	noun	the person who brings the lawsuit into court
remitter (ree-*mit*-er)	noun	person who submits a matter for judgment
testimony (*tes*-tih-moh-nee)	noun	oral evidence offered by a sworn witness on the witness stand in court

Word	Part of Speech	Definition
venue (*ven*-yoo)	noun	the area in which a court may hear or try a case
verdict (*vur*-dikt)	noun	the judge or jury's formal finding on a matter submitted to court

The Latin root *corp* means "body." Several important legal words come from this root, including the phrase *habeas corpus* (hay-bee-uhs *kor*-puhs). Literally, the phrase means "you have the body." A writ of habeas corpus is used in some criminal proceedings to order the court officer to bring the detained person to court to determine the lawfulness of his or her imprisonment. Therefore, a writ of habeas corpus safeguards individuals from being unlawfully taken into custody.

Given the corp connection, you may be able to figure out the definition of the term *corpus delicti*. Literally, the phrase means "body of the crime." It is used to refer to facts that show that a crime has taken place.

Talkin' the Talk

As the days pass without the jury reaching a resolution, the jurors are getting increasingly cranky. Elsie and Elmer are especially vocal in their opposition. Our cantankerous buddies complain to each other as they munch on some cookies during their break. Feel free to listen in.

Elsie: Now we're *deadlocked*. That's a pretty kettle of fish.

Elmer: *Deadlocked* — it sounds just as bad as it is. Our deliberations are at a complete standstill.

Elsie: Did you hear the rumors of a *suspended sentence*? That would mean the court would decide to delay imposing punishment.

Elmer: If we ever reach a decision, the judge could *commute* it, so it would be reduced.

Elsie: Gimme another cookie. I sure need it.

Legal Latin

Many legal terms on leases, wills, deeds, and other official documents are in Latin. Some legal terms even appear on bills of sale. Use the following table to figure out some seemingly obscure legal lingo.

Term	Definition
a fortiori (ay for-shee-*or*-eye)	all the more
a priori (ay pry-*or*-eye)	something based on theory, logic, or fixed rules
ad hoc (ad *hok*)	for this purpose only
ad litem (ad *ly*-tum)	for the purposes of the legal action
ad valorem (ad vah-*lor*-em)	in proportion to value
bona fide (*boh*-nih fyd)	in good faith; real
caveat (*kav*-ee-aht)	let him beware; warning
caveat emptor (*kav*-ee-aht *emp*-tor)	let the buyer beware
certiorari (ser-shee-uh-*rer*-ee)	a writ order from a higher court requesting the record of a case for review
seriatim (sir-ee-*ay*-tim)	one after another

Hailing the Chief: Words about Government

The U.S. legal system has given English some strange but important terms. For example, ever hear the phrase *lame duck*? When applied to cartoons, it likely means that Donald Duck had his wing clipped in a hit-and-run. When applied to politics, however, a *lame duck* is an elected official who, because of term limits, retirement, or defeat, won't be returning to office after the end of his or her present term of office. Presidents serving in their second term are not eligible to run for a third term and are, therefore, "lame duck" Presidents. *Pork-barrel* is another odd political term. It refers to government spending that primarily benefits a specific person, group, or interest.

Knowing the basic terms used in government can help you better understand the news when you read it, hear it, or even see it being made.

Governmental terms with multiple meanings

Table 16-5 shows some political nouns that are especially confusing because they mean one thing when applied to general interests and quite another when applied to government and politics.

Table 16-5		Political Terms with Multiple Meanings
Word	*General Meaning*	*Political Meaning*
cabinet	dresser; bureau; cupboard	group of key presidential advisors
lobby	foyer; entryway	to attempt to persuade government officials to support or oppose particular policies or pieces of legislation
rider	person who rides	a clause added to a piece of legislation that is generally unrelated to the rest of the bill
whip	rod with a lash attached to one end	political party official in a legislative body charged with the duty of encouraging party members to vote with their parties on crucial legislation

Making sense of political terms

The end of the 20th century and the beginning of the 21st century were interesting periods in American politics. Americans experienced impeachment proceedings against a President (Bill Clinton) and a hair-raising presidential election (between Al Gore and George W. Bush) that took weeks to resolve.

During all this coverage, and regardless of which side you were on (and even if you weren't on any side and just wanted the thing to end), you couldn't help but get bombarded with terms and concepts relating to U.S. politics. Even when the action isn't as rollicking, you're still likely to encounter other political terms. After all, who can say no to C-SPAN? Table 16-6 lists some common political terms.

Table 16-6		Words about Politics and Government
Word	*Part of Speech*	*Definition*
bipartisanship (by-*par*-ti-san-ship)	noun	cooperation between two parties (in the U.S., it would be cooperation between Republicans and Democrats)
caucus (*kaw*-kus)	noun	meeting of leaders of a political party to decide on policy, candidates, and so on, prior to a general, open meeting
census (*sen*-sus)	noun	an official, periodic, counting of the population
deficit (*def*-ih-sit)	noun	amount by which spending exceeds funds during a fiscal year
delegate (*del*-eh-get)	noun/verb	a representative who is authorized or sent to speak and act for others / to give authority to a person acting as one's agent
discretionary spending (dis-*kresh*-en-air-ee *spen*-ding)	noun	spending that Congress can raise, lower, cut, or keep even at will
filibuster (*fil*-ih-bus-ter)	noun/verb	making of long speeches, introduction of irrelevant issues, and so on, in order to stop or delay a bill from passing in the Senate / to engage in a filibuster
initiative (ih-*nish*-ih-tiv)	noun	right of legislature to introduce new legislation; right of a group of citizens to introduce a matter for legislation
laissez faire (lez-ay *fair*)	noun	a "hands-off" approach to the economy characterized by minimal governmental interference
patronage (*pay*-treh-nij)	noun	power to appoint to office or grant favors, especially political favors
soft money	noun	political contributions given to a political party but not designated for any particular candidate
subsidy (*sub*-si-dee)	noun	grant of money from one government to another; government grant given to a private enterprise that benefits the public
surplus (*sur*-plus)	noun	amount by which available funds exceed spending

Word	Part of Speech	Definition
trustee (trus-*tee*)	noun	nation that has the authority over a trust territory
veto (*vee*-toh)	noun/verb	order prohibiting some proposed act; to reject a bill (Latin for "I forbid.")

A word that no elected official wants applied to him or her is *impeachment* (im-*peech*-ment). This noun refers to the process by which members of the executive branch or the judiciary are formally charged with crimes that could be grounds for removing them from office. A trial takes place after the impeachment to determine the fate of the impeached individual. Nasty stuff, boys and girls.

Chapter 17

Doctoring Your Words: Medical Terms

In This Chapter

▶ Exploring roots used in medical terminology

▶ Matching doctors and their specialties

▶ Mastering words that describe sickness and health

▶ Using medical lingo when you visit your health care providers

Sometimes it seems as though you go in a big circle when it comes to medicine. But the number of medical treatments — and medical terms — created in the past century show that medicine has come a long way, indeed. To be an informed medical consumer, you *must* know the language of the profession. It's the best way to make sure that you and your loved ones are getting the treatment you need — and deserve. In this chapter, I help you master many terms that pertain to your medical needs.

Talking about Your Body

Most medical terms can be broken down into multiple word parts: a root, prefix, suffix, and perhaps a linking vowel or two. For example, *pericarditis* can be divided into three parts:

1. The prefix, *peri-*, means "surrounding."

2. The root, *card,* means "heart."

3. The suffix, *-itis,* means "inflammation."

Therefore, *pericarditis* is an inflammation of the area surrounding the heart — or an inflammation of the outer layer of the heart, anatomically known as the pericardium.

Medicine and the gods

A number of medical terms and conditions come to English by way of Greek gods and goddesses. For example, in his winged cap and sandals, Hermes (the Roman "Mercury"), son and messenger of the supreme Greek god Zeus, was among the busiest of the gods. When not carrying tidings or leading the dead to Hades, he was the god of roads, fraud and cunning, commerce, and luck. Hermes' serpent-entwined staff is still the emblem of the medical profession. The staff is known as the *caduceus* (kuh-*dew*-see-us). To the ancient Greeks, a snake's ability to shed its skin was a symbol of renewal and fresh strength, and hence, the healing power of medicine.

Narcissists — people who are obsessed with their looks — are named after Narcissus, a handsome youth in Greek mythology. Narcissus refused all offers of love, including that of the nymph Echo. Aphrodite punished him for his indifference by having him fall in love with his own reflection in a forest pool. Unable to possess his reflection, Narcissus pined away and was changed into the flower that now bears his name.

The modern psychological term *narcissism,* meaning immoderate love of oneself, was coined by Austrian psychiatrist and pioneer of psychoanalysis, Sigmund Freud (1856–1939).

Psychology, the science of the mind, gets its name from Psyche, a beautiful girl in Greek mythology who was desired by Eros, the god of love. He forbade her to look at him because he was a god. When she disobeyed him by lighting a lamp in the dark, he abandoned her. Eventually she joined the immortals and was reunited with Eros. She was worshipped as the personification of the human soul.

Medical terms always consist of at least one root, although they may contain more. The root conveys the essential meaning of the word, as in *pericarditis.* The root *card* refers to the heart, so any prefix or suffix added to the root makes it more specific. Therefore, if you add the prefix *brady-* (slow), you get *bradycard,* which means "slow heart." Add the suffix *-ia* (abnormal state) to get *bradycardia,* which means "slow heart rate."

Table 17-1 lists several medical roots and their meanings.

Table 17-1		Body Language		
Root	*Meaning*	*Example*	*Part of Speech*	*Definition*
arteri/arterio	artery	arterial (ar-*teer*-ee-al)	adj.	having to do with blood vessels that carry blood from the heart to the rest of the body

Root	Meaning	Example	Part of Speech	Definition
arthr	joint	arthritis (arth-*ry*-tis)	noun	inflammation of the joints
bronch	throat	bronchitis (bron-*ky*-tis)	noun	inflammation of the bronchial tubes
cardio	heart	cardiovascular (kar-dee-oh-*vas*-kyoo-ler)	adj.	pertaining to the heart and blood vessels
chiro	hand	chiropractor (*ky*-roh-prak-ter)	noun	licensed professional who manipulates joints, especially the spine, to improve nerve function
cranio	skull	cranium (*kray*-nee-um)	noun	bones forming the enclosure of the brain
derm	skin	epidermis (ep-ih-*der*-mis)	noun	outermost layer of skin in vertebrates
digit	finger, toe	digital (*dij*-ih-tel)	adj.	pertaining to a finger or toe
gastr	stomach	gastrointestinal (gas-troh-in-*tes*-teh-nal)	adj.	of the stomach and intestines
hemo/hema	blood	hematology (hee-muh-*tol*-eh-jee)	noun	study of the blood, blood-forming tissues, and blood disease
laryng	larynx; the organ of voice	laryngitis (lar-in-*jy*-tis)	noun	inflammation of the muscles and cartilage in the throat
neur	nerve	neurology (noor-*al*-eh-jee)	noun	study of the structure and diseases of the nervous system
odont	tooth	orthodontist (*or*-theh-*dahn*-tist)	noun	dentist who straightens teeth
ophthalm	eye	ophthalmic (ahp-*thal*-mik)	adj.	pertaining to the eye

(continued)

Table 17-1 (continued)

Root	Meaning	Example	Part of Speech	Definition
oste	bone	osteoporosis (ah-stee-oh-peh-*roh*-sis)	noun	bone disorder characterized by a reduction in bone density
pneum	lung	pneumonia (new-*mohn*-yah)	noun	inflammation or infection of alveoli of the lungs
pulmo	lung	pulmonary (*pul*-meh-nair-ee)	adj.	pertaining to the lungs

Choosing a Specialist

Some medical specialties are easy to tell apart, but many are a little more difficult to distinguish. Professionals who deal with eye care and mental health demonstrate this:

- **Ophthalmologists and optometrists:** *Ophthalmologists* (ahp-thal-*mahl*-ih-jists) are medical doctors who identify and heal diseases of the eye. They can prescribe drugs and perform surgery, as well as examine eyes and sell corrective lenses. *Optometrists* (ahp-*tahm*-ih-trists) are not medical doctors. An optometrist has a degree in eye care and can test vision and prescribe and sell eyeglasses and contact lenses. Optometrists, who may write "O.D." after their name, can detect eye diseases, but they cannot prescribe medicines or perform surgery, as ophthalmologists can.

- **Psychiatrists and psychologists:** A *psychiatrist* (sy-*ky*-ih-trist) is a medical doctor who specializes in treating mental disorders. Patients see these doctors for extended therapy dealing with mental illness or trauma. *Psychologists* (sy-*kol*-ih-jists) are not medical doctors, but they are trained to deal with mental and emotional processes and conditions.

Table 17-2 lists a wide variety of doctors and their areas of expertise. Familiarity with these words can make it easier to know just what kind of medical specialist to call when you need one.

Table 17-2	Medical Specialists
Doctor	*Specialty*
allergist (*al*-er-jist)	doctor who treats sensitivity to pollen, food, pets, and so on (You consult an allergist if you have hay fever or are allergic to peanuts, for example.)
anesthesiologist (an-es-thee-zee-*ahl*-ih-jist)	doctor who reduces pain and renders patients unconscious (An anesthesiologist is present during surgery to administer the anesthetic.)
audiologist (aw-dee-*ahl*-ih-jist)	hearing specialist
epidemiologist (ep-eh-dee-mee-*ahl*-ih-jist)	doctor who specializes in infectious diseases (Epidemiologists usually do research and track outbreaks of major contagious diseases.)
geriatric specialist (jer-ee-*ah*-trik)	doctor who specializes in the medical problems of older people (Geriatric specialists treat a full range of medical conditions in the aged.)
internist (*in*-tern-ist)	doctor who specializes in internal medicine, which includes the diagnosis and treatment of nonsurgical diseases
oncologist (on-*kol*-ih-jist)	doctor who treats cancer
orthopedist (or-theh-*pee*-dist)	doctor who deals with deformities, diseases, and injuries of the bones
otolaryngologist (oh-toh-lar-in-*gahl*-ih-jist)	doctor who treats conditions of the ear, nose, and throat (often called ENT — ear, nose, and throat — specialists, for short)
pathologist (path-*ol*-ih-jist)	doctor who studies body tissue (Doctors send slides of growths and masses to these specialists for analysis.)
periodontist (per-ee-ih-*dahn*-tist)	dentist who treats diseases of the bones and tissue that support the teeth
plastic surgeon (*plas*-tik *sur*-jun)	doctor who repairs or restores injured, deformed, or destroyed parts of the body (Plastic surgeons also perform nose jobs and tummy tucks.)
podiatrist (poh-*dy*-ih-trist)	doctor who treats and prevents foot disorders
radiologist (ray-dee-*ahl*-ih-jist)	doctor who deals with x-rays
surgeon	doctor who specializes in surgery
urologist (yoo-*rahl*-ih-jist)	doctor who deals with problems of the urinary system

Several types of doctors deal with women's reproductive health and the health of their children:

- **Gynecologist** (gy-neh-*kol*-ih-jist): Specializing in female reproductive organs, a gynecologist is the person women see for yearly checkups and Pap smears.

- **Neonatologist** (nee-oh-nay-*tol*-ih-jist): A neonatologist is a doctor who specializes in treating very young infants (usually up to two months old).

- **Obstetrician** (ahb-steh-*trih*-shun): An obstetrician actually delivers babies. All obstetricians are gynecologists, but gynecologists are not obstetricians unless they deliver babies.

- **Pediatrician** (pee-dee-eh-*trih*-shun): This type of doctor treats infants and children.

Talkin' the Talk

Little Billy suspects that he broke his toe trying to kick his brother, Little Willy, out the window. Although the pain serves Little Billy right, he still needs to find a doctor. Follow Little Billy's adventures as he attempts to get medical help while deceiving his Sainted Mother. Little Billy hops to the Emergency Medical Care facility at the end of the block.

Little Billy: Excuse me, I think I broke my toe trying to drop kick my brother to Mars. I need to see an *obstetrician.*

Nurse: Child, an *obstetrician* delivers babies. Since you're hopping on one foot and holding your toe, perhaps you need an *orthopedist.*

Little Billy: Okay, I'll take the orthopedist.

Doctor: First, we'll x-ray your foot. For that, you need a *radiologist.* Then maybe we'll get you a *psychologist* or a *psychiatrist* to see why you were trying to drop kick your brother to Mars.

Little Billy: I don't need a head doctor. I just wanted to see if Little Willy could fly. He can't.

Poor Little Billy — if only he knew the terms for doctors and their specialties. We must send him a copy of this book. He can read it while he's grounded.

Determining What Ails You

Epidemiologist. Otolaryngologist. Oncologist. With all these interesting names, doctors must treat some pretty fancy diseases, right? Table 17-3 lists just a few of the conditions that you may want to consult your medical practitioner about.

Table 17-3	Medical Conditions
Word	*Definition*
alopecia (al-eh-*pee*-shah)	hair loss
anorexia nervosa (an-ah-*rex*-ee-ah ner-*voh*-sah)	eating disorder characterized by an extreme aversion to food and obsession with losing weight
asthma (az-muh)	chronic disorder marked by recurrent attacks of distressed breathing
lymphadenitis (lim-fah-den-*eye*-tis)	inflammation of the lymph nodes
bulimia (byoo-*lee*-mee-ah)	eating disorder characterized by the gorging of large quantities of food followed by self-induced vomiting
cirrhosis (sir-*roh*-sis)	disease in an organ of the body, especially the liver, marked by excessive tissue formation
congenital (kon-*jen*-ih-tal)	condition originating before birth
diabetes mellitus (dy-eh-*bee*-teez muh-*ly*-tus)	disease characterized by an insulin deficiency
insomnia (in-*sahm*-nee-uh)	abnormal inability to sleep
schizophrenia (skit-seh-*free*-nee-ah)	mental disorder characterized by a distortion of reality in addition to delusions and hallucinations

The suffix *-itis* means "inflammation." For example, *dermatitis* is a "skin inflammation," *gastritis* is a "stomach inflammation," *gingivitis* is a "gum inflammation," *meningitis* is the "inflammation of the lining of the brain," and *phlebitis* is the "inflammation of a vein."

Decoding Medical Lingo

If you're watching a TV drama about doctors, it doesn't matter whether you understand exactly what's being said. But when you're sitting in a doctor's office and he or she is talking about your child, your parent, or you, understanding the doctor is a must.

Kind and gentle medical terms

Modalities of therapy. Capillary hemangiomas. Spontaneous involution. Believe it or not, doctors bandy about complicated terms as though the terms actually mean something. And, believe it or not, they do — but only to other doctors. At some point in your life, you may have to deal with a medical specialist — and their language, as the preceding terminology shows, can be very intimidating. So what do you do when you have to talk to a doctor who uses complex medical terms? First, you ask them to put everything in plain English:

Modalities of therapy? It means "treatments."

Capillary hemangiomas? It refers to strawberry birthmarks.

Spontaneous involution? It means "disappearing on its own."

Table 17-4 can help you get a grasp of some basic, benign medical terms that you actually may not mind hearing your doctor say . . . until you get the bill, of course!

Table 17-4		Benign Medical Terms
Word	*Part of Speech*	*Definition*
antibiotic (an-ty-by-*ah*-tik)	noun	bacteria-killing substance
antidote (*an*-teh-doht)	noun	remedy that acts against a poison
antiseptic (an-tih-*sep*-tik)	noun	substance that prevents infection or decay by killing germs
asymptomatic (ay-simp-teh-*ma*-tik)	adj.	without symptoms
benign (bih-*nyn*)	adj.	harmless; not malignant

Word	Part of Speech	Definition
coagulate (koh-*ag*-yoo-layt)	verb	to thicken or clot, or to cause to do so (as in blood)
convalescence (kon-veh-*les*-sens)	noun	gradual recovery; period of recovery
diagnosis (dy-ag-*noh*-sis)	noun	decision or opinion based on an examination
plasma (*plaz*-ma)	noun	fluid portion of the blood
prognosis (prog-*noh*-sis)	noun	prediction of the probable course of a disease and the chances of recovery
remission (ree-*mih*-shun)	noun	disappearance of disease symptoms
suture (*soo*-chur)	verb/noun	joining two edges together by stitching, or similar means; a stitch
therapy (*ther*-ah-pee)	noun	treatment of disease

A *CAT scan* (computed axial tomography) is an x-ray image of an organ — often the brain. CAT scans help doctors view the body by providing a computer reconstruction of multiple images at different planes. An *MRI* (magnetic resonance imaging) is a scan of the body that uses magnetic energy, rather than radiation, to view an organ or body part. An MRI is especially useful for visualizing soft tissue. Still another way of seeing what's going on inside a body is a *sonogram*, which creates a visual image from sound waves. Sonograms are often used to determine the gender of a baby before birth.

Medical terms to come to terms with

It's true that medical jargon all too often makes simple and relatively harmless things sound scary. After all, most lay people would quake at a diagnosis of *acute paronychia* only to feel immense relief to discover that it's an infected hang nail.

Still, many medical terms are a bit more worthy of their scary sounding names. Hearing one of the terms in Table 17-5 may make you sit up a little straighter. If your doctor applies one of the following words to you, you may want to do some additional research on your condition.

Preoccupying manias and frightening phobias

The root *mania* means a "compulsion" or "preoccupation with." *Phobia* means "fear." While doing research for this book, I was astonished to discover the number of fears people have. Although the following lists show the most common fears, I also discovered some very strange revulsions indeed. For example, *arachibutyrophobia* is the fear of peanut butter sticking to the roof of your mouth. I'm not making this up — honest!

Word	Preoccupation with
gamomania (gam-oh-*may*-nee-ah)	marriage
gynecomania (gy-nuh-koh-*may*-nee-ah)	women
kleptomania (klep-toh-*may*-nee-ah)	stealing
megalomania (meg-ah-loh-*may*-nee-ah)	self-greatness
mythomania (mith-ah-*may*-nee-ah)	lies
phagomania (fag-oh-*may*-nee-ah)	eating
plutomania (ploo-toh-*may*-nee-ah)	wealth
pyromania (py-reh-*may*-nee-ah)	fire
xenomania (zen-oh-*may*-nee-ah)	foreigners
zoomania (zoh-*may*-nee-ah)	animals

Word	Fear of
acrophobia (ak-roh-*foh*-bee-ah)	heights
chronophobia (kron-oh-*foh*-bee-ah)	time
demophobia (dem-oh-*foh*-bee-ah)	people
entomophobia (en-toh-moh-*foh*-bee-ah)	insects
ergophobia (er-goh-*foh*-bee-ah)	work
gerontophobia (jer-un-teh-*foh*-bee-ah)	old people
hematophobia (hem-ah-tah-*foh*-bee-ah)	blood
necrophobia (nek-reh-*foh*-bee-ah)	corpses

Word	Fear of
nyctophobia (nik-tah-*foh*-bee-ah)	night
pedophobia (ped-ih-*foh*-bee-ah)	children
theophobia (thee-ih-*foh*-bee-ah)	God
thermophobia (ther-meh-*foh*-bee-ah)	heat

Table 17-5		Medical Terms that Cause Concern
Word	**Part of Speech**	**Definition**
aneurysm (*an*-yoor-iz-em)	noun	sac formed by an enlarged weakened wall in arteries, veins, or the heart
carcinogenic (kar-sin-oh-*jen*-ik)	adj.	cancer-producing
comatose (*koh*-ma-tohs)	adj.	unconscious; in a coma
concussion (kon-*kuhs*-shun)	noun	brain injury due to violent blow or impact
hematoma (hee-meh-*toh*-ma)	noun	collection of blood, usually clotted, outside a blood vessel
incision (in-*siz*-zhun)	noun	cut, as in surgery
lacerated (*las*-er-ay-ted)	adj.	torn, as in a wound
lesion (*lee*-zhun)	noun	injury
melanoma (mel-eh-*noh*-ma)	noun	malignant skin tumor
migraine (*my*-grayn)	noun	intense, recurring headache
toxic (*tox*-ik)	adj.	poisonous
ulcer (*ul*-sur)	noun	open sore, as in the stomach lining

Talkin' the Talk

Marissa is visiting Jordan, who recently delivered her first child through *caesarean section* (surgical operation for delivering a baby through the abdomen) and is still on family leave.

Marissa:	Hey, you! How's the convalescence going? You look good.
Jordan:	I'm so tired. I swear, being up all night with a baby is more exhausting than insomnia.
Marissa:	Have you been back to your OB [short for obstetrician]?
Jordan:	Yes, and she says everything's healing the way it should. The incision looks good, and the sutures are almost all gone.
Marissa:	How's the baby doing?
Jordan:	He's fine. Stanley's worried, though.
Marissa:	About what?
Jordan: (snickering)	He's afraid the baby has congenital alopecia.
Marissa:	Because the baby's bald?!
Jordan:	No, because Stanley is.

Chapter 18

Acquiring Shopping and Eating Language

In This Chapter

▶ Discovering terms for antiques and collectibles

▶ Trying on clothing words

▶ Dining on words

*E*veryone shops. Whether you love to shop or hate to shop, you've proba-bly already spent a good portion of your life in grocery, discount, and department stores. And you're undoubtedly familiar with the vocabulary you need to buy ordinary, everyday things. After all, what are the three most important words to any shopper? You got it — *coupon, credit,* and *sale.* But shopping for special things (like antiques, gourmet items, and clothing), or in special ways (like online), calls for its own vocabulary. The words you need are in this chapter.

I also give you vocabulary for food and food dishes. Why? Because everyone eats, too (everyone that is, except a few models and movie stars). And, despite what your physician may say, the most important food words are not *low-fat, low-calorie,* and *low-cholesterol.*

Cashing In with Collectibles

Many people collect something — stamps, figurines, rocks, fine art, or sausage grinders. You name it, and someone, somewhere, is probably collecting it. You have your serious collectors for whom amassing memorabilia (mem-uh-ruh-*bil*-ee-uh), or collectible items, is a full-time hobby. And you have your dab-blers who collect here and there when something catches their eye.

In addition to these bona fide collectors, you also have people who don't want to collect so much as they want to own a bit of history. For example, in 1998, the baseball Mark McGwire hit for his record-shattering 70th homerun sold for $3 million. In 1999, a *Titanic* boarding pass went for $110,000. (According to auctioneer Alan Gorsuch, it is the only known complete *Titanic* pass. The original owner, 19-year-old Anna Sofia Sjoblom, ended up safe and sound on lifeboat #16, with the pass still pinned to the inside of her coat.)

The world of collectibles and antiques has its own language, and the words in this section can help you understand that language.

Collecting words, or words for collectors

Prices for many desirable objects are rising faster than flood waters during a Midwestern spring. You can get baseball cards for the price of a pack of gum (usually less than a dollar). But let those cards become collector's items, and you may have to pay into the thousands. So, if you want to get the best deals at flea markets, garage sales, swap meets, antique stores, and online auctions, take a peek at the nouns in Table 18-1.

Table 18-1	Words for Collectors
Word	*Definition*
daguerreotype (duh-*ger*-oh-typ)	photograph created by an old-fashioned photographic process on a plate of metal treated with chemicals
ephemera (ee-*fem*-er-ah)	any printed matter that was meant to be used for a short time but has been kept by collectors, such as postcards, posters, and programs
incunabula (in-kyoo-*nab*-yoo-luh)	printed book produced before 1500; work of art or memento from an early era (**Note:** *Incunabula* is actually a Latin word that means "cradle" or "birthplace" — so its English meaning is related to, but different than its Latin meaning.)
illuminated books (ih-*loo*-muh-nayt-id bookz)	books with hand-painted pictures
lithograph (*lith*-ah-graf)	type of print made from a flat plate
pewter (*pyoo*-ter)	alloy containing mostly tin
porcelain (*por*-seh-lin)	high quality, translucent and white ceramic ware (used primarily for dishes and ornaments)
provenance (*prahv*-ah-nens)	record of all former owners of a piece of artwork (having the provenance usually makes an artwork more valuable)

Talkin' the Talk

Flea markets and swap meets are great places to find bargains on collectibles, but the tension can build as collectors jockey for the best buys. Stake your ground and start grabbing as they're gabbing.

Carmen:	Move over and gimme me that record. I'm a *discophile.*
Miranda:	So you collect records. Big deal. I'm a *philatelist* (fih-*lah*-tel-ist), and your records are blocking my stamps.
Manuel:	You're obviously a *philistine* (*fil*-ih-steen), totally lacking in culture. I can't believe they let you people in.
Carmen:	Yeah? So what are you doing here?
Manuel:	I specialize in *breweriania* (*broo*-er-ay-nee-uh). I collect beer cans and barrels.
Miranda:	Oh *that's* really classy. My uncle collects those, too. You know what my aunt calls them? Trash.
Manuel:	How *dare* you, you . . . you . . .
Carmen:	. . . Stamp-stealing harpy?
Marcella: (coming to break up the fight that ensues)	Hey! Hey! Break it up! Who's going to pay for this damage?

Cybershopping: Terms for buying and selling memorabilia online

The familiar advertising slogan "Let your fingers do the walking" has taken on a whole new meaning since the start of the Internet explosion. No matter what you want to buy, you can find it for sale on the Web. This has been a real *boon* (blessing) for collectors, especially those who live in isolated places or collect unusual items. The terms in Table 18-2 all pertain to shopping for online collectibles.

The perfect wedding gift

People in the Middle Ages rarely tolerated their enemies, so poison sales were brisk. Because of the constant danger of poisoning, wealthy people had a servant whose duty was to sample food and drink for the master. If the servant didn't keel over, the master could eat.

In Spain, a special word was created for such precautionary measures — *salvo,* meaning "to save or protect." (The word *salvo* is still used in English to describe a discharge of artillery or armaments.) Because the master's food was served on a separate tray, the tray came to be called a *salvo.* As poisoning passed out of general fashion, the term *salvo* came to be connected with the tray alone, which today we call a *salver.* Remember this the next time you shop for a *salver!*

Table 18-2	Terms for Buying at Online Auctions	
Word	**Part of Speech**	**Definition**
auction (*awk*-shun)	noun/verb	public sale at which property or goods are sold to the highest bidder; to offer for purchase by competitive bidding
bid shilling (bid *shil*-ing)	noun	bidding used by the seller to fraudulently increase the price of the thing for sale
eBay	noun	world's biggest online auction Web site
escrow service (*es*-kroh *sur*-vis)	noun	third-party service used to protect the buyer and seller in an auction
FAQs	noun	abbreviation for "frequently asked questions;" answers to common questions about a Web site
feedback	noun	comments used to describe the reliability of buyers and sellers
proxy bidding (*prox*-see *bid*-ing)	noun	bidding that increases automatically until the buyer's maximum bid is achieved by the auction
reserve price	noun	lowest price a seller is willing to accept for an item
sniper (*sny*-per)	noun	person who bids on an item moments before the auction closes and closes other bidders out

Let the buyer beware

The ancient Latin phrase *caveat emptor* (*kav-ee*-at or *kay*-vee-at *emp*-tor) has been warning buyers to beware for centuries. It's good advice, especially relevant when you're shopping at online auction Web sites: Always check the site first. The largest online auction sites are middlemen that bring together buyer and seller. Therefore, just because an online auction house has a great reputation, it doesn't mean that you won't get burned. Remember that you're not trading with the site; you're trading with the person who uses the site. To protect yourself, consider the following suggestions:

✔ Make sure you clearly understand the bidding procedures before you place a bid.

✔ Resist the temptation to jump right into the action.

✔ Spend some time online at the auction site before you bid.

✔ Factor in the fees. Some auction sites are free, but others charge a percentage of the winning bid. Nail down the site fees (as well as shipping fees) before you buy. You may discover that a "great buy" is a stinker by the time you add on site fees, shipping, and handling.

Make online auctions fun instead of frightening.

Dressing for Success: Terms for Clothes

You can't buy only the things you like, such as collectibles, antiques, and computer equipment. Sometimes you have to bite the bullet and shop for more mundane things, like clothing.

Ordinary words for ordinary clothes

If you're relatively new to English, the names of particular items can be a bit confusing. Not because the words are unfamiliar, but because their use is determined by custom. (Although the rules have gotten much more relaxed over the past few years.) Consider the following examples:

✔ Men wear *trousers* and *pants.* Women wear *slacks.* All of these words refer to long pants not made of denim. Anyone can wear *jeans,* which specifically means "pants made of denim."

Pants and *slacks* can be used interchangeably for men and women nowadays. *Trousers* has largely fallen out of use. These words just illustrate the point that English is ever changing.

✔ Men wear *shirts* (and so do women). Women wear *blouses.* Anyone can wear a *top.*

- Everyone (well, almost everyone, I suppose) wears *underwear,* also called *undergarments.* But if you're in the company of people over a certain age, you use the term *unmentionables* (if you mention it at all).

  Nowadays, men wear *boxers* or *briefs;* women wear *panties.* But in the 1800s, men wore the panties. Yep. You read that right. Panties were drawers for men and were so named because they were the diminutive of pants, a male article of clothing. So what did the women wear under their clothes? Actually, probably nothing. In fact, underwear for women and children wasn't recorded until the early 1900s.

- You can find a whole slew of words for shoes: *mules, pumps, flats, saddle oxfords, wingtips, loafers, sneakers,* and *tennis shoes,* just to name a few. With the exception of sneakers and tennis shoes, you can't use the words interchangeably. Each word represents a particular style of shoe, as the following table shows.

Word	*Definition*
mule	woman's lounging slipper that doesn't cover the heel
pump	woman's shoe with a moderate to high heel
flat	woman's flat-heeled shoe
saddle oxfords	white shoes with a band of black or brown leather across the instep
wingtip	man's dress shoe, characterized by a decorative piece of leather and peaked toward the tongue, with perforations on it
sling back	woman's open-heeled pump that has a strap across the top of the heel
loafer	leather shoe with a broad flat heel (often called a *penny loafer* because they traditionally include a decorative slot in the center that you can insert a penny into)
sneaker	canvas or leather shoe with a rubber sole, used for play and sports (also called a *tennis shoe*)

Searching out named clothing

If you're like me, shopping for clothing is not a chore at all — especially when you get to shop for fun clothing or clothing for special occasions. The following list provides some words for items of clothing that bear the name of a person or place.

Putting on the Ritz

Men, what do you do when you get a wedding invitation that says *tailcoat* required? You rest easy, for now you know that a *tailcoat* (also called *tails, dress coat, cutaway, swallow-tailed coat*) is a coat with the front portion cut away at the waist, and long, tapering tails. The rest of the outfit includes an Oxford gray coat with striped pants, a pearl gray vest, and a tie. A tailcoat is the most formal outfit men can wear. *White tie* calls for a tailcoat accented with a white bow tie.

Next on the formal scale is *formal dress* — a tuxedo or tailcoat. *Black tie*, which used to mean a black bow tie and a tuxedo, comes next. Now, however, men can wear a bow tie and *cummerbund* (*kum*-ur-bund), a thick belt-sash, of any color.

Semiformal dress means that men can wear anything from a dark business suit to a tuxedo. It's also called *evening wear* or *evening clothes*.

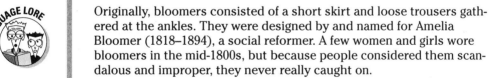

✔ **bikini** (bih-*kee*-nee): An itty-bitty two-piece bathing suit. The name was chosen by designer Louis Reard, in 1946, because he hoped the abbreviated garment would have the same explosive effect as the atomic bomb detonation that had occurred a few days earlier on the tiny reef of Bikini in the Pacific. Reard's hopes proved prophetic, as the bikini shows no signs of declining in popularity.

✔ **bloomers** (*bloom*-erz): Loose, knee-length underpants designed for girls and women.

Originally, bloomers consisted of a short skirt and loose trousers gathered at the ankles. They were designed by and named for Amelia Bloomer (1818–1894), a social reformer. A few women and girls wore bloomers in the mid-1800s, but because people considered them scandalous and improper, they never really caught on.

✔ **knickers** (*nik*-erz): Knee-length loose pants. Named for Diedrich Knickerbocker, the pen name of American writer Washington Irving. These pants were a popular fashion for both men and boys in the early 1800s; later, they became the attire of boys too young for long pants. Today, very few people wear knickers. (In Britain, *knickers* is the slang term for women's panties.)

✔ **cardigan** (*kar*-dih-gan): A sweater that opens down the front. It was named for James Udenell, seventh earl of Cardigan (1797–1868), who wore buttoned woolen sweaters while commanding the Light Brigade of the Cavalry during the Crimean War.

✔ **Levi's** (*lee*-vyz): Blue jeans. Named for Levi Strauss, the man who created denim blue jeans.

✔ **leotard** (*lee*-ah-tard): One-piece garment that covers only the torso. Leotards are also a close-fitting leg covering, or tights. Named for Jules Leotard, a 19th-century French trapeze artist who wore tights.

✔ **tuxedo** (tux-*see*-doh): Black dinner jacket with satin lapels. Named for the place where tobacco millionaire Griswold Lorillard first wore the dinner jacket without tails — the Tuxedo Park resort near Tuxedo Lake, New York.

✔ **wellingtons** (*wel*-ing-tunz): Tall, waterproof boots. Named for Arthur Wellesley, Duke of Wellington (1769-1852), the Iron Duke. We can only suppose that his feet were always dry, even on the battlefield.

Chowing Down: Terms for Food

Do you live to eat or eat to live? I confess: Strolling through a gourmet (goor-*may*) food store always gives me a little thrill of pleasure. Tables 18-3, 18-4, and 18-5 list some delicious treats from around the world that can now be found in American shops and restaurants. Knowing these words can help you order with confidence in gourmet shops and restaurants, and at different social events. Best of all, the words can ensure you some really good eats and tasty treats! (All the words are nouns.)

Beginning at the beginning: Appetizers

An *appetizer* is food or drink served before a meal. Contrary to what your boorish Uncle Max might think, appetizers aren't supposed to fill you up. They're supposed to stimulate your appetite. If you ever want to branch away from the onion rings and fried cheese, Table 18-3 lists a few appetizers you may want to try:

Table 18-3	Appetizers
Word	*Definition*
antipasto (an-tih-*pahs*-toh)	plate of cured meats, olives, marinated vegetables, and cheese
canapé (*kan*-ah-pay)	small open sandwiches served as snacks
caviar (*kav*-ee-ar)	salted fish eggs, usually of sturgeon or salmon
foie gras (fwah-*grah*)	enlarged liver of a force-fed goose or duck, often made into a meat paste
fondue (fon-*doo*)	dipping sauce, often made with cheese or chocolate
gazpacho (gahz-*pah*-choh)	cold vegetable soup, of Spanish origin

Other words for appetizers include the French words *hors d'oeuvre* (or-*durv*) and *aperitif* (uh-per-uh-*teef*). An *hors d'oeuvre* is food you eat before a meal; an *aperitif* is the liquor you drink before a meal. The English synonym of aperitif is *cocktail*.

Enter the entrees

In America, an entrée (*on*-tray) is the main dish. Whether the dish is spaghetti pie, roast duck, or peanut-butter-and-jelly, the entrée is the food you build your meal around.

The United States has always been a multicultural place. Like most multicultural places, you can treat yourself to similar foods prepared in different ways. Take, for example, the idea of a meat- or vegetable-filled pastry. If you know where to look and what to ask for, you can take a culinary trip around the world just by eating meat or veggie pies, as Table 18-4 shows.

Table 18-4	Pastry-Based Entrees from Many Lands
Word	*Definition*
burrito (buh-*reet*-oh)	Mexican dish consisting of a flour tortilla wrapped around a filling of meat, cheese, fried beans, and so on (A *chimichanga* [chim-ee-*chan*-guh] is the same thing deep fried.)
calzone (kal-*zohn*/kal-*zoh*-nay)	Italian turnover filled with a combination of meat, vegetables, and cheese, usually served with marinara sauce.
dim sum (dim sum)	fried or steamed pastry filled with meat or vegetables; Chinese dumplings
empanada (em-peh-*nah*-dah)	small savory pie from Spain and South America, filled with meat, seafood, or vegetables
potpie (pawt-*py*)	American concoction of meat and/or vegetables baked in a crust — sometimes just a top crust
shepherd's pie (*shep*-erdz py)	meat pie baked with a layer of mashed potatoes serving as a top crust

Not quite pastry, a *falafel* (fuh-*lahf*-ul) is a deep-fried chickpea patty that comes to the United States from the Middle East.

Diving into dessert

What's the use of eating while you're out, if you can't splurge on dessert? Sure, you can always go for the ice cream sundae (ice cream covered with syrup, fruit, nuts, and whipped cream) or the carrot cake, but why not try something different? Table 18-5 lists a few desserts that you may have bypassed for fear that your caloric sacrifice would have been for naught.

Table 18-5	Yummy Desserts
Word	*Definition*
biscotti (bih-*skaht*-ee)	dry Italian cookies
cannoli (kah-*noh*-lee)	crisp Italian tube-shaped pastry filled with sweetened cheese
flan (flahn)	Spanish custard covered with a burnt-sugar syrup
gelato (jeh-*laht*-oh)	Italian sherbet
Linzer torte (*lin*-zer tort)	Austrian almond pastry filled with raspberry jam
marzipan (*mahr*-zih-pan)	colored almond paste candy, shaped into figures of animals, fruits, and vegetables
strudel (*strood*-el)	a German pastry made of a very thin sheet of dough covered with apple slices, cherries, cheese, and so on, rolled up, and baked
tart (tart)	a small, fruit- or jam-filled pastry

Chapter 19

Expanding the Language: Recent Additions

* *

In This Chapter

▶ Discovering brand-new words

▶ Understanding how new words are formed

▶ Using freshly coined words when you need them

* *

Anyone can create new words. President Thomas Jefferson created the word *belittle,* which means "to disparage or ridicule." Other words created in the past include such familiar goodies as *groundhog, lightning rod,* and *seaboard* — as well as many, many more. Shakespeare himself created many of the words he used — among them *bedroom, olympian* (characteristic of the gods), *bandit, premeditated* (to think of and plan beforehand), and *madcap* (zany, which, by the way, is another of Shakespeare's words) — and look where it got *him.* There's even a word that means "newly created word" — *neologism.* Creating new words keeps English fresh, vital, and alive — and ever-changing.

As you can imagine, dictionary editors at Webster's New World, for example, aren't particularly happy-go-lucky about the changes that language brings. The influx of new words keeps them scrambling. They are constantly collecting new words, which they feed into a database. The editors then sift through these words to decide which ones merit inclusion in their dictionary.

Fortunately, you don't face the challenge that dictionary editors do. You don't have to verify that a word is actually a word or evaluate whether it merits official acceptance as a bona fide, real-life, no-questions-about-it word. You just have to know what the words mean. That's where this chapter can help.

Sputnik appeared in the dictionary faster than any other word in history, says David Barnhart, editor of the *Barnhart Dictionary.* In 1957, six hours after the Russian satellite was launched, Barnhart's father stopped the presses and added the word to the dictionary.

Combining Old Words to Make New Words

Many new words are created by combining two existing words. This process of blending two words to create a new word is so common that it even has a name: a *portmanteau word*. (Pronounced port-*man*-toh, it's a term for a suitcase, especially the kind that opens up to reveal two halves.)

Unlike a compound word, in which two complete words are combined intact (*eye* and *ball* form the compound *eyeball*), portmanteau words are formed by blending the two words. For example, the English writer Lewis Carroll blended the words "chuckle" and "snort" to create a new word: *chortle.* It means "chuckle, to utter with glee."

Looking at common blended words

English has several common portmanteau words. More recent words created this way are *motel* (from the words *motor* and *hotel), bookmobile* (from *book* and *automobile*), and *ebonics* (from *ebony* and *phonics*), which is a term for Black English vernacular. Table 19-1 lists other more modern portmanteau words. (For information on how compound words are formed and a list of common compound words, head to Chapter 10.)

Table 19-1		Common Portmanteau Words		
Word +	*Word* =	*New Word*	*Part of Speech*	*Definition*
advertise	editorial	advertorial (ad-ver-*tor*-ee-al)	noun	advertisement created to resemble an article or report
fantastic	fabulous	fantabulous (fan-*tab*-yoo-lus)	adj.	marvelously good
female	emcee	femcee (*fem-see*)	noun	mistress of ceremonies
psychotic	drama	psychodrama (sy-koh-*drah*-ma)	noun	therapy in which patients act out situations related to a personal problem or a problem related to a group of patients
spoon	fork	spork	noun	utensil with both bowl and tines

Word	+ Word	= New Word	Part of Speech	Definition
television	evangelist	televangelist (tel-eh-*van*-jeh-list)	noun	person who conducts religious services on television
hocus-pocus	bunkum	hokum (*hoh*-kum)	noun	crude humor or trite comment used to get emotional response from someone
prim	sissy	prissy (*pris*-ee)	adj.	fussy, finicky
smoke	fog	smog (smog)	noun	dark, heavy fog resulting from smoke and chemical fumes
cremated	remains	cremains (kree-*maynz*)	noun	ashes of a cremated body

Speaking a bit of slanguage

Slanguage is a word blended from *slang* and *language*. You can probably guess what it means: slangy speech or writing. Table 19-2 describes some fascinating new words that have been created through this blending or portmanteau process.

Table 19-2		Brand-New Portmanteau Words		
Word	+ Word	= New Word	Part of Speech	Definition
campus	police	campos (*kam*-pohs)	noun	campus police who patrol a university's grounds
funk	kinetics	funkinetics (fun-kih-*net*-ix)	noun	energetic form of step aerobics that mixes exercise and soul music
information	entertainment	infotainment (in-foh-*tayn*-ment)	noun	television programming of news presented in a dramatic or sensational style
meander	Neanderthal	meanderthal (mee-*an*-dur-thawl)	noun	annoying person moving slowly and aimlessly in front of another person who is in a hurry

(continued)

Table 19-2 (continued)

Word +	Word =	New Word	Part of Speech	Definition
sarcasm	catastrophe	sarcastrophe (sar-*kas*-truh-fee)	noun	event occurring when a person attempts and fails to use humorous sarcasm
slacker	academy	slackadem (*slak*-uh-dem)	noun	student majoring in humanities or social sciences due to a perceived lack of work or effort
stalker	paparazzi	stalkerazzi (stawk-er-*raht*-zee)	noun	tabloid photographer who pursues celebrities night and day, dogging their every move

New Words Galore: Neologisms

A neologism is simply a new word. Some words are so new, in fact, that they're still waiting to be included in the dictionary. Here are some examples:

- An *attack fax* (noun) is an aggressive fax.

- A *freeman* (noun) is a unit that measures the amount of plagiarism in a text. The word was coined in the late 1990s during a successful copyright-infringement suit.

- To *mad-dog* (verb) is to stare at someone as though to spark a fight. It seems likely that the shift in meaning from a noun ("a rabid dog") to a verb is the work of Los Angeles gangs.

- *Rug-ranking* (noun) is a policy that assigns secretarial status and pay on the basis of the boss's status rather than on secretarial skills required for the job. The earliest known usage of this word was the late 1990s.

- *Urban yoga* (noun) is a new form of exercise, also known as "power yoga." This coinage is similar to words like *urban guerrilla, urban homesteading, urban renewal,* and *urban sprawl.*

The neologisms in Table 19-3 are hot out of the headlines. They're so hot that they're *sizzlin'.* Or perhaps I can say that because these words have plenty of *mojo* (energy, power), they'll soon become part of your *wordrobe* (your vocabulary). If I'm wrong, these could be the *losingest* words ever, an adjective that means "lagging behind the rest." It's all up to you. Use 'em . . . or the language will lose 'em.

Talkin' the Talk

Amy and Kate are sharing tales of their nieces and nephews' amazing and adorable antics. Listen in as they invent a whole new word.

Amy:	I love my nieces and nephews, but they can sure be a handful.
Kate:	I know what you mean, and saying 'nieces and nephews' all the time sure is a mouthful.
Amy:	Does some other language have a single word for both?
Kate:	Not that I know of. I don't think Spanish or French does.
Amy:	Well, we can make up our own word.
Kate:	Great idea! I've always called my brothers and sisters my 'siblings' to avoid having to say 'brothers and sisters,' and because *sibling* is such a fun word. Can we do something with 'sibling'?
Amy:	Well, nieces and nephews are the offspring of your siblings, but "offlings" doesn't sound very nice.
Kate:	How about "sibsprings"?
Amy:	I like it! It's cute, it's collective.
Kate:	And it's not gender-specific.
Amy:	All right then. If the two of us start using it, even just in our over-sized families, it'll spread around the country in no time.

Table 19-3		Useful Neologisms
Neologism	*Part of Speech*	*Definition*
Analysisparalysis (uh-*nal*-eh-sis-pah-*ral*-eh-sis)	noun	decision-making ability paralyzed by overexposure to overwhelming amounts of information
anime (an-ih-*may*)	noun	Japanese animation, used chiefly in cartoons and video games
audiophile (*aw*-dee-oh-fyl)	noun	one who loves and collects audio equipment and media
domo (*doh*-moh)	noun	downwardly mobile professional
ego-surfing (*ee*-goh *sur*-fing)	verb	searching the Internet for listings of your own name
fashionista (fash-un-*ee*-sta)	noun	devotee of the cutting edge of haute couture (also called *fashion victim*)
futique (few-*teek*)	adj.	stylishly futuristic
mall rats	noun	teenagers who hang around shopping malls
pluggers	noun	people who lead very bland, boring lives but nonetheless always try hard and cope with their situations
pooper-scooper (*poop*-er *scoop*-er)	noun	scooping device on a long pole used to collect pet waste
post-rock	noun	experimental music that combines rock, jazz, avant-garde, classical, and so on
starter marriage	noun	first marriage
supertwin	noun	any child born of a multiple birth of three or more

If you come upon a new word in your reading or daily conversation with friends and colleagues, I strongly recommend that you put off making it part of your lexicon immediately. Don't use it until you've seen or heard it in several other situations. Not only will this help you know how to use the word properly, but it will also help you verify that it is indeed a new word and not something the writer or speaker misunderstood and mangled!

A few of my favorites

I love lists! Here are some of my favorite neologisms. Warning: My list is highly idiosyncratic.

Neologism	Part of Speech	Definition
back story	noun	events of a character's life prior to the start of a fictional story (The word is also used to mean "background.")
benedict	noun	newly married man who has long been a bachelor (The term was formed from the Shakespearean character of the same name in *Much Ado About Nothing*.)
garden burger	noun	vegetarian patty
fro-yo	noun	frozen yogurt
noah's arking	verb	wearing pants that are far too short (This replaces earlier nouns for such pants: "high-waters" and "floods.")
potus, vpotus, flotus	noun	acronyms for the President of the United States, Vice President, and First Lady
shopgrifting	verb	to "rent" an article for free by buying it and then returning it within 30 days for a full refund
speel	noun	informal speech (also *spiel*)
videophile	noun	person who loves and collects videos

Does the concept of coining words make you uncomfortable? Not to worry! Just take an existing word and adapt it to your needs. The catch: Enough people have to agree with you to make the word into a meaningful sound bite. (Notice how I sneaked in newly coined "sound bite"?)

New business words

Alvin Toffler's neologism *future shock* (an inability to cope with the rapid changes of modern society) has stood the test of time to become an accepted part of our lexicon. Table 19-4 shows 10 new words coined from the business realm. Will they last? Who can tell! Check back in a few years to see which ones have entered English . . . and which ones have gotten *downsized, rightsized, excessed,* or just plain *axed!*

Table 19-4		Newly Created Business Words
Neologism	**Part of Speech**	**Definition**
c.l.m. (career limiting move)	noun	used among workers to describe ill-advised activity (For example, trashing your boss while he or she is within earshot is a serious c.l.m.)
funged	adjective	epithet for when someone bungles an important task (Coined in honor of criminalist Dennis Fung, the term was first used by journalists covering the O.J. Simpson civil trial.)
irritainment (ir-ih-*tayn*-ment)	noun	entertainment and media spectacles that are annoying but compelling
narfistic (nahr-*fiss*-tik)	noun	idea or concept that works fine when you think about it, but is very difficult to express to someone else
prairie-dogging	verb	when someone yells or drops something loudly in an office with cubicles, and people's heads pop up over the walls to see what's going on
retail elephant	noun	a business that dominates or monopolizes an area
rubber-chicken circuit	noun	fund-raising dinners attended by politicians and business people (The term refers to the standard unappetizing, rubbery chicken served at such dinners.)
telescam (*tel*-eh-skam)	noun	illegal money-making schemes conducted by phony telemarketers
zine/'zine (zeen)	noun	periodical printed by amateurs; a non-formal, homemade magazine (A *fanzine* is a publication produced by or for devotees of a specific subject, celebrity, or musical group.)

Talkin' the Talk

Jeffrey Gen X is moaning to his mother about his tough life on the job. They're chatting on a cell phone, so you can switch on your baby monitor and pick up their frequency. It makes listening in on private conversations a breeze.

Jeffrey:	Maaaaa, I hate my McJob!
Ma:	Jeffrey, what's with this *McJob* nonsense? So you have a low-paying, low-prestige job in a service-related field and little opportunity for advancement. I told you to study harder in college.
Jeffrey:	Maaaaa, I'm just a *microserf*.
Ma:	So you're an oppressed worker in the new economy. I was an oppressed worker in the old economy. Work isn't supposed to be fun. If it was, they'd call it play.
Jeffrey:	Maaaaa, I sit in my cube in the *cube farm* and get *dilberted* all day long.
Ma:	So you sit in an office filled with cubicles. You think you're exploited and oppressed by your boss. You always were a *stress puppy* — you thrive on being stressed-out and whiny.

Compiling new computer terms

The advent of computers brought with it a whole new vocabulary. Some words were just out-and-out new. *Input* and *output,* for example, were coined to describe what you put into a computer and what you got out of it. Other words took on completely different meanings: Bug, mouse, desktop, and monitor are just a few of many ordinary words that have specialized meanings in the computer age.

The following sections give you the words you need to know if you're on the Internet or using e-mail. For a list of general computer terms, head to Chapter 14.

Table 19-5 lists several neologisms. They all relate to computers, which is not surprising, since the computer industry accounts for many of the new words formed every day. Some of these words, like *modem* and *snail mail*, have already passed into common usage. Others, such as *globoboss* and *troll*, are cutting-edge usage.

Table 19-5		Newly Created Internet Terms
Neologism	*Part of Speech*	*Definition*
cometised (*kahm*-ih-tyzd)	adj.	used to describe Netscape Navigator when it freezes or jams (The word is based on the observation of a "shooting star" or comet that appears on the Netscape button in the upper right corner of a Netscape browser.)
cybersquatter (*sy*-ber-skwaht-er)	noun	person who registers well-known company names as Internet addresses in order to sell them for a profit to the companies involved
globoboss (*gloh*-boh-boss)	noun	cosmopolitan executive who can perform well across the globe
home page	noun	the first document you come to at a Web site
hotlists	noun	lists of frequently used Web sites and URLs (addresses)
hypertext (*hy*-per-text)	noun	information on a Web page that is linked together and can be accessed by clicking on a highlighted word or symbol
links	noun	hypertext connections between Web pages (also called *hotlinks* and *hyperlinks*)
macintrash (*mak*-in-trash)	noun	derogatory reference to Macintosh computers
microphobes (*my*-kroh-fohbz)	noun	opponents of Microsoft
mouse potato	noun	person who sits for hours in front of a computer, the online version of the "couch potato"
netizen (*net*-ih-zun)	noun	someone who is comfortable navigating the Internet (The word was formed from "Internet" and "citizen.")

Neologism	Part of Speech	Definition
search engine	noun	program that helps users find information in text-oriented databases
snail mail	noun	standard system of mail delivery in which letters, documents, and packages are physically transported from one location to another, in contrast to e-mail
troll	noun	person who sends messages to a newsgroup (sort of like an e-mail bulletin board with thousands of different categories) to spark emotions and cause controversy
Web browser	noun	software that allows a user to access Web sites
Webmaster	noun	person in charge of administrating a Web site
Web rage	noun	anger provoked by slow Internet access (The word grew out of another neologism, "road rage.")

An *Internet Service Provider* is a company that provides access to the Internet. The best-known ISPs are the commercial online services such as America Online, CompuServe, Prodigy, and MSN. However, many national companies such as AT&T and MCI, as well as regional and local companies, provide Internet access. ISPs usually charge a monthly subscription rate and offer unlimited access to e-mail and the Internet.

Amazing e-mail facts

Did you know that . . .

- ✔ About one-third of all Americans send messages over the Internet. (*1999 World Almanac*)

- ✔ E-mail is currently the most popular and widely used resource on the Internet. (*1999 World Almanac*)

- ✔ Americans now send 2.2 billion e-mail messages a day, compared with 292 million pieces of first-class mail. (*U.S. News and World Report*)

- ✔ Traffic on the Internet doubles every 100 days. (UUNET, Internet backbone)

- ✔ Around the world, about 100 million people use the Internet. (*1999 World Almanac*)

- ✔ It is estimated that by the year 2005, about a billion people will be connected to the Internet. (*1999 World Almanac*)

E-mailing expressions

E-mail is formed by blending the words "electronic" and "mail" (see the earlier section "Combining Old Words to Make New Words" for more on blended words). Basically, if you have a personal computer and an e-mail program, you can send messages electronically to other people with a computer and an e-mail application.

Table 19-6 shows a half-dozen new words that have been formed as a result of e-mail. They may or may not make the cut to commonly accepted usage. Your use of these words will determine which ones eventually make it into the "major-league" dictionaries.

Table 19-6	Newly Created E-Mail Words	
Neologism	*Part of Speech*	*Definition*
cyberspace (*sy*-ber-spays)	noun	online environment
emoticon	noun	symbol, usually found in e-mail messages, that uses punctuation marks to resemble a human expression (The word is a blend of "emotion" and "icon.")
flame	noun/verb	personal attack within a newsgroup or e-mail message; the act of criticizing or insulting someone in an e-mail or newsgroup message
hackers	noun	people who use their computer knowledge for illicit purposes, such as gaining access to computer systems without permission, and tampering with programs and data
netiquette (*net*-ih-kit)	noun	etiquette rules of cyberspace (The word was formed from "Internet" and "etiquette.")
spam	noun/verb	multiple posts of the same message to the same or different Usenet newsgroups or to an e-mail account (The messages are usually advertisements.); the act of sending multiple copies of a useless message to a newsgroup or e-mail account
spider	noun	person or computer program that searches the Web for new links and adds them to search engines

E-breviations

In a quest to make e-mail even quicker, a whole crop of *e-breviations* — some already common *IRL* (in real life)— have sprung up. They have come to represent an entirely new online vocabulary. The following list contains the most common e-breviations. If you use them, be prepared to translate for your less-savvy correspondents.

afaik	as far as I know	fwiw	for what it's worth
afk	away from keyboard	gg	got to go
atm	at the moment	hhoj	Ha! Ha! Only joking!
b	be	imho	in my humble opinion
b4	before	imnsho	in my not-so-humble opinion
bbiaf	be back in a few minutes	j/k	just kidding
bcnu	be seeing you	lol	laugh out loud
brb	be right back	oic	Oh, I see!
btw	by the way	r	are
c	see	rotfl	rolling on the floor laughing
cul	see you later	ttyl	talk to you later
f2f	face to face	ttfn	ta-ta for now
focl	falling off the chair laughing	u	you
fwd	forwarded	y	why

Chapter 20

Exploring Words from Real and Mythical People and Places

In This Chapter

▶ Exploring *eponyms,* words from people's names

▶ Discovering *toponyms,* words from place names

▶ Acquiring words from animals and myths

The names of people are sometimes remembered when the people themselves are long forgotten. The same is true of places. This immortality comes through language. In this chapter, I share some fascinating and useful *eponyms* (words from people's names) and *toponyms* (words from place names). Enjoy words from animals and mythology, as well.

What's in a Name? A Lot When It's an Eponym!

A surprising number of useful words come from (or are assumed to come from) people's names. Such words are called *eponyms* (*ehp*-uh-nimz). Common eponyms include the following:

✔ **Caesarean** (suh-*zehr*-ee-an): This adjective describes a method of delivering a baby by operating through the abdomen. It's believed that Julius Caesar, the Roman Emperor and military strategist, was born this way, and hence, the procedure got his name.

✔ **Herculean** (hur-*kyoo*-lee-an): This adjective means "having extraordinary strength" or "being tremendously difficult." The term is derived from the mythical hero Hercules, who possessed prodigious strength and successfully completed the Twelve Labors, feats so difficult that they were nearly impossible.

✔ **malapropism** (*mal*-ah-prop-izm): A malapropism is a humorous misuse of a word or phrase. This word comes from Mrs. Malaprop, a fictional character in the comedy *The Rivals* (1775), by Richard B. Sheridan.

As you can see from these examples, eponyms can come from real names, as well as from fictional and mythological characters. The section "Words from Myths and Literature," later in this chapter, is devoted solely to these words.

A rose by any other name: Eponyms with positive connotations

Just as most words have various connotations (an implied or suggested meaning), so do eponyms. Some, like *begonia* — a flower named after Michel Begon, the French governor of Santo Domingo who died in 1710 — are positive or at least neutral. Others, like chauvinism (*shoh*-vin-iz-um), which means "intense, fanatical nationalism" and is named after Nicolas Chauvin, a French soldier devoted to Napoleon, are negative.

Table 20-1 lists several eponyms that originated from the names of historical figures. Each word in this list has a positive connotation. The next section lists eponyms with negative connotations.

Good or bad? Depends when you ask

Over time, the connotation of words sometimes changes. Take, for example, the word *dunce*, which comes from the name of the dazzlingly brilliant 13th-century theologian John Duns Scotus, whose once widely accepted ideas were strongly ridiculed by the 16th-century humanists. Today the term *dunce* has come to refer to someone who is not intelligent.

Another word whose connotation has changed over time is *silhouette* (sil-oh-wet). This word comes from Etienne de Silhouette, the finance minister of France under Louis the Fifteenth.

The Seven Years' War and Louis XV's costly mistress Madame de Pompadour left France poised on the brink of bankruptcy. By 1759, hoping for a miracle, Madame de Pompadour convinced Louis XV to replace the finance minister with a friend of hers, Etienne de Silhouette. The new appointee immediately instituted a series of stringent, and somewhat ridiculous, reforms. The nobility poked fun at many of the petty regulations, especially the rules calling for coats without folds and snuffboxes made of wood. At the same time, the ancient art of tracing the outlines of shadows went through a revival. Because these shadow profiles replaced many costly paintings, they sneeringly came to be called *à la Silhouette*. Silhouette lost his job within the year, but his name has become permanently attached to this art form.

Table 20-1		Eponyms with Positive Connotations	
Eponym	*Part of Speech*	*Definition*	*Origin*
algorithm (*al*-gor-rith-um)	noun	set of rules for solving a mathematical problem	Arabic mathematician al-Khowarizmi
braille (bray-el)	noun	writing system for the visually-impaired	inventor Louis Braille
derby (*der*-bee)	noun	type of hat	Edward Stanley, 12th earl of Derby
epicure (*ep*-ih-kyoor)	noun	expert in food	the Greek philosopher Epicurus
mackintosh (*mah*-kin-tosh)	noun	raincoat	Charles Mackintosh, its British inventor
macadam (mah-*kad*-um)	noun	type of road surface	John McAdam, its inventor
marcel (mar-*sel*)	verb	permanent waves set in hair	a 19th-century hairdresser of the same name
maverick (*mav*-er-ik)	noun	unbranded calf; independent person	Samuel Maverick, a Texas pioneer who didn't brand his cattle
mentor (*men*-tor)	noun	trusted teacher or guide	Mentor, Odysseus's friend and his son Telemachus's teacher
mesmerize (*mez*-mer-ize)	verb	hypnotize	inventor, Franz Mesmer
pasteurize (*pass*-chur-rize)	verb	method of sterilizing milk	inventor, Louis Pasteur
thespian (*thes*-pee-in)	noun	term for an actor or actress	the Greek poet Thespis
wisteria (wis-*teer*-ee-uh)	noun	flowering plant	Casper Wistar, an American doctor
zeppelin (*zep*-uh-lin)	noun	rigid, lighter-than-air flying ship	inventor, Count von Zeppelin
zinnia (*zin*-ee-uh)	noun	brightly colored flower	Johann Gottfried Zinn, a German physician and botanist

Name change, anyone? — Eponyms with negative overtones

Quite a few unfortunate souls gave their names to words whose connotations are negative. Take, for example, the word *gerrymander* (*jehr*-ee-man-dur). This verb means "to rig election districts" and is named for Elbridge Gerry, an early 19th-century statesman and governor of Massachusetts whose party benefited from such rigged districts.

Gerrymander is also a portmanteau word (see Chapter 19 to find out about this type of word). It's a combination of Gerry's last name and the word *salamander* — the area that had been created by manipulating the election district to favor Gerry's party looked like a salamander in the editorial cartoons of the time.

Following are a few eponyms that originated from the names of historical figures. This time, however, each word has a negative connotation:

- **bowdlerize** (*boud*-lur-ize); verb: To bowdlerize means "to edit a literary text in a priggish manner," and it's named after Thomas Bowdler. Bowdler took it upon himself to edit what he considered the "dirty parts" out of Shakespeare's play. His aim was to remove all "words and expressions . . . which cannot with propriety be read aloud to the family." He published his new edition of Shakespeare's works in 1818. Both he and his book were widely and publicly ridiculed. The word *bowdlerize* still carries negative overtones. Poor fellow; all he was trying to do was protect the public from the naughty bits in the Bard!

- **guillotine** (*gil*-uh-teen); noun: The inventor of the original close shave, Dr. Joseph Guillotin suggested a beheading machine as a way of ensuring humane executions. In 1791, after Dr. Guillotin had retired from his position in France's National Assembly, Antoine Louis actually designed the machine. The guillotine was first used in 1792 to behead a thief; soon after, it was used to execute aristocrats during the phase of the French Revolution called "The Terror."

- **Machiavellian** (mak-ee-uh-*vel*-ee-un); adj.: This word comes from the name of the Florentine political philosopher Niccolo Machiavelli (1469–1527) whose masterpiece, *The Prince,* argued that a ruler can justifiably use any means, however unethical, unscrupulous, or illegal, to secure and maintain a strong central government. Machiavelli's name has since become a synonym for cunning and deception in the pursuit of power.

- **martinet** (mart-in-*et*); noun: In 1660, Colonel Jean Martinet created a military drill to whip France's soldiers into shape. Martinet proved to be such an exacting taskmaster that his name came to be applied to any officer intent on maintaining military discipline. In English, a *martinet* is a strict disciplinarian, especially a military one.

✔ **boycott** (*boy*-kot); verb: Boycott means "to join together in protest, as in a strike." The term dates back to 1880, when, in an attempt to break the death grip of Ireland's absentee landlords, the great Irish leader Charles Stewart Parnell advocated that anyone who took over land from which a tenant had been evicted for nonpayment of rent should be punished "by isolating him from his kind as if he was a leper of old." Parnell's suggestion was applied soon after on the estate of the Earl of Erne. Unable to pay their rents, the tenants tried to secure a lower rate. When the estate manager, Charles Boycott, refused, the tenants not only refused to pay, but they also intercepted Boycott's mail and humiliated him in public. This treatment came to be called a *boycott.*

Good book, good words: Eponyms from the Bible

Sixty miles south of Baghdad, in modern Iraq, you can see the crumbling mounds of the ancient city of Babylon. According to Genesis 11:7, the ancient people of Babel tried to build a tower to heaven. They were punished for their presumption by losing the power of intelligent speech. The result provides English with the word *babble,* which means "a meaningless confusion of words and sounds."

Several other biblical stories, characters, and places lend their names to English words. Table 20-2 lists a few of them. Use the words to make your language both precise and colorful.

Table 20-2		Eponyms from the Bible	
Eponym	*Part of Speech*	*Meaning*	*Allusion*
Armageddon (ahr-mah-*ged*-en)	noun	conflict characterized by wholesale slaughter and mass destruction, the outcome of which is usually so conclusive that renewed conflict is impossible	place where the final battle between good and evil will be fought on Judgment Day (Revelation 16:14–16)

(continued)

Table 20-2 *(continued)*

Eponym	Part of Speech	Meaning	Allusion
Jezebel (*jez*-eh-bel)	noun	wicked woman	after the wife of King Ahab, who installed prophets of Baal and ordered the slaughter of the prophets of God: under her sway, Ahab, who had the capacity to be brave, chivalrous, and conscientious, became one of the most wicked kings of Israel (1 Kings 16:31)
Jonah (*joh*-nuh)	noun	person thought to bring bad luck	from the Old Testament prophet who, by disobeying God's command, caused a storm to endanger the ship he was traveling in: he was cast overboard from his ship and swallowed by a fish (Jonah 1:4)
Judas (*joo*-dus)	noun	traitor	from Judas Iscariot, the disciple who betrayed Christ
maudlin (*mawd*-lin)	adj.	tearfully emotional	from the practice of representing Mary Magdalene in paintings as a penitent sinner with eyes swollen and red, weeping
Philistine (*fil*-ih-steen)	noun	person more interested in material than intellectual values; uncultured person	from the tribe of people who challenged the Hebrews for dominance of Palestine: they were eventually conquered by the Hebrew King David
simony (*sy*-muh-nee)	noun	act of buying or selling of ecclesiastical preferments	Simon the sorcerer (Simon Magus), who offered to pay the Apostle Peter to teach him the wondrous cures he had seen him perform: Simon did not understand that Peter's feats were miracles rather than magic (Acts 8:9–24)

When you use an eponym from the Bible — or from mythology or literature, for that matter — you're making an *allusion* (uh-*loo*-zhun), a figurative or symbolic reference. As such, these types of words pack more punch than ordinary words because the connotations are so powerful and deep. For example, the actual definition of a Judas is "a traitor." The connotation, however, implies a betrayer of the worst kind — one who betrays from a position of trust and often under the pretense of friendship.

We now use the term *jeroboam* (jer-ah-*boh*-em) to refer to "a wine bottle having a capacity of about three liters." Historically, Jeroboam was the first king of the Biblical kingdom of Israel, described in I Kings 11:28 as "a mighty man of valor," who, three verses later, "made Israel to sin." Some historians trace today's use of *jeroboam* to the king, reasoning that because an oversized bottle of wine can cause sin, it too is a jeroboam!

Words from Places: Toponyms

Just as words come from people's names, so they come from place names. Such words are called *toponyms.* The word *canary,* for example, is a toponym. It comes from the Canary Islands, about 60 miles off the northwest coast of Africa. In addition to identifying a little songbird, the word *canary* is a slang term for a police informer. (*Canary yellow* is a bright yellow color.)

Toponyms are words formed from place names. The word *toponym* comes from the Greek words *topos* (place) and *onoma* (name).

Placing place names

Table 20-3 lists ten toponyms, words that come from the names of places. As you can see from the list, even though the origin of the word is a place, many of these are not locations at all. For example, a *chautauqua* is a type of meeting named after the place where these meetings first occurred. Furthermore, the few that are places (like Shangri-La) aren't real places; instead they represent mythical or symbolic locations.

Table 20-3		Place Names that Became Words	
Toponym	*Part of Speech*	*Definition*	*Source*
bedlam (*bed*-lem)	noun	any scene or place of wild uproar	the popular name for the Hospital of St. Mary of Bethlehem, an insane asylum in London
chautauqua (shah-*taw*-kwah)	noun	educational institutions that usually traveled, held meetings in tents, and offered entertainment in the form of lectures and dramatic performances	Chautauqua, New York, where this meeting style was founded in the 1800s
Mecca (*mek*-ah)	noun	any place considered the center of activity or the goal of its followers	place (Mecca, Saudi Arabia) where Muhammad was born and the holy city of the Islamic religion
Shangri-La (*shan*-grih-*lah*)	noun	imaginary place where life is nearly perfect	fictional setting of English novelist James Hilton's utopian novel, *Lost Horizon* (1933)
shanghai (*shang*-hy)	verb	to bring in by deceit and force	from Shanghai, China, where, in earlier days, unwilling sailors were often drugged and kidnapped to work on ships that made this city a port of call
Utopia (yoo-*toh*-pee-ah)	noun	a perfect place	from the name of Sir Thomas More's 1516 work in which he describes an imaginary country having ideal laws and social conditions (*Utopia* literally means "nowhere.")
Valhalla (val-*hal*-uh)	noun	place for people deserving special honor or glorification	in Norse mythology, Valhalla is the hall in which Odin, the chief god, receives the souls of the men who died in battle
Waterloo (*wot*-ur-loo)	noun	disastrous defeat	from Napoleon's crushing defeat at Waterloo, Belgium, in 1815

Toponym	Part of Speech	Definition	Source
Xanadu (*zan*-uh-doo)	noun	any place of great beauty and luxury	region in China that Samuel Taylor Coleridge refers to in his poem "Kubla Khan" (1797): in the poem, Xanadu is the location of Kubla Khan's pleasure garden

In the late 1400s, a small band of Osmanli Turks established the Ottoman Empire. The court became famous for its luxurious furnishings. Among the most noteworthy pieces of furniture was a small seat, which the French dubbed an *ottomane.* The English translated this to *ottoman,* the term we use today to describe a small stool or footrest.

Sparkling toponyms about gems and colors

What put the *rhine* in *rhinestone*? The Rhine River, of course! Originally, *rhinestones* were a variety of rock crystal found in this part of Germany. By 1800, the term *rhinestone* had come to be applied to the imitation diamonds being produced. Today, the term has also come to be applied to anything artificial or excessively showy, such as the title character in the movie *Rhinestone Cowboy.*

As you can tell from this brief story, toponyms also provide us with useful words for precious gems and colors. As you read the words in Table 20-4, link them to their histories to make them easier to remember.

Table 20-4		Toponyms for Jewels and Gems	
Toponym	**Part of Speech**	**Definition**	**Source**
agate (*ag*-it)	noun	semiprecious quartz	Achates River in Sicily
alabaster (*al*-ah-bas-ter)	noun/adj.	usually white and translucent gypsum; being white	Alabstron, Egypt
chartreuse (shar-*trooz*)	adj.	yellowish-green	color of the liqueur made by the Carthusian monks in Grenoble, France

(continued)

Table 20-4 *(continued)*

Toponym	Part of Speech	Definition	Source
copper (*kop*-er)	noun	reddish metal	island of Cyprus
magenta (mah-*jen*-tah)	adj.	deep reddish-purple	Magenta, Italy, where a bloody battle was fought
turquoise (*tur*-koiz)	noun/adj.	blue-green colored gemstone; bluish green	country of Turkey (*Turquoise* is a French adjective meaning "Turkish.")

Talking with Words from Animals

It's exceedingly rare to hear animals describe people, but not at all strange to hear people describe animals. Further, we often use words drawn from the names of animals to talk about our fellow citizens. Images adapted from the animal kingdom, such as *fishy* and *chameleon,* add precision and flavor to speech and writing. Table 20-5 lists other such words.

Table 20-5   **Words from Animals**

Toponym	Part of Speech	Definition
bull-headed	adj.	headstrong, stubborn
eely	adj.	slick or slippery
hangdog	adj.	silent, sullen, dejected
horse-faced	adj.	having a long, ugly face
lamblike	adj.	meek, gentle
peacock	noun	boastful or strutting person

A lot of descriptive words are formed by taking a root and adding *-ine.* When you do this with animal names, you get words like *bisontine* (like a bison), *giraffine* (like a giraffe), *elephantine* (like an elephant), *falconine* (like a falcon), and so on. The tricky part is that, a lot of times, the root is the Latin or Greek word for the animal, which may not bear much resemblance to the English word. So here's a list to help you figure out whether you should be insulted or grateful when someone says you're *leonine.*

aquiline (eagle)

bovine (ox/cow)

canine (dog)

cervine (deer)

corvine (crow)

delphine (dolphin)

equine or chevaline (horse)

feline (cat)

hippotigrine (zebra)

leonine (lion)

leporine (hare)

lupine (wolf)

lutrine (otter)

ovine (sheep)

picine (woodpecker)

piscine (fish)

porcine (pig)

ranine (frog)

tigrine (tiger)

ursine (bear)

vespine (wasp)

vulpine (fox)

Talkin' the Talk

Mildred the Moose and Hector the Hippo are happily settled in the local zoo. To pass the time of day, Mildred and Hector chew the fat about some humans of their acquaintance. Here's what they have to say. Feel free to eavesdrop, but don't listen too closely because you're not allowed to bother the critters.

Mildred: The new zookeeper certainly is pig-headed.

Hector: Indeed. He's stubborn and won't listen to anyone's advice, even mine.

Mildred: And such a tiny man, too. Remember our last keeper? He was some *behemoth.*

Hector: Ah, such an enormous man. He was a giant among men. It's a shame that he was such a *chameleon.*

Mildred: True, true. He was always changing his mind. Pay one-price admission one day, separate tickets the next.

Hector: These humans are odd creatures, no? I never cease to be amazed by them.

Animal packs

In addition to gaining animal words to describe people, English has also adopted special words to describe groups of animals. The following table shows some of the most useful of these words. They'll come in handy when you have to identify animals.

Word	Animal Group		
brood	chickens	gam	whales
covey	game birds	murder	crows
drove	sheep or oxen	pride	lions
flock	birds	shoal; school	fish
gaggle	geese	stable	horses
		swarm	bees

Words from Myths and Literature

English has taken many words from literature and myths, just as we've raided the names of people and places. For example, *hygiene* (the science of establishing good health) was named for Hygeia, the Greek goddess of health. The goddess of health is often shown feeding a snake, a symbol of good health.

Following are other terms that, like hygiene, come from mythology or literature:

- ✔ **Adonis** (ah-*don*-is): This noun for a handsome man comes from a Greek myth. In the story, Adonis is the studmuffin adored by Aphrodite and Persephone.

- ✔ **gargantuan** (gar-*gan*-choo-an): This adjective means "enormous" and comes from Gargantua, the huge hero of Francois Rabelais' satire *Gargantua (1535)*.

- ✔ **laconic** (lah-*kon*-ik): This adjective means "concise, terse, or undemonstrative." The word comes from Laconia, a region in ancient Greece associated with the Spartans, a people who were known for their bravery, self-discipline, and stoicism in the face of difficulties or suffering.

- ✔ **hymen** (*hy*-men): This noun refers to the membrane that closes the opening to the vagina. It gets its name from the Greek god of marriage, Hymen.

- ✔ **iris** (*eye*-ris): This noun refers to the colored part of the eye. It takes its name from Iris, the Greek goddess of the rainbow.

✔ **Procrustean** (proh-*krus*-tee-an): According to the Greek myth, Procrustes was a bandit who made his living waylaying unsuspecting travelers. He tied everyone who fell into his trap to an iron bed. If they were longer than the bed, he trimmed their legs to make their bodies fit; if they were a tad too short, he stretched their bodies. As a result, the adjective *procrustean* has come to mean "tending to produce conformity through violent or arbitrary means."

✔ **mercurial** (mur-*kyoor*-ee-al): This adjective means "unpredictable and volatile," as well as "quick-witted and sprightly" — all characteristics of Mercury, a Roman god of commerce, as well as a messenger for the other gods.

✔ **tantalize** (*tan*-tah-lyz): This verb means "to torment by offering some-thing and then withholding it." The words comes from the legend of Tantalus, a king who offended the gods by (in addition to other lesser crimes) murdering his own son and serving him as a meal to the gods. As punishment, Tantalus was send to Hades where he was condemned to stand chin-deep in water with a bough of grapes hanging just over-head. Whenever he stooped to drink or reached overhead to eat, the water and food receded.

✔ **vulcanize** (*vul*-kah-nyz): This verb means "to strengthen rubber by heat-ing it" and comes from Vulcan, the Roman god of fire and the forge. He was also a metalworker for the gods.

Table 20-6 lists other words from mythology.

Table 20-6		Words from Myths	
Word	*Part of Speech*	*Definition*	*Source*
amazon (*am*-ah-zon)	noun	strong or masculine woman	mythical tribe of women warriors
ambrosia (am-*broh*-zah)	noun	especially delicious or fragrant food or drink	food that conferred immor-tality to the Greek and Roman gods
cornucopia (kor-neh-*koh*-pee-ah)	noun	horn of plenty; any un-ending supply	horn of plenty containing an endless supply of food and drink given by Zeus to Amalthea
harpy (*har*-pee)	noun	greedy person; mean-tempered, shrewish woman	repulsive mythological birds, with the heads of maidens and long claws, who could snatch away the souls of the living

(continued)

Table 20-6 (continued)

Word	Part of Speech	Definition	Source
martial (*mar*-shul)	adj.	warlike	Mars, the Roman god of war
saturnine (*sat*-er-nyn)	adj.	gloomy	Titan Saturn, father to Jupiter and several other Roman gods, who, when defeated by his children, was confined with the other Titans in Tartarus
Venus (*vee*-nus)	noun	beautiful woman	Roman goddess of beauty, Venus

Some words from myths and literature begin with capital letters, while others are lowercase. This example shows a term being misused in writing:

Correct: What an Adonis! Is he seeing anyone?

Incorrect: What an adonis! Is he seeing anyone?

Unfortunately, there's no rule for capitalization when it comes to toponyms from myths and legends; it's just something you have to memorize. Be on the lookout for capital and lowercase letters when you encounter words from myths and stories.

Part V
The Part of Tens

The 5th Wave   By Rich Tennant

In this part . . .

These short and sweet chapters give you ten (or more) tidbits that can help you fine-tune your vocabulary. I warn you about types of language to avoid, explain the differences between some of the more confusing word pairs, and clarify some of the trickier bits of English for nonnative speakers.

Consider these chapters your dessert after an all-you-can-ingest word buffet and enjoy!

Chapter 21

Don't Go There: Language to Avoid

In This Chapter

▶ Staying away from phrases and terms that offend

▶ Being aware of expressions that obscure meaning

▶ Avoiding common pitfalls

*E*veryone occasionally says the wrong thing at the wrong time. It happens when your memory fails you, your tongue gets ahead of you, or your mind wanders. That's life. You plow ahead and hope that your audience knows what you meant to say and forgives you for your blunder.

Some mistakes, however, are a lot harder to forgive and forget. Not only do these types of errors color your message, but they also affect how your audience perceives *you*. In this chapter, I give you 10 of the most common — and dangerous — vocabulary pitfalls.

Ageist Vocabulary

Ageism is discrimination against people of a particular age — it's generally aimed at the elderly. Such language includes words and phrases that stereotype older folks as "doddering fools" or "past their prime." Be sure to use vocabulary that doesn't discriminate. For example, use *senior citizen* instead of *old person, geezer,* or *gramps.*

Bureaucratic Language

Bureaucratic language is stuffy and overblown. It uses far more words than are necessary. If you want to say *covered,* for example, don't say *covered over very completely.* Similarly, don't say *revert back to its original state and form* when you simply mean to say *revert.*

Bureaucratic language is the reason the U.S. Tax Code is about a million pages long and nearly impossible to read. It's also the mark of an immature writer — ask any English teacher who has had to evaluate the requisite five-page theme comprised of nearly three pages of fluff.

Doublespeak

Doublespeak is evasive vocabulary that confuses meaning. A classic example of doublespeak is the word *disinformation,* which simply means "information that is known to be false." In other words, "a lie." Using *revenue enhancement* to describe taxes is another example of doublespeak.

Unlike bureaucratic language or euphemistic language (which obscures meaning simply by being unclear), doublespeak is *intended* to obscure the truth. People who use doublespeak are generally trying to hide something.

Empty Words

Some words have been used so much that they've lost their meaning. For example, *fantastic, awesome, nice, terrific, wonderful, fabulous,* and *marvelous* have all lost their potency by being thrown about as catchall expressions meaning "good." If the latest flick at the cineplex doesn't actually inspire dread, veneration, or wonder, it isn't an awesome movie. And if Mom's potato salad isn't bizarre or otherworldly, it isn't fantastic, no matter how tasty it may be.

The point here isn't to completely give up using these words, but to use them more carefully.

Inflated Language

Inflated language makes the ordinary seem extraordinary. Folks who use inflated language are generally trying to impress people. For example, with inflated language, a mechanic becomes an *automotive internist,* and an elevator becomes a *vertical transportation system.*

Why use a cumbersome phrase or a long word when a simple phrase or short word will do just as well, and usually better? You may think you sound smarter, but your audience is likely to see you as pretentious or silly.

Euphemisms

People use euphemisms to make a point in such a way that they don't actually have to say words that they're uncomfortable saying or conjure images that may be just a bit too graphic. You hear euphemisms most often when people are talking about things that are potentially embarrassing or uncomfortable, such as nudity, body parts, sex, and bathroom activities.

A euphemism for nudity, for example, is *in the altogether,* and a euphemism for sex is *making love.* To get an idea of the many (often creative) euphemisms parents come up with for bodily functions and body parts, just hang around a baby changing station for a while.

It's okay to use euphemisms to spare someone's feelings, especially in delicate situations, as when you say, "I'm sorry your sister passed away" rather than "I am sorry your sister died." But avoid euphemisms that obscure meaning.

Language Biased Against the Handicapped

Always focus on people, not their conditions. Avoid terms such as *abnormal, afflicted,* and *struck down.* Instead, use *atypical.*

If you describe a person by only one characteristic, you are essentially cataloging that person by the one trait that *you* see as his or her defining characteristic.

Jargon

Suppose that you ask your sister what she did over the weekend and she answers: "We went to the FTX site, grounded our gear, located our grid coordinate, and prepared for a frontal assault." Chances are — unless you're in the army, too — that you may wonder what the heck she just said. What she said, in plain English, is this: "We went to the campground, dropped our backpacks, looked at a map to see where we were, and got ready for an attack by the enemy."

The reason that you probably didn't understand what she said is because she used *jargon,* the specialized vocabulary that a particular group uses. Jargon is a great verbal shortcut — if you're talking to people in the same group or profession. If you're not, you may as well be speaking in another language.

Always consider your purpose and audience before deciding whether a word is jargon in the context of your material. For example, a baseball fan would easily understand the terms *shutout* and *homer,* but these terms are jargon to a nonfan like me.

Racist Vocabulary

First, never use any racial epithet. Second, unless race is germane to the conversation (and it usually isn't), don't identify people by their ethnicity. Third, if you must identify a person's ethnic background, make sure you use the preferred term. Here's the catch: The preferred term changes. For example, a hundred years ago, black people were known as *colored.* Fifty years later, the term *Negro* was used. Today, the preferred terms are *African American* and *black* (which you will also see capitalized: *Black*). Similarly, the term *Asian* is preferred over *Oriental. Inuit* is preferred over *Eskimo. Latino* and *Latina* are the preferred designations for Mexican Americans, Puerto Ricans, Dominicans, and other people with Central American and Latin American backgrounds.

Finally, some terms and phrases have racist histories. For example, *jew down* and *gyp* allude to the offensive stereotypes of Jewish people as money-grubbers, and Gypsies as thieves. Don't use these types of terms.

Sexist Language

Sexist language assigns qualities to people on the basis of gender. It reflects prejudiced attitudes and stereotypical thinking about the sex roles and traits of both men and women. Sexist language causes legal problems and perpetuates sexist attitudes. Here are some general guidelines:

- ✔ Avoid using *he* to refer to both men and women.

- ✔ Avoid using *man* to refer to men and women.

- ✔ Avoid expressions that exclude one sex. For example: Use *humanity* or *humankind* rather than *mankind.* Use the *average person* rather than the *common man.*

- ✔ Just as you don't refer to a grown man as a boy, don't refer to a grown woman as a girl.

It sometimes takes a bit of time and effort to avoid sexist language, but this woman, at least, appreciates your efforts.

Chapter 22

Distinctions Worth Making

- -

In This Chapter

▶ Discerning the differences in sound-alike words

▶ Seeing differences in similarly spelled words

▶ Distinguishing between words with similar meanings

▶ Figuring out how many words to use

- -

Certain word combinations plague both native and nonnative English speakers. These word combinations are problematic because they either sound alike or have similar meanings but are used in different ways. This chapter lists a few of the most problematic, starting with *imply* and *infer*.

As a speaker or writer, you *imply;* as a listener or reader, you *infer. Imply* means "to hint or suggest," which is an action only someone speaking or writing can accomplish. And to draw a conclusion from information presented, which is what you do if you infer something, is an action you can take only as a listener or reader — someone else has to give you information. So, if I *imply* that a strong vocabulary can help you get ahead in your job and in your life, you can *infer* that I think words are valuable.

Sound-Alike Words

English boasts a number of word pairs that sound very similar but have dissimilar meanings. I list a few of these couples in this section.

Accept and except

Accept is a verb meaning "to receive" or "to approve." Example: They had trouble *accepting* a genius in their family.

Except is a verb meaning "to leave out" or "to exclude." Example: When Marta said that she'd eat anything, she always *excepted* squid.

Conscious and conscience

Conscious is an adjective meaning "able to feel and think" or "in a normal waking state." Example: Sheila appeared alert and *conscious* during her minor medical procedure.

The noun *conscience* means "a knowledge or sense of right and wrong." Example: I can sleep with a clean *conscience,* knowing that I did the right thing.

Sit and set

Sit and *set* have the same relationship that *lie* and *lay* have: You actively *lie* yourself down, and you *lay* an object down. To *sit* is to put yourself in a sitting position; to *set* is to place an object somewhere — whether it's in a sitting position or not. Example: *Set* your bag down and come *sit* next to me.

What a Difference a Letter (Or Two) Makes

It's no surprise that one little letter can have a major impact. The word pairs in this section can be tricky because they look alike and sometimes sound similar, but their meanings are very different.

Affect and effect

As a verb, *affect* (uh-*fekt*) means "to influence" or "to produce an effect." Example: The news affected her mood. *Affect* (*af*-ekt) is also used as a noun meaning "feeling" or "emotion." This meaning is commonly used in psychology. Example: The medicine caused the patient to experience a lack of *affect.*

As a noun, *effect* means "result," "consequences," or "outcome." Example: The news had a profound effect on her mood. As a verb, *effect* means "to make happen" or "to bring about." Example: She *effected* important changes during her term as president. Both are pronounced "eh-*fekt.*"

Allusion and illusion

Allusion (ah-*loo*-shun) is a noun meaning "an indirect reference" or "the act of hinting at something." Example: Luis's *allusion* to the movie was very witty.

Illusion (ih-*loo*-shun) is a noun meaning "misleading image" or "misunderstanding." Example: The heat shimmering on the road created an optical *illusion* of water.

Beside and besides

The preposition *beside* means "at or by the side of," "alongside," or "near." Example: I found my car keys right *beside* my wallet. You can also use *beside* to compare things. Example: *Beside* your wonderful garden, my poor plants seem scrawny.

The adverb *besides* means "in addition to." Examples: *Besides* Tony, who wants pineapple on the pizza? And, do you want onions *besides*?

Describe and prescribe

Describe is a verb meaning "to tell what something is like." Example: Describe the coat for us.

Prescribe is a verb meaning "to lay down as a rule or course to be followed." Example: The doctor *prescribes* medicine for people to take.

Farther and further

These two comparative forms of *far* are basically interchangeable as both adjectives and adverbs meaning "more distant or remote." Example: Jupiter is *farther* from the sun than Venus, and Neptune is *further* from the sun than either of them.

However, *further* is more commonly used to mean "to a greater extent" and "in addition" or "additional." Example: I need to run *further* tests before I can be certain.

Immigrate and emigrate

The distinction here is one of geographic direction. *Emigrate* is a verb meaning "to move away from one's country." Example: She *emigrated* from Colombia to America. *Immigrate* is a verb meaning "to move to another country." Example: It can be hard to adjust when you *immigrate* to a new homeland.

Lose and loose

Lose is a verb meaning "to mislay," "to get rid of," or "to bring to ruin." Example: Don't *lose* that article telling you how to *lose* weight.

Adding an *o* gives you the adjective *loose,* which has many meanings, most of which are closely related to "free" or "not restrained." Example: I put my *loose* change in a bowl and use it for mad money when I want to cut *loose.*

Raise and rise

As a verb, *raise* means "to lift or elevate." Example: I was too shy to *raise* my hand. It also means "to increase in degree," as in *raising* your voice. As a noun, a *raise* is a pay increase, and getting one would sure raise my spirits.

Rise is an active verb whose more commonly used meanings are "to stand" or "to get up after sleeping." Example: Every morning I *rise* in anticipation of a wonderful day. When you talk about the sunrise, you use *rise* as a noun.

Uninterested and disinterested

Uninterested is an adjective meaning "indifferent" or "not interested." Example: Eva seemed uninterested in the information.

Disinterested is also an adjective that can mean indifferent, but it is more often used to mean "not influenced by personal motives" or "unbiased." Example: Anna is perfect as a mediator because she's completely *disinterested.*

Words with Similar Meanings

English is full of synonyms that mean almost, but not quite the same thing. Tradition, more than any other factor, often dictates how you use certain words. I include a few of the more confusing pairs in this section.

Aggravate and annoy

Aggravate (*ag*-ruh-vayt) is a verb meaning "to make worse." Example: Too much exercise can aggravate back problems. Sometimes people use *aggravate* colloquially (or informally) to mean "to irritate" or "to annoy." That usage is fine among friends, but don't use *aggravate* when you mean "to irritate" in formal speech and writing. Instead, use *annoy,* which means "to bother or harass."

Amount and number

Use *amount* when you're describing something that *can't* be counted. Use *number* when you're describing something that *can* be counted. For example, you can count sand castles, but not grains of sand. So, the former is measured in number (a large *number* of sand castles), and the latter is measured by *amount* (a great *amount* of sand).

Note for nonnative speakers: A singular noun follows *amount*. Example: You have to measure the right *amount of flour* if you want your cake to turn out. A plural noun follows *number*. Example: The *number of stars* in the sky is astronomical.

Authentic and genuine

Authentic and *genuine* are synonyms. That is, they mean sort of the same thing. However, if something is *genuine*, it's the real thing; if something is *authentic,* it tells the truth about its subject. The diamond your honey gave you this weekend is *genuine,* and your story of the proposal is *authentic.*

Between and among

Use *between* when you talk about only two people or things, as in "Franchesca was forced to choose between the brie and the cheddar." Use *among* when you discuss three or more people or things, as in "It is difficult to choose *among* all the delicious cheeses."

Healthful and healthy

Healthful is an adjective meaning "wholesome." *Healthy* is also an adjective, meaning "having good health" or "resulting from good health." Example: Adopting a *healthful* lifestyle helps make you a *healthy* person.

Oral and verbal

There is a very fine distinction between *oral* and *verbal*. *Oral* means "spoken" and "by mouth" or "having to do with the mouth." Examples of the former meaning: We will now hear the *oral* arguments. The *oral* exam will commence. Example of the latter meaning: Her teeth were so crowded that she needed *oral* surgery. *Verbal* can also mean "spoken." Example: We made a *verbal* agreement. However, it more precisely means "having to do with words" — even written words.

Precede and proceed

Both of these words are verbs. *Precede* means "to come before in time, place, order, rank, or importance." Example: I insist that you *precede* me through the door. "Age before beauty," I always say.

Proceed means "to go on, especially after an interruption." Example: Ignore the blare of the car alarm and just *proceed.*

Unique and unusual

Unique items are one of a kind and may be rare or *unusual,* but not all unusual items are unique. Example: His *unusual* sense of humor is part of what makes my Uncle Michael so *unique.*

One Word or Two?

Compound words, which I cover in Chapter 10, are two (or more) words put together to form one new word. Compound words are very handy, but sometimes figuring out when two words should be one word and when they should stay as two is confusing. One thing that may help is realizing that a compound word is generally a different part of speech than its two-word twin. I give you a few examples in the following list.

- **Everyday and every day:** *Everyday* is an adjective meaning "suitable for ordinary days" or "common." As two words, *every day* is an adverb indicating frequency. Example: Laura wears her *everyday* clothes *every day* — even on Sundays.

- **Everyone and every one:** *Everyone* is a pronoun, and *every* is an adjective that modifies *one.* If you can substitute *everybody,* use *everyone.* Example: It will be excellent if we can get *everyone* to eat *every one* of these eggs.

- **Into and in to:** *Into* and *in* are both prepositions, and both indicate about the same thing, though *into* generally indicates movement. So, as with so much of English, you have to pay attention to context.

    You separate *in* and *to* when *in* acts as a preposition and *to* is part of the verb. Example: You're just giving *in to* temptation if you go *into* the ice cream shop. (*On to* and *onto* have similar distinctions.)

Paying attention to the purpose the words serve in a sentence can help you decide whether they should be one word or two.

Chapter 23

Ten Techniques for Nonnative Speakers

In This Chapter

▶ Discovering common English quirks

▶ Using tips for proper English

*W*hen English is your second language, you face the special challenges of learning characteristics of English that native-born English speakers take for granted. This chapter lists 10 ways to help you deal with some of the most baffling problems that English vocabulary can pose for second-language speakers.

A or An

Often, it's the little words rather than the big ones that trip up second-language speakers. *A* and *an* are small but crucial words. Although both *a* and *an* refer to a single person, place, or thing, *a* is used before words that begin with a consonant sound, and *an* is used before words that begin with a vowel sound. Remember that the vowels are *a, e, i, o, u,* and sometimes *y;* the consonants are all the other letters in the alphabet. However, it's not enough to identify vowels and consonants, because their sounds can be created by other letters, as the following shows:

Words with Consonant Sounds	*Words with Vowel Sounds*
a history lesson ("h" sound)	an honest man (no "h" sound)
a one-horse town ("w" sound)	an only child ("o" sound)

Check out the "The and A" section farther along in this chapter for more tips on how to use these articles.

Degree of Comparison

Adjectives and adverbs, words used to describe things or actions, have different forms to show *degree* (or amount) of comparison:

- ✔ The *positive* degree is the basic form of the word without any comparison being made.

- ✔ The *comparative* degree is used to compare two things. Often, these words end in *-er* or use *more,* but never both.

- ✔ The *superlative* degree is used to compare three or more things. Often, these words end in *-est* or use *most,* but never both.

To see how degrees of comparison work, consider these examples: *fast* (positive), *faster* (comparative), *fastest* (superlative); *quickly* (positive), *more quickly* (comparative), and *most quickly* (superlative).

Some adjectives and adverbs do not follow this pattern. The following words pose special challenges for nonnative speakers:

Positive	*Comparative*	*Superlative*
good	better (not gooder)	best (not goodest)
bad	worse (not badder)	worst (not baddest)
late	later	last or latest

You may also find the following usage tips helpful:

- ✔ Use *more* and *most* to form the comparative and superlative degrees of all modifiers with three or more syllables. For example: *more popular, most popular; more affectionate, most affectionate.*

- ✔ Don't use *more* and *-er* together to form a comparative (*more happier,* for example). Similarly, don't use *most* and *-est* together to form a superlative (*most nicest,* for example).

- ✔ Use the comparative degree when you're comparing two things. For example: Of the two sisters, the younger one is smarter. Use the superlative degree when you're comparing three or more things. For example: Of the seven children, he is the youngest.

Count Nouns

Some English nouns name items that can be counted, such as *newspaper, street,* and *idea.* You say "I have a newspaper" or "I have a hundred newspapers from the past year," for example. In other words, count nouns are plural or singular nouns that indicate number.

Noncount Nouns

English has other nouns that identify objects thought of as a whole. Therefore, these objects are not divided into separate parts that can be counted. Examples include *sand, blood, beef, salt, sugar, rice,* and *traffic*. These words are never preceded by *a* or *an* and are never plural. Table 23-1 shows more noncount nouns.

Table 23-1	Noncount Nouns
Category	*Examples*
abstract ideas	advice, equality, health, fun, information, news, peace, respect
food	bread, butter, macaroni (mak-uh-*roh*-nee), pork
gases	air, helium (*hee*-lee-um), smog, steam
languages	Arabic, Chinese, Japanese, Spanish
liquids	coffee, gasoline, water
pastimes	chess, homework, housework, soccer
things	aluminum (uh-*loo*-muh-num), clothing, furniture, jewelry, luggage, mail, money, vocabulary

Nouns That Can Be Both Count and Noncount

Some nouns can be count nouns or noncount nouns, depending on the way you use them in your speech and writing. If the noun names something that can be taken individually or as a whole, it can be used both ways. For example:

Count: You have *a* hair on your shoulder.

Noncount: Luis has black hair.

Nouns as Adjectives

Adjectives are words that describe a noun or pronoun. It sounds easy enough, but in English, words are used as different parts of speech all the time. Sometimes a word is a noun and sometimes it's an adjective. Consider this sentence for example:

> We went to the train station to ride a train.

Train is used twice in this sentence, once as an adjective and once as a noun. How do you tell the difference? You use the context: The first *train* is an adjective because it describes the kind of station. The second *train* in the sentence is a noun.

Adjectives do not have plural forms. When you use an adjective with a plural noun, don't make the adjective plural. For example: the *train* (not *trains*) stations and the *yellow* (not *yellows*) flowers.

Plurals

Many nouns form regular plurals (more than one) by adding *-s* or *-es,* as in *coat/coats* or *fox/foxes.* Nouns whose singular ends in *-y* normally form their plural by changing *-y* to *-ies:* one *city,* two *cities.* Other nouns have irregular plurals, which means that making the plural isn't as simple as adding an *-s* or *-es.* Examples of irregular plurals include *foot/feet* and *leaf/leaves.*

If you're not sure whether a noun is plural, look it up in a dictionary. If no plural is given for a singular noun, add *s* to form the plural.

Proper Nouns

Proper nouns name specific people, places, or things. For example: *Emperor Hirohito, Mexico,* and *Jell-O.* Always capitalize proper nouns.

Most proper nouns do not require an article (a, an, the). For example, We visited (not *the*) Mt. Fuji. There are several exceptions, however, such as *the Rocky Mountains, the Great Lakes,* and *the Amazon.*

The and A

The and *a* or *an* precede nouns: the house, a horse, an appendectomy (ap-un-*dek*-tuh-mee), for example. Which one you use depends on whether you're referring to a specific thing or a nonspecific thing.

✔ Use *the* to refer to a specific person, place, or thing. For example: *the* soccer game (one specific game), *the* sari (one specific sari), and *the* tortilla (one specific tortilla).

✔ Use *a* or *an* to indicate any item in a group. For example: *a* kitten (not any particular kitten) or *an* apple (any apple).

Note the subtle difference in meaning in the following sentences:

The house burned down. (A statement about a particular house)

A house burned down. (A general statement that doesn't specify which house)

Who, Which, That

Who refers only to people: He is the man *who* delivered the package.

Which refers only to things: *Which* package was it?

That refers to both people and things: *That* package came from my aunt *that* lives on the West Coast.

Some people (my editor among them) strongly object to referring to humans as "that." So you may want to change your referent according to your audience.

Index

• Symbols and Numerics •

: (colon), as context clue, 40
— (dash), 40, 155
- (hyphen). *See* hyphens

• A •

a/an, 315, 319
a lot/allot, 135
a- prefix, 82, 88–89, 91
abbreviation, 79
abbreviations, 62. *See also* e-breviations
abducted, 68
-able/-ible suffix, 102–103, 116, 200
ablution, 103
abridged dictionary, 22
abstract, 216
-ac suffix, 107
accept, 307
accrue, 232
acquisition, 232
acquit, 238
acr/acro root, 70
acronyms, 62
acrophobia, 70, 260
The ACT For Dummies, 199
act- prefix, 98
action, 98
acute paronychia, 259
ad- prefix, 82
adamant, 106
address, 48, 91
adjectives. *See also* part of speech
  definition of, 1–2, 117
  nouns as, 318
  suffixes indicating, 13, 116
adjudicator, 242

admiral, 193
adobe, 176
adolescent, 111
Adonis, 298
adverbs. *See also* part of speech
  definition of, 1–2, 117
  suffixes indicating, 116
advertorial, 274
advisory, 108
affect, 308
affirmation, 103
affixes, 101. *See also* prefixes; suffixes
ag- prefix, 98
agate, 295
-age suffix, 103, 114
ageist vocabulary, 303
aggravate, 311
aggravated assault, 241
aid/aide, 135
AIDS, 62
ail/ale, 135
ain't, 59
air/heir/err, 135
aithros root, 82
-al suffix, 13, 107
alabaster, 295
albacore, 191
albino, 178
alchemy, 192
alcove, 192
algebra, 192
algorithm, 289
alias, 238
all, compound words beginning with, 154
allergist, 255
allowed/aloud, 136
allusion, 309
alopecia, 257
already/all ready, 136

alt root, 79
altar/alter, 136
altimeter, 70, 224
altitude, 79
altogether/all together, 136
amazon, 299
amber, 191
ambrosia, 299
The American Heritage Dictionary of the English Language, 22
Amish, 32
among, 312
amoral, 88
amount, 311
amount. *See* number
an- prefix, 66
-an suffix, 108
analogy test questions, 202, 203–207
analysisparalysis, 278
-ance suffix, 102, 114
anchovy, 175
anesthesiologist, 255
aneurysm, 261
Anglo-Saxon prefixes, 99–100
animals, words derived from, 296–298
anime, 278
anitpasto, 270
ann root, 78
annihilate, 78
anniversary, 78
annoy, 311
annual, 78
annual report, 216
annuity, 230
anorexia, 112
anorexia nervosa, 257
-ant suffix, 106
ante- prefix, 88, 98

antecedent, 98

anteroom, 98

anthro root, 71

anthropology, 71

anthropomorphism, 71

anti- prefix, 88–89

antibiotic, 258

anticlimactic, 89

antidote, 258

antihero, 89

antipathy, 88

antiseptic, 258

antonyms
  on standardized tests,
      201–202, 204, 207–208
  in a thesaurus, 24, 25, 26
  using, 126–127

aperitif, 270

aplomb, 35

apocryphal, 35

appeal, 238, 240

appearance, 244

application, 222

approach, 91

aquarium, 111

aqueduc 78

-ar suffix, 110

arabesque, 108, 171

Arabic, 190–194

arachibutyrophobia, 260

arassein root, 96

arbitrator, 110

arbor root, 12, 13, 66

arborist, 13, 110

arc/ark, 136

arcade, 180

arch- prefix, 94

arch root, 70

archaeology, 94

archbishop, 70, 94

arche-/archae- prefix, 94

archetype, 94

archy root, 65, 66, 72, 75

argument, 102

-arium suffix, 111

Armageddon, 291

arraign, 244

arrivederci, 178

arroyo, 176

arteri/arterio root, 252

arterial, 252

arteriosclerosis, 39

arthr root, 253

arthritis, 253

-ary suffix, 110, 111

ascent/assent, 136

aspic, 170

assault, 241

assets, 228

aster/astro root, 71

asterisk, 71

asthma, 257

astro- prefix, 94

astronaut, 71, 94

asymptomatic, 258

-ate suffix, 12, 103, 115

ATM, 228

attack fax, 276

attorney, 238

atypical, 88

auction, 266

audience
  choosing words for, 51–52,
      53–54, 123–124
  levels of vocabulary for,
      10–11. *See also*
      everyday English;
      formal diction;
      standard English

audio root, 66

audiologist, 255

audiophile, 278

audit, 234

authentic, 311

auto- prefix, 94, 95

automobile, 95

autonomy, 72, 75, 94

avalanche, 168

avenue, 173

aviary, 111

avocado, 175

awry, 34

• *B* •

babushka, 195

back story, 279

backup, 223

bacteria, 40

bail, 238

bail/bale, 136

bailiff, 244

bailiwick, 35

balance, 228

balcony, 180

balloon loan, 232

bandit, 182

bandolier/bandoleer, 182

bankrupt, 228

banquet, 34

banshee, 188

baptism, 112

barometer, 224

barrack, 182

bas-relief, 171

base/bass, 137

battalion, 182

battery, 241

bear market, 231

beau/bow, 137

béchamel, 170

bedlam, 294

Bedouin, 193

begonia, 288

being, state of, suffixes
      indicating, 105–107

beliefs, Greek roots for,
      74–76

benchmark, 224

bene- prefix, 98

benedict, 279

benediction, 98

benefactor, 98

beneficial, 98

beneficiary, 230

benign, 258

berth/birth, 137

beside(s), 309

between, 312

bi- prefix, 93

biannual, 78

bias crime, 241

bible, eponyms from,
      291–293

biblio root, 71

bibliophile, 71

bicycle, 93

bid shilling, 266
biennial, 78
bikini, 268
bio- prefix, 95
bio root, 73
biography, 95
biology, 73
bipartisanship, 248
birth/berth, 137
biscotti, 271
blanket, 225
blarney, 187
blasé, 35
bleeding, 225
blended words. *See*
    compound words;
    portmanteau words
blind copy, 217
blintz, 189
bloomers, 268
boar/bore, 137
board/bored, 138
body, vocabulary for,
    251–254
Boggle, 19
boilerplate, 217
Bolshevik, 195
bon mot, 168
bond, 230
books. *See* publications
born/borne, 138
borscht, 189
bouillon, 170
boulevard, 173
bounce, 228
bourgeois, 168
bow/beau, 137
bowdlerize, 290
boycott, 291
bradycardia, 252
braille, 289
brake/break, 138
bravado, 178
bravo, 179
bread/bred, 138
break/brake, 138
brev root, 79
Brewer's Dictionary of
    Phrase and Fable, 61

bridal/bridle, 138
British English, 185
brogue, 187
bronch root, 253
bronchitis, 253
bronco, 176
brotherhood, 106
budget, 228
bulimia, 257
bull-headed, 296
bull market, 231
bullets, 217
buoy, 32
bureau, 173
bureaucratic language,
    303–304
burglary, 241
burlesque, 172
burnout, 218
burrito, 271
business casual, 218
business vocabulary
  for business documents,
    216–217
  for engineering, 223–224
  importance of knowing,
    215–216
  jargon, 221–225, 305–306
  neologisms, 279–285
  for publishing and
    printing, 225
  for software and
    hardware, 221–223,
    281–285
  for the workplace,
    217–221
businesses, tests required
    by, 11. *See also*
    standardized tests
buy/by, 138

• C •

caballero, 176
cabaret, 172
cabinet, 247
cache, 35
caduceus, 252
Caesarean, 287

cal root, 69
calzone, 271
camphor, 191
campos, 275
canapé, 270
cannoli, 271
cantata, 179
canteen, 173
canyon, 176
capillary hemangiomas, 258
capit root, 66
capital, 231
capital/Capitol, 138
capital offense, 241
capitalization and
    pronunciation, 30–31
carafe, 191
carat/carrot, 139
carcinogenic, 261
card root, 251
cardiac, 107
cardigan, 269
cardio root, 253
cardiograph, 75
cardiovascular, 253
cards, index, 17–18, 28
carn root, 66, 69
casserole, 170
CAT scan, 259
cata- prefix, 91, 96
catacomb, 91, 180
catalogue, 91
cataract, 96
catharsis, 106
caucus, 248
cavalier, 182
caviar, 270
CD-ROM, 222
CD-ROM
    dictionaries on, 23, 24
    thesauruses on, 26
CD-RW, 222
cede/seed, 146
cell/sell, 139
Celtic, 32
Celtic, 187–188
census, 248
cent/scent, 139
centr root, 79

centric root, 67
centrist, 79
certificate, 231
certificates of deposit, 231
chaise, 173
challah, 189
chaparral, 176
charlatan, 168
charlotte, 170
chartjunk, 218
chartreuse, 295
chateau, 173
chautauqua, 294
chauvinism, 288
chemistry, 191
chic, 168
chicle, 40
chile, 175
chiro root, 253
chiropractor, 253
chortle, 274
chromo-/chroma- prefix, 95
chromo/chroma root, 70
chromosphere, 70, 95
chron- prefix, 95
chron root, 69, 70
chronicle, 70
chrono root, 66
chronological, 95
chronophobia, 260
chronos root, 94
churlish, 108
chutney, 195
cide root, 67
circum- prefix, 90–91
circumambulate, 91
circumference, 91
circumscribe, 91
circumstantial evidence, 244
circumvent, 91
cirrhosis, 257
citadel, 182
citation, 238
cite/sight/site, 146
civet, 191
clan, 188
claustrophobia, 72, 96
clearance, 102

CliffsTestPrep
SAT I/PSAT, 199
CliffsTestPrep LSAT, 199
c.l.m. (career limiting
    move), 280
closed compound words,
    152–153, 313
clothing, vocabulary for,
    267–269
co-/col-/com-/con- prefix,
    89–90
co-pay, 90
co-worker, 90
coagulate, 259
coarse, 132
cocktail, 270
cohabit, 90
collaborate, 90
collectible, 103
collectibles, vocabulary for,
    263–265
colleen, 188
colloquial diction. *See*
    everyday English
collusion, 241
colon, as context clue, 40
colonnade, 181
colors
    connotations of, 130
    toponyms about, 295–296
comatose, 261
comedian, 110
cometised, 282
communication, vocabulary
    helping with, 11
comparative degree, 316
comparison
    suffixes indicating,
        107–108, 117
    words indicating, 316
competency tests, 11. *See
    also* standardized tests
complacent, 76
complement/compliment,
    139
compote, 171
compound words
    closed, 152–153, 313
    definition of, 14, 151–152

examples of, 156–166
hyphenated,
    152, 153–154, 157
multiword, 155, 313
comprehension,
    improving, 29
comprehension test
    questions, 202, 210–212
compress, 90
computers, vocabulary for,
    221–223, 281–285
con- prefix, 89–90
concave, 90
concierge, 173
concussion, 261
condition, suffixes
    indicating, 111–112
conductor, 224
confectioneries, 39
conference, 102
congenital, 257
conjugating verbs, 104
conjunction, 90
conjunction, 117
connotation, 127–130, 202.
    See also denotation
conscience, 308
conscious, 308
consonants, pronunciation
    of, 3, 30
consort, 90
contempt of court, 244
contentious, 45
context
    colons and dashes as
        clues, 40
    contrast clues, 45
    inferential clues, 42–44
    knowledge required for
        standardized tests, 201
    restatement clues, 38–40
    transitions as clues, 40–42
    using to determine
        meaning, 37–38,
        46–47, 47–50
contra- prefix, 98
contraband, 98
contractions, 54, 57
contrary, 98

contrast, as context
clue, 45
convalescence, 259
convocation, 103
copper, 296
cornucopia, 299
corp root, 245
corpus delicti, 245
corral, 176
corridor, 181
cosmo- prefix, 96
cosmopolitan, 74, 96
Cossack, 195
cotillion, 172
council/counsel, 139
count nouns, 316–317
counter- prefix, 100
counterintuitive, 100
counterproductive, 100
course, 132
CPU, 222
cracy root, 75
crag, 188
cranio root, 253
cranium, 253
craze, 47
credence, 43, 44
credit, 228
cremains, 275
crêpe, 171
crescendo, 179
croquette, 171
crossword puzzles, 20
croupier, 172
crouton, 168
cuisine, 171
culprit, 238
culture, 218
cur- prefix, 98
current, 39, 98
custody, 238
-cy suffix, 105
cyberspace, 284
cybersquatter, 282

• D •

-d/-ed suffix, 101, 104, 115
dacha, 195

daguerreotype, 45, 264
darjeeling, 195
dash, 40, 155
database program, 222
day trader, 232
days of the week, 162
de-emphasize, 85
de- prefix, 83, 85
dear/deer, 139
debit card, 228
debone, 85
deca- prefix, 93
Decalogue, 93
decertify, 85
decommission, 85
decompose, 85
decorum, 184
decrease, 85
deduction, 233
defendant, 244
defense, 238
deficit, 248
definition. *See* denotation;
meaning
degrade, 78
degree
prefixes indicating, 92
suffixes indicating,
113, 117
words indicating, 316
dehydrate, 73
delegate, 248
dem root, 71
demagogue, 71
democracy, 71
demographics, 71
demophobia, 260
denotation, 127–130. *See
also* connotation;
meaning
dénouement, 34
dependent, 234
deposition, 244
derail, 85
derby, 289
derm root, 253
dermatitis, 257
dervish, 193
describe, 309

desert, 19
desktop, 220
desperado, 178
desperation, 47
dessert, 19
deterrent, 68
dethrone, 85
deviant, 106
di- prefix, 93
diabetes mellitus, 257
diagnosis, 259
dialect. *See* vernacular
dichotomy, 93
dict root, 77
dictate, 77
dictator, 77
diction. *See* everyday
English; formal diction;
standard English
dictionary
choosing, 22
electronic dictionary, 24
example entry in, 23–24
print dictionary, 22–24
pronunciation guides in, 2
dictum, 77
die/dye, 139
digit root, 253
digital, 253
digraph, 30
diligent, 106
dim sum, 271
dining, vocabulary for,
269–272. *See also* food
diphthong, 30
dis-/di-/dif- prefix, 82
dis- prefix, 88–89
disagree, 89
discord, 89
discreet/discrete, 140
discretionary spending, 248
diseases, vocabulary
for, 257
disinterested, 310
dispelled, 68
doctors, vocabulary
for, 254–256
-dom suffix, 105–106
domo, 278

Don, 178
Doña, 178
dorado, 175
dors root, 79
dorsal, 79
doublespeak, 304
download, 222
dox root, 65, 66
duct root, 78
ductile, 78
duenna, 178
duet, 179
dummy, 225
duo- prefix, 93
duplex, 93
DVD, 222
dy- prefix, 66
dye/die, 139

• E •

e-breviations, 285
e-mail, vocabulary for, 283–285
e- prefix, 98
easterly, 111
eBay, 266
economic, 47
-ed suffix, 101, 104, 115
education, 11. *See also* standardized tests
eely, 296
effect, 308
effluent, 106
ego-surfing, 278
elaborate, 47
élan, 34, 169
elect, compound words ending with, 154
electronic dictionary, 24
electronic thesaurus, 26
elegant, 45
elicit/illicit, 140
elixir, 191
elongate, 98
em- prefix. *See* in- prefix
emigrate, 310
eminent, 46–47
eminent/imminent, 142

emoticon, 284
empanada, 271
empathize, 86
empty words, 304
en- prefix. *See* in- prefix
-en suffix, 103, 115
-ence/-ance suffix, 102
encouragement, 102
engineering vocabulary, 223–224
English. *See also* vocabulary; words
everyday. *See* everyday English
formal. *See* formal diction
influences from other languages, 12. *See also* specific languages
learning as second language, 315–319
oddities in, 14–15
standard. *See* standard English
English Grammar For Dummies, 117, 216
enn root, 78
ensemble, 173
enslave, 86
-ent suffix, 106
entomb, 86
entomologist, 110
entomology, 75
entomophobia, 260
epergne, 173
ephemera, 264
epics, 40–41
epicure, 289
epidemic, 38
epidemiologist, 255
epidermis, 253
eponyms, 287–293
equilibrium, 224
-er suffix, 109, 110, 117
ergophobia, 260
-erly suffix, 111
err/air/heir, 135
-es suffix, 101, 104–105
escargot, 171
-escent suffix, 111

escrow service, 266
-esque suffix, 108
-est suffix, 117
etiquette, 168
etymology
books about, 61
definition of, 22
in dictionary entry, 23–24
meanings changed over time, 52, 53
using to learn words, 26–27, 167
eu- prefix, 95
eulogize, 95
-eum suffix, 112
euphemisms, 305
euphonious, 95
euphoria, 95
everyday English, 10, 54, 57–59
everyday/every day, 313
everyone/every one, 313
ex- prefix, 98
except, 307
exchange, 98
exemption, 234
exile, 41
expressions. *See* idioms
extradite, 238
eye, compound words beginning with, 161–163

• F •

fabrication, 224
facade, 173
fact root, 77
factory, 77
fair/fare, 140
fakir, 193
fantabulous, 274
FAQs, 266
farther, 309
fashionista, 278
faux pas, 169
favoritism, 218
faze/phase, 140
febrile, 32

feedback, 216, 266
felony, 240
femcee, 274
fer root, 78
-ferous suffix, 112
festive, 112
figure, 220
filibuster, 248
fin root, 79
finale, 179
financial vocabulary,
    227–235
finish, 79
flame, 284
flan, 271
flash cards, 17–18, 28
flight risk, 218
florid, 112
flotus, 279
flow chart, 216
foie gras, 270
fondue, 270
font, 217
food
    compound words
        for, 157–158
    French words for, 170–171
    Spanish words for, 175
    vocabulary for, 269–272
forcible, 103
formal diction, 10, 53, 54–55
forte, 179
forward/foreword, 141
fracas, 32, 182
fraud, 234, 241
fray, 39
freedom, 106
freeman, 276
French, 12, 168–174
fricassee, 171
friendship, 106
frieze, 181
fro-yo, 279
-ful suffix, 105, 114, 116
funct root, 78
functional, 78
functionary, 110
funged, 280

funkinetics, 275
furrier, 110
further, 309
futique, 278
future perfect tense, 104
future tense, 104
-fy suffix, 112

• **G** •

gala, 182
galore, 187
gam root, 75
gamble/gambol, 141
game, 48
games, word, 17–20, 21
gamomania, 260
gamut, 34
garage, 168
garden burger, 279
gargantuan, 298
gastr root, 253
gastritis, 257
gastrointestinal, 253
gauche, 169
gazpacho, 270
gecko, 36
gefilte fish, 189
gelato, 271
gems, toponyms
    about, 295–296
gen root, 73
geneticist, 110
genetics, 73
genteel, 169
genuine, 311
geo root, 67, 71
geography, 71
geology, 71
ger root, 70
geriatric, 70
geriatric specialist, 255
German, 12
Germanic language, 12
gerontophobia, 260
gerund, suffixes
    indicating, 104
gigantic, 106

gilt/guilt, 141
ginger, 195
gingivitis, 257
glass ceiling, 218
globoboss, 282
glossary, 216
*The GMAT For
    Dummies*, 199
gods and goddesses, roots
    for, 80, 252
gold, phrases using, 234
GOOD job, 218
goodness, 106
gorilla/guerilla, 141
government vocabulary,
    246–249
governorship, 107
grad root, 78
gradual, 78
grammar
    books about, 117, 216
    ignored in nonstandard
        usage, 59
graph root, 65, 69, 75
gratis, 184
GRE (Graduate Records
    Exam), 207
Greek
    influences on English, 12
    medical terms from, 252
    prefixes, 93–96
    roots, 69–76, 80
gross income, 234
grotto, 181
guerilla/gorilla, 141
guide words, in
    dictionary, 24
guillotine, 290
guilt/gilt, 141
gutter, 220
gyn root, 73
gynecologist, 73, 256
gynecomania, 260

• **H** •

habeas corpus, 245
hacienda, 176

hackers, 284

hair, compound words beginning with, 163–164

hairdresser, 110

half, compound words beginning with, 156–157

handicapped, languaged biased against, 305

hangdog, 296

hard copy, 217

hard drive, 222

hardware, vocabulary for, 221–223, 281–285

harem, 193

harpy, 299

hart/heart, 142

hate, 123, 126

hazard, 192

healthful, 312

healthy, 312

hearsay, 244

heart/hart, 142

hegemony, 32

heir, 231

heir/air/err, 135

helio root, 74

heliotrope, 74

helping verb, 104

hematology, 253

hematoma, 261

hematophobia, 260

hemo/hema root, 253

hepta- prefix, 93

heptagon, 93

Herculean, 287

hexa- prefix, 93

hexagon, 12, 93

Hindu numeral system, 194

history of words. *See* etymology

hobbies, 15, 17

hokum, 275

hombre, 178

home, compound words beginning with, 159–160

home page, 282

homicide, 74

homo/homi root, 74

homogenous, 74

homonym, 74

homonyms

creating puns with, 148–149

definition of, 15, 132

differentiating with a thesaurus, 26

inferring meaning from context, 47–50

list of, 134–148

using, 134

homophones

creating puns with, 149

definition of, 15, 131–132

differentiating with a thesaurus, 26

list of, 134–148

using, 134

-hood suffix, 106

horo root, 70

horoscope, 70

hors d'oeuvre, 270

horse-faced, 296

hotlists, 282

hydrangea, 73

hydrate, 73

hydro/hydr root, 72–73

hydrometer, 224

hydrophobia, 73

hydroplane, 73

hydroponics, 73

hydropower, 73

hydrosphere, 73

hydrotherapy, 73

hymen, 298

hyper- prefix, 95

hyperactive, 95

hyperbaric, 95

hypercritical, 95

hypertext, 282

hyphens

after prefixes, 84, 85

in compound words, 152, 153–154, 157

in pronunciation guides in this book, 2

uses of, 155

hypo- prefix, 82, 91

hypodermic, 91

hypothermia, 91

-ia suffix, 112

-ian suffix, 110

-ible suffix, 102–103, 116

-ic suffix, 106

ichthy root, 74

ichthyology, 74

icons used in this book, 5–6

-id suffix, 112

ideas, Greek roots for, 74–76

ideo root, 75

ideology, 75

idioms, 59–62, 163

-ier suffix, 110

ignominious, 77

ignore, 89

il- prefix, 99

-ile suffix, 108

illegible, 89

illegitimate, 86

illicit/elicit, 140

illiterate, 99

illnesses, vocabulary for, 257

illuminate, 99

illuminated books, 264

illusion, 309

illustrious, 46–47

im- prefix, 99

immigrate, 310

imminent/eminent, 142

immobile, 86

immodest, 89, 99

impeachment, 249

impeccable, 89

impel, 78

imperfect, 86

imperiled, 68

implacable, 76
import, 99
impresario, 179
in- prefix, 67, 82, 84, 86, 88–89
in toto, 184
inactive, 86
inane, 86
incessant, 86
incision, 261
incognito, 182
inconsiderate, 89
incredible, 68
incunabula, 264
index cards, 17–18, 28
Indian, 195, 196
indict, 244
-ine suffix, 108, 296–297
inextricable, 43, 44
infancy, 105
inference, as context clue, 42–44
inflated language, 304
informal English. *See* everyday English
infotainment, 275
infra- prefix, 98
infrared, 98
-ing suffix, 104
ingrate, 89
initially, 47
initiative, 248
inscribe, 78
insomnia, 257
insouciant, 32
inter- prefix, 98
intercom, 98
interest, 231
interest charge, 228
interjection, 117
internal reports, 216
Internet. *See also* Web sites
  online dictionary, 24
  online shopping, vocabulary for, 265–266
  online thesaurus, 26
  vocabulary for, 281–285
internist, 255
into/in to, 313

intransitive verbs, 23
intrigue, 182
investment vocabulary, 230–233
ir- prefix, 99–100
iris, 298
Irish. *See* Celtic
irradiate, 99
irrefutable, 99
irregular, 99
irrepressible, 86
irresolute, 99
irritainment, 280
IS, 222
-ish suffix, 108
-ism suffix, 112
ISP, 222, 283
-ist suffix, 13, 66, 110–111
Italian, 178–182
italic text, used in this book, 2
-ite suffix, 103, 110–111, 115
-itis suffix, 112, 251, 257
it's/its, 142
-ity suffix, 114
-ive suffix, 112
-ize suffix, 103, 115

• J •

jargon, 221–225, 305–306
ject root, 78
jeroboam, 293
Jezebel, 292
jocund, 34
jokes. *See* puns
Jonah, 292
journal, for vocabulary words, 27, 28
Judas, 292
judge advocate, 242
judgment, 112
judicial, 242
jurisdiction, 242
jurisprudence, 242
jurist, 243
jus/jur root, 242
jus sanguinis, 243
justify, 220

• K •

kata- prefix, 96
khaki, 36
kinetic, 224
kingdom, 105
kleptomania, 260
knickers, 268
knish, 189
kreplach, 189

• L •

la dolce vita, 178
lacerated, 261
"lack of something" analogies, 205
laconic, 298
laissez faire, 248
lamblike, 296
lame duck, 246
language. *See* vocabulary; words
languages. *See* specific languages
larceny, 241
lariat, 176
laryng root, 253
laryngitis, 253
larynx, 36
lasso, 176
Latin
  influences on English, 12, 183–186
  legal terms, 246
  plurals, 104, 185–186
  prefixes, 93–94, 97–99
  roots, 76–79, 80
latke, 189
lay/lei, 142
lead/led, 143
legal vocabulary, 237–246
legato, 179
lei/lay, 142
leotard, 269
leprechaun, 188
lesion, 261
-less suffix, 116

lessen/lesson, 142
lethal, 46
levee, 38
levels of vocabulary
 (diction), 10–11. *See
 also* everyday English;
 formal diction;
 standard English
Levi's, 269
liability, 231
libel, 241
library, 111
libretto, 179
lightness, 106
likeness, suffixes
 indicating, 107–108
likewise, 108
Lincolnesque, 108
lineal root, 67
links, 282
Linzer torte, 272
literature, words from,
 298–300
lithograph, 264
litigation, 239
live art, 225
load/lode, 143
loath, 36
lobby, 247
location, prefixes
 indicating, 90–91
loch, 188
loggia, 181
logy/ology root, 75
loose, 310
lose, 310
lovable, 102
love, 123, 126
lox, 189
Luddite, 110
-ly suffix, 108, 114, 116
lymphadenitis, 257

• *M* •

macabre, 32
macadam, 289
Machiavellian, 290
macintrash, 282

mackintosh, 289
mad-dog, 276
MADD, 62
made/maid, 143
maestro, 179
magenta, 296
magni root, 79
magnify, 79, 112
mail/male, 143
mail merge, 222
mal-/male- prefix, 98
malapropism, 288
malevolent, 98
malfeasance, 244
mall rats, 278
malodorous, 98
manageable, 102
mandible, 36
mandolin, 179
mania root, 260
manias, vocabulary for, 260
mansard, 173
manslaughter, 241
manufacture, 77
marabou, 191
marauders, 41
marcel, 289
marinade, 175
maritime, 42
market, 232
marquee, 172
martial, 300
martinet, 290
marzipan, 272
masque, 172
matri root, 67
matrimony, 106
matzo, 189
maudlin, 292
mausoleum, 34
maverick, 289
meanderthal, 275
meaning. *See also*
 connotation;
 denotation
 altered by prefixes and
 suffixes, 67, 81, 101
 determining from context.
 See context

 determining from
 etymology, 26–27, 167
 in dictionary entry, 23–24
 and pronunciation, 30–31
measurement
 Greek roots for, 69–70
 instruments for, 224
meat/meet/mete, 143
Mecca, 294
med root, 79
medal/mettle, 143
median, 79
medical vocabulary
 for the body, 251–254
 general medical terms,
 258–262
 from Greek, 252
 manias and phobias,
 260–261
 medical conditions, 257
 medical specialties,
 254–256
megalomania, 260
melanoma, 261
memo, 216
memory tricks. *See*
 mnemonics
meningitis, 257
-ment suffix, 102, 112, 114
mentor, 289
mercurial, 299
meringue, 171
*Merriam-Webster's
 Collegiate
 Dictionary*, 22
*Merriam-Webster's Pocket
 Dictionary*, 22
Merriam-Webster's Word
 Game of the Day, 20
mesmerize, 289
metamorphosed, 46
metamorphosis, 71
meteorologist, 111
meter root, 69, 70
mettle/medal, 143
mezzanine, 181
micro- prefix, 95
microbe, 95
microphobes, 282

microscope, 95
migraine, 261
minaret, 192
minutes, 220
mis- prefix, 95
misdemeanor, 95, 240
misnomer, 77
mispronunciation, 31–35
misspell, 95
mistake, 95
mnemonics, 18–19
M.O. (modus operandi), 218
modem, 222
monarchy, 72, 75
money-market funds, 231
money, phrases using, 233
money, vocabulary for. *See* financial vocabulary
mono- prefix, 93
monologue, 93
monsoon, 192
-mony suffix, 106
morph root, 71
morphology, 71
Morris Dictionary of Word and Phrase Origins, 61
mosque, 192
mouse potato, 282
MRI, 259
multi root, 79
multimedia, 223
multiply, 79
multiword compound words, 155, 313
museum, 112
music, Italian words about, 179–180
mustang, 176
mut root, 200
mutual funds, 231
MVP, 62
mythomania, 260
myths, words from, 298–300

• *N* •

NAACP, 62
nabob, 195

narcissism, 252
narfistic, 280
NASA, 62
NASDAQ, 232
NATO, 62
nature, Greek roots for, 72–74
nautes root, 94
necrophobia, 260
negotiable, 232
neighborhood, 106
neo root, 70
neologisms, 273, 276–285
neonatologist, 256
neophyte, 70
-ness suffix, 106, 114
nest egg, 232
net income, 234
netiquette, 284
netizen, 282
neur root, 253
neurology, 253
The New Shorter Oxford English Dictionary, 22
newly created words, 273, 276–285
niche, 32
nihil root, 78
nihilism, 78
noah's arking, 279
nom root, 72, 75
nomenclature, 77
nomin/nomen root, 76–77
nominal, 77
nominate, 77
nominee, 77
nomos root, 94
nonchalance, 169
noncount nouns, 316–317
nonnative speakers, techniques for, 315–319
nonstandard usage, 59
nouns. *See also* part of speech
as adjectives, 318
count and noncount, 316–317
definition of, 1, 117

proper, 318
suffixes indicating, 13, 114
nov- prefix, 93
novelty, 107
novena, 93
number, 311
number
Hindu (Arabic) numeral system, 194
nouns that can be counted, 316–317
prefixes indicating, 92–94
suffixes indicating, 101, 104–105, 113, 318
numismatist, 111
nyctophobia, 261
nym root, 72, 75
NYSE, 232

• *O* •

ob- prefix, 98–99
obdurate, 32
obedient, 98
"object to function" analogies, 205
observatory, 108
obstetrician, 256
obstruction, 99
oct- prefix, 93
octet, 93
odium, 184
odont root, 253
odoriferous, 112
OED. See The Oxford English Dictionary
-oid suffix, 108
Old English, 100, 162
Old German, 12
ology root, 75
omni root, 79
omniscient, 79
oncologist, 255
online dictionary, 24
online shopping, vocabulary for, 265–266
online thesaurus, 26
onym root, 72, 75

onyma root, 72, 82
operational, 224
ophthalm root, 253
ophthalmic, 253
ophthalmologist, 254
optometrist, 254
-or suffix, 110
oral, 312
orama root, 75
ornith root, 74
ornithology, 74
ortho- prefix, 66
orthodontist, 253
-ory suffix, 108
-ose/-ous suffix, 105
oste root, 254
osteoporosis, 254
otolaryngologist, 255
ottoman, 191
-ous suffix, 13
over- prefix, 100
overarching, 100
overdrawn, 100
overreaching, 100
ovoid, 108
The Oxford English
    Dictionary, 22, 23

• P •

pagination, 225
pail/pale, 144
paleo root, 70
paleogeology, 70
Pan-American, 92
pan- prefix, 92
panacea, 80
panache, 182
pandemic, 92
panic, avoiding during
    test-taking, 213–214
panorama, 75
paper loss, 232
paper profit, 232
parasol, 182
parity, 107
paronychia, 259
part of speech. See also
    specific parts of speech

in analogy test questions,
    203, 204
definition of, 1, 117
in dictionary entry, 23
suffixes indicating, 13,
    101, 113–117
of synonyms, 125–126
in thesaurus entry, 25
"part to whole" analogies,
    204–205
past perfect tense, 104
past tense, suffixes
    indicating, 104
pasteurize, 289
pastoral, 107
patch, 223
patent medicines, 39
path root, 75
pathologist, 255
patio, 176
patronage, 248
PC, 220
peace/piece, 144
peaceable, 102
peacock, 296
ped root, 72
pedal, 74
pedestal, 181
pedestrian, 74
pediatrician, 72, 74, 256
pedo/pedi root, 74
pedometer, 224
pedophobia, 261
pel/puls root, 78
pend root, 78
pendulous, 78
pendulum, 78
penta- prefix, 93
pentagram, 93
people
    Spanish words for,
        177–178
    suffixes indicating,
        109–111
    words derived from. See
        eponyms
per- prefix, 99
per se, 184
perambulate, 99

performance review, 219
peri- prefix, 95, 251
pericarditis, 251
perimeter, 95
periodontist, 255
perjury, 241
personal references, in
    formal diction, 54, 55
personality tests, 11. See
    also standardized tests
pestilence, 46
pewter, 264
phagomania, 260
phase/faze, 140
phenomenon, 46–47
phil- prefix, 96
phil root, 72, 76
philanthropy, 72, 96
philatelist, 111
Philistine, 292
phlebitis, 257
phob- prefix, 96
phob root, 72
phobia root, 260–261
phobias, vocabulary for,
    260–261
physicians, vocabulary for,
    254–256
phyt root, 74
phytology, 74
pianoforte, 179
piazza, 181
piece/peace, 144
pimento, 175
pirouette, 172
plac root, 76
placate, 76
place
    effect on
        connotations, 128
    suffixes indicating,
        111–112
    words derived from. See
        toponyms
"place for" analogies, 206
placid, 76
plaid, 187
plain/plane, 144
plaintiff, 244

plait/plate, 144
plasma, 259
plastic surgeon, 255
play, compound words
    beginning with,
    164–165
plie, 172
pluggers, 278
plurals, 23
  Latin, 104, 185–186
  suffixes indicating,
    104, 318
plutocracy, 75
plutomania, 260
pneum root, 254
pneumonia, 254
podiatrist, 255
pogrom, 195
pointillism, 172
polit root, 74, 96
political vocabulary,
    246–249
poly- prefix, 92
polygamy, 75
polyglot, 92
polygon, 92
polynomial, 92
pompano, 175
pool, 48
pooper-scooper, 278
porcelain, 264
pork-barrel, 246
portico, 181
portmanteau words,
    14, 274–276
positive degree, 316
post- prefix, 99
post-rock, 278
posthumous, 35
postpone, 99
potpie, 271
potpourri, 35
potus, 279
Powerpoint, 217
prairie-dogging, 280
pre-owned, 87
pre- prefix, 84, 87–88
precede, 87, 312

precursors, 46
precut, 87
predestine, 87
preface, 87
prefix, 88
prefixes. *See also specific*
    prefixes
  adding to roots, 68
  altering meaning of
    words, 67, 81
  Anglo-Saxon, 99–100
  common, 83–94
  definition of, 13, 68, 81–82
  Greek, 93–96
  indicating degree, 92
  indicating location, 90–91
  indicating number, 92–94
  knowledge required for
    standardized tests, 200
  Latin, 93–94, 97–99
  when to hyphenate, 84, 85
  words acting as, 100
prehistoric, 87
prelude, 87
premarital, 87
premeditated, 87
prepositions, 117
prescribe, 309
presence/presents, 144
present participle, suffixes
    indicating, 104
present perfect tense, 104
present tense, 104
preset, 87
prima donna, 179
principal, 134
principle, 134
print dictionary, 22–24
print thesaurus, 25–26
printing, vocabulary
    for, 225
prissy, 275
pro tempore, 184
proceed, 312
procrastinate, 219
Procrustean, 299
prognosis, 259
proletariat, 43, 44

pronouns, 117
pronunciation
  common mistakes
    in, 31–35
  in dictionary entry, 23
  improving, 35–36
  multiple pronunciations
    for one word, 32
  rules for, 29–31
pronunciation guides, 2–3
proof, 225
proper nouns, 318
prot root, 70
prototype, 70
provenance, 264
proxy bidding, 266
pseudo- prefix, 82, 96
pseudonym, 72, 75
pseudoscience, 96
psychiatrist, 254
psycho root, 71, 75
psychodrama, 274
psychologist, 111, 254
psychology, 71, 75, 252
psychosis, 71
ptarmigan, 188
pubescent, 111
publications
  about grammar, 117, 216
  about idioms and word
    histories, 61
  about test
    preparation, 199
  dictionaries, 22, 23, 24
  thesauruses, 25, 26
publishing, vocabulary
    for, 225
pueblo, 176
puerile, 108
pulmo root, 254
pulmonary, 254
puls root, 78
pulse, 224
puns, from homonyms and
    homophones, 148–149
pyr root, 74
pyrogenic, 74
pyromania, 260

• Q •

quad- prefix, 93
quadrangle, 93
quagmire, 36
quality control, 224
quantity. *See* number
quay, 188
quixotic, 174
quotidian, 35

• R •

racist vocabulary, 306
raconteur, 169
radar, 62
radiologist, 255
ragout, 171
raise, 310
RAM, 223
rancho, 176
*The Random House
    Webster's College
    Dictionary*, 22
rapport, 169
rapture, 112
rash, 48
ratify, 112
re- prefix, 83, 84–85
reacquaint, 84
read/reed, 144–145
reading, 15, 17, 27–28
reading comprehension
    test questions,
    202, 210–212
reallocate, 84
reattach, 84
rebellion, 103
recertify, 84
recommission, 84
rectitude, 112
recur, 84
redo, 84
refer, 85
referral, 68
regardless, 100
regionalism. *See* vernacular

reject, 78
remission, 259
remitter, 244
remuneration, 36
renegade, 178
renumber, 85
repartee, 169
repeat, 85
replace, 85
repulsion, 68
reserve price, 266
residence/residents, 145
resigned, 48
restatement, as context
    clue, 38–40
retail elephant, 280
retractable, 68
reverence, 102
revert, 85
ribald, 36
rider, 247
right/rite/write, 145
rise, 310
rodeo, 176
Roget's online
    thesaurus, 26
ROM, 223
Romance languages, 167.
    See also French; Italian;
    Spanish
Romans, 77, 80. *See also*
    Latin
roots. *See also specific roots*
    definition of, 13, 65–66
    determining meaning
        from, 67
    forming words with, 66–69
    Greek, 69–76, 80
    knowledge required for
        standardized tests, 200
    Latin, 76–79, 80
rote/wrote, 145
rotunda, 181
roulette, 172
rubber-chicken circuit, 280
rug-ranking, 276
Russian, 195

• S •

-s/-es suffix, 101, 104–105
sail/sale, 145
salon, 173
salutation, 217
salvo, 182
sans-serif, 217
sarcastrophe, 276
saturnine, 108, 300
scent/cent, 139
schizophrenia, 257
scholar, 110
school, 11. *See also*
    standardized tests
schwas, in dictionary
    pronunciation guides, 2
Scottish. *See* Celtic
Scrabble, 19, 21
scrib root, 78
scribble, 78
scuba, 62
search engine, 283
SEC, 62
sed/sess root, 79
sedate, 79
Seed/cede, 146
seisms, 46
self, compound words
    beginning with, 154
sell/cell, 139
senior citizens, vocabulary
    describing, 303
sentence completion test
    questions, 202, 208–210
sentence structure, 55, 56,
    57. *See also* context
serif, 217
serious tone, 54, 55, 56
sess root, 79
set, 308
sexist vocabulary, 306
sexual harrassment, 219
shallot, 32
shaman, 39, 195
shamrock, 187
shanghai, 294
Shangri-La, 294

sheik, 193
shepherd's pie, 271
-*ship* suffix, 106–107
shoes, vocabulary for,
    267–268
shopgrifting, 279
shopping, vocabulary for,
    263–269
sideward, 112
sierra, 176
sight/site/cite, 146
silhouette, 288
Silicon Valley, 219
simony, 292
sinusitis, 112
-*sion*/-*tion* suffix, 114
-*sis* suffix, 106
sit, 308
skimming, 29
slackadem, 276
slander, 242
slang, 57–59, 275–276
slanguage, 275–276
slash, used in this book, 3
slush pile, 225
smog, 275
snafu, 62
snail mail, 283
snake, 49
sniper, 266
snow, compound words
    beginning with,
    164–165
social situations,
    vocabulary helping
    in, 11
socialite, 111
sod, 39
soft money, 248
software, vocabulary for,
    221–223, 281–285
solarium, 111
sole/soul, 146
soma root, 74
somatic, 74
-*some* suffix, 108
sonogram, 259
sophistry, 75
sophy/soph root, 75

soprano, 179
spam, 284
Spanish, 12, 174–178
spare, 49–50
specialties, medical,
    vocabulary for, 254–256
speech, part of. *See* part of
    speech
Speed Scrabble, 21
speel, 279
spelling
    altering when adding
        suffixes, 115
    and pronunciation, 30
    words with same spelling
        and pronunciation. *See*
        homonyms
    words with similar
        spelling, 14
spider, 284
spontaneous involution, 258
Spoonerism, 34
spork, 274
spreadsheet program, 223
stalkerazzi, 276
stampede, 176
standard English, 10,
    54, 55–56
standardized tests
    analogy questions on, 202,
        203–207
    antonym questions on,
        201–202, 204, 207–208
    avoiding panic during,
        213–214
    books about, 199
    building vocabulary for,
        27–29
    preparation for, 212–213
    reading comprehension
        questions on, 202,
        210–212
    required by schools and
        businesses, 11
    sentence completion
        questions on, 202,
        208–210
    vocabulary skills needed
        for, 199–202

starter marriage, 278
state of being, suffixes
    indicating, 105–107
stationary, 19, 134
stationery, 19, 134
status quo, 184
stiletto, 182
stock, 231
structures
    Italian words about,
        180–181
    Spanish words about, 176
strudel, 272
stucco, 181
sub- prefix, 91
subhuman, 91
subordinate, 91
subpoena, 239
subsidy, 248
subterranean, 91
suburban, 108
suffixes. *See also specific*
    suffixes
    adding to roots, 68
    adding to words, 115
    altering meaning of words,
        67, 101
    definition of, 13, 68
    indicating a person,
        109–111
    indicating action, 102, 103
    indicating degree, 113, 117
    indicating likeness or
        comparison,
        107–108, 117
    indicating number,
        101, 104–105, 113, 318
    indicating part of speech,
        13, 101, 113–117
    indicating place or
        condition, 111–112
    indicating state of being,
        105–107
    indicating verb tense,
        101, 104
    knowledge required for
        standardized tests, 200
suite/sweet, 145–146
sultan, 193

sun, compound words beginning with, 160–161
super, compound words containing, 153
super- prefix, 92
supercilious, 92
superlative degree, 316
supertwin, 278
surgeon, 255
surplus, 248
surrealism, 172
sustainable, 102
suture, 259
sweet/suite, 145
swindle, 242
syllables, 3, 32–33
symbiosis, 90
symmetrical, 90
sympathy, 75
syn-/sym- prefix, 82, 89–90, 94
synchronize, 94
synonyms
  analogy questions involving, 203–204
  benefits of using, 122
  choosing, 125–126
  knowledge required for standardized tests, 201–202
  not being exact substitutes, 123–124
  reasons for using and not using, 124
  in a thesaurus, 24, 25, 26
synopsis, 90

• T •

table, 220
tail/tale, 147
tamale, 175
tamarind, 191
tantalize, 299
tarantella, 179
tarragon, 191
tart, 272

tax vocabulary, 233–235
tele- prefix, 96
telecommunication, 96
telepathy, 96
telephone, 96
telescam, 280
televangelist, 275
ten/tin root, 79
tenet, 79
tense, verb. *See* verb tense
term root, 65, 79
terminal, 79
terra firma, 185
terrine, 171
terrorism, 242
testimony, 244
tests. *See* standardized tests
tetra- prefix, 93
tetrahedron, 93
that/who/which, 319
the, 318, 319
their/there/they're, 146
theo- prefix, 96
theo root, 75
theology, 75, 96
theophobia, 261
therapy, 259
thermo root, 74
thermometer, 224
thermophobia, 261
thermostat, 74
thesaurus, 24–26. *See also* antonyms; synonyms
thesis, 106
thespian, 289
threw/through, 147
throne/thrown, 146
thug, 195
tildes, in dictionary pronunciation guides, 2
time, effect on connotations, 128
tin root, 79
-tion suffix, 114
to/too/two, 146
toady, 28
toile, 168
tomato, 32

tone
  effect on connotations, 128
  in everyday English, 57
  in formal diction, 54, 55
  in standard English, 56
toponyms, 293–296
toreador, 178
tort, 237
torte, 237
tortilla, 175
toxic, 261
train, 48
trans- prefix, 200
transfer, 78
transformer, 224
transistor, 224
transition, 46
transitions, as context clue, 40–42
transitive verbs, 23
treason, 242
tri- prefix, 93
trim size, 225
tripod, 93
triumvirate, 12
troll, 283
trompe l'oeil, 172
troubadour, 172
trustee, 249
Tsar, 195
tsunamis, 39
-tude suffix, 112
tundra, 195
turquoise, 296
tuxedo, 269
-ty suffix, 107
"type of" analogies, 204
typeface, 217

• U •

ulcer, 261
ultra- prefix, 92
ultramarine, 92
ultraviolet, 92
umlaut, in dictionary pronunciation guides, 2
un- prefix, 13, 67, 83, 86–87

unabridged dictionary, 22
unambiguous, 87
unbuckled, 87
uncensored, 87
unclad, 87
under- prefix, 100
underage, 100
underhanded, 100
underscore, 100
uni- prefix, 93
unicycle, 93
uninterested, 310
unique, 312
unjustified, 87
unruly, 87
unswerving, 87
unusual, 312
Upwords, 19
urban yoga, 276
-ure suffix, 112
urologist, 255
Utopia, 294

• *V* •

vain/vane/vein, 147
Valhalla, 294
valise, 182
vandalism, 242
vaquero, 176
vaudeville, 172
vehement, 35
vein/vain/vane, 147
vendetta, 182
vengeance, 46
vent root, 66
venue, 245
Venus, 300
verb tense
  suffixes indicating,
    101, 104
  of synonyms, 125
verbal, 312
verbs. *See also* part of
    speech
  conjugating, 104
  definition of, 1, 117
  helping, 104

intransitive, 23
  suffixes indicating, 115
  transitive, 23
verdict, 245
vernacular, 57, 59
vested interest, 219
veto, 249
vial/vile, 147
vid/vis root, 79
videophile, 279
vignette, 36
villa, 181
virus, 223
visual, 79
vocabulary. *See also* words
  ageist, 303
  benefits of improving, 11
  biased against
    handicapped, 305
  bureaucratic, 303–304
  for business. *See* business
    vocabulary
  for computers, 221–223,
    281–285
  for dining. *See* food
  doublespeak, 304
  for government, 246–249
  improving, 15, 17–29
  inflated, 304
  jargon, 221–225, 305–306
  for legal matters, 237–246
  levels of, 10–11. *See also*
    everyday English;
    formal diction;
    standard English
  for medicine. *See* medical
    vocabulary
  for money and finances,
    227–235
  racist, 306
  sexist, 306
  for shopping, 263–269
  for taxes, 233–235
  tests for. *See* standardized
    tests
vodka, 195
vor root, 69
vowels, pronunciation
    of, 2–3, 30

vpotus, 279
vulcanize, 299

• *W* •

waist/waste, 147
waive, 239
-ward suffix, 112
warrant, 239
Waterloo, 294
way/weigh, 147
weak/week, 147
weather/whether, 148
Web browser, 283
Web rage, 283
Web sites
  online dictionaries, 24
  online *Oxford English
    Dictionary*, 23
  online thesauruses, 26
  word games, 20
Webmaster, 283
*Webster's 3rd New
    International
    Dictionary*, 22
*Webster's New World College
    Dictionary*, 22
*Webster's New World
    Dictionary and
    Thesaurus*, 25
weigh/way, 147
wellingtons, 269
Welsh. *See* Celtic
whether/weather, 147
which/who/that, 319
whine/wine, 148
whip, 247
white-collar crime, 242
white space, 217
who/which/that, 319
whose/who's, 148
windfall, 231
wine/whine, 148
-wise suffix, 108
wisteria, 289
witness, 239
wizened, 35
word processor, 223

Word Safari Web site, 20
words. *See also* vocabulary
  acting as prefixes, 100
  from animals, 296–298
  blended. *See* portmanteau
    words
  changing over time, 52, 53
  choosing, 51–52. *See also*
    audience
  compound. *See*
    compound words
  context of. *See* context
  elements of, 13. *See also*
    prefixes; roots; suffixes
  empty, 304
  euphemisms, 305
  games using, 17–20, 21
  history of. *See* etymology
  idioms. *See* idioms
  meaning of. *See* meaning
  from myths and literature,
    298–300
  newly created. *See*
    neologisms
  with opposite meanings.
    See antonyms
  from other languages. *See*
    specific languages
  part of speech. *See* part of
    speech
  from people's names. *See*
    eponyms
  from places. *See*
    toponyms
  pronunciation of. *See*
    pronunciation
  relationship between,
    201–202
  with same meanings. *See*
    synonyms
  with same pronunciation.
    See homophones
  with same pronunciation
    and spelling. *See*
    homonyms
  with similar meanings,
    311–313
  with similar
    pronunciation, 307–310
  with similar spelling, 14
  slang. *See* slang
  vernacular. *See* vernacular
worrisome, 108
worsted, 32
writ, 239
write/right/rite, 145
writing ability, testing, 200
wrote/rote, 145

• *X* •

Xanadu, 295
xenomania, 260

• *Y* •

-y suffix, 105, 115, 116
yearly, 108
Yiddish, 188–190
your/you're, 148

• *Z* •

zealous, 35
zeppelin, 289
zine, 280
zinnia, 289
zoo root, 74
zoology, 74
zoomania, 260